JACKFRUIT
and
WILD HONEY

JACKFRUIT
and
WILD HONEY

by

Barbara Graham

ISPCK, DELHI
1996

Jackfruit and Wild Honey—Published by the Indian Society for Promoting Christian Knowledge (ISPCK), Post Box 1585, Kashmere Gate, Delhi–110006.

Cover Design by Gregor Graham

Laser Typeset at **ISPCK**, Post Box 1585, 1654 Madarsa Road, Kashmere Gate, Delhi–110006. * Phone: 2966323, Fax: 011-2965490.

Printed at Cambridge Press, Kashmere Gate, Delhi–110,006.

Contents

SKETCH TITLES

Church of South India Hospital Chikballapur.
Outpatient Department.
Part 1 Chap 3.

Bargaining for wood.
Note solid wooden wheels.
Part 1 Chap 4.

Wood to market to buy the day's food.
Part 1 Chap 4.

Gopuram at Gopal's temple.
Part 1 Chap 6.

Fruit stall at the bus stand.
Part 1 Chap 20.

Lancing an abscess rural style. (in cart)
Part 2 Chap 6.

Lining up for milk powder Rural Dispensary.
Part 2 Chap 7.

The evening task! Hand-feeding the oxen.
Part 2 Chap 9.

Irrigating the fields. (canti-lever well)
Part 2 Chap 10.

Is the patch anaesthetic? (Dr. Graham, Sabhapathy and patient)
Part 2 Chap 11.

Admiring the pigs.
Part 2 Chap 13.

Taking skin-clippings from an H.D. patient. (Sabhapathy and patient)
Part 2 Chap 13.

"Don't muzzle the ox that treads the corn."
Part 2 Chap 16.

Irrigation works Maddurenahalli.
Part 2 Chap 18.

Measuring out the grain.
Part 2 Chap 18.

(The words in brackets I have added to avoid any confusion.)

ACKNOWLEDGEMENTS

I owe a debt of thanks to my late husband Dr Keith Graham for his support and advice, particularly on matters medical, and to my late mother for keeping my letters which have been a valuable reference.

There are many others who have helped with information and encouragement to whom I am most grateful : friends in India and the late Mrs. Eleanor Cutting; Dr. Cecil Cutting's book "Hot Surgery" for some details of the Cholera epidemic; members of the Sunnybank Writers Group for their useful criticism and interest; friends who read the rough draft and especially Mrs. Delys Carver who did proof-reading.

A very special thank you to our son, Gregor, for painting the cover and drawing the illustrations.

Last but not least, thanks to Mrs. Betty Robinson for all the work she had done to make this ready for publication.

FOREWORD

In 1987 I revisited India. Dr. Leslie Robinson who has been Medical Superintendent of the C.S.I.Hospital, Chikballapur since 1967 and his wife Betty said "When are you going to write Sabhapathy's story?" I have been working on it ever since.

In February 1951, due to the escalation of the war in Korea, my husband Dr.Keith Graham and I came out of China where he had been working as a Medical Missionary with the London Missionary Society over a period of thirteen years.

We spent five months at home in Australia, then set sail with our baby daughter, Fiona, for India where Keith had been appointed to work in the Wardlaw Thompson Hospital(later Church of South India Hospital) Chikballapur.

Our first year was spent in Bangalore learning Telugu, one of the major south Indian languages.

Due to a crisis in the hospital at Jammalamadugu we were sent to work there for two years. Our son Gregor was born in 1953 and we moved to Chikballapur in late 1954. Our third child Heather was born in 1955.

Dr. Cutting, L.M.S.Missionary, was in charge of the hospital and had been looking forward to our arrival so that he could do more rural medical work but after a year he became ill and had to return to the U.K.for surgery.

The rural medical work continued. Each Wednesday the hospital car held clinics at various spots down the Gauribidanur road (see map), one week turning off to the left, the next week to the right, to cover a larger number of villages.

It was at this time that we first met Sabhapathy. He had just taken one year's leave of absence from his position as a Revenue Inspector in Kolar District in order to help people in the villages fight for their rights.

Sabhapathy was for more than thirty years closely associated with the work of the hospital as he moved around the villages of the area. For the fourteen years my husband was Medical Superintendent of the hospital we had a close association with him and after our transfer further north remained in contact. In the anecdotes which make up the second part of the book I am referred to as amma. We were fortunate to have a very reliable ayah to look after the children. She had come to us in Jammalamadugu at the age of 16 and became virtually part of the family.

Our cook, Doramma, was a delightful woman who at 24 had six children. While we were on furlough in 1958-9 she died tragically and when we returned in January '60 with our third daughter, Carol, we sent three of her older children to boarding school at Gangasandra and gradually took on the younger two as well. These are the children referred to in the story.

As a missionary wife I was variously employed, from poisoning rats to managing a municipal nursery school and a rural boarding school and doing paramedical work. During this time I came to know the local people well and developed a love for India and its people.

The suffixes attached to names can be confusing. In India people are not generally spoken to by name without attachment of a suffix which shows various degrees of respect.

The suffix 'garu' shows the highest respect and is used for both sexes.

The language spoken in the area is mixed, as many of the villages are basically Telugu speaking, but because they are now part of Karnataka state, the official language, and that taught in schools, is Kannada.

Suffixes attached to men's names are appa(Kan.) and ayya(Tel.) used when addressing your superiors or to show respect. Anna is the common mode of address when speaking to peers. It means simply elder brother.

Amma is commonly used as suffix to a woman's name to show respect while akka means elder sister and is used among peers.

Before we left India in 1974 Sabhapathy told me his life story. I have filled in the background from my own knowledge of India. It is Part One of this book. Part Two relates incidents in which we were personally involved or of which we got to know. In 1987 I revisited India. The Prologue relates my first return to Sabhapathy's village.

SYNOPSIS

E.R.SABHAPATHY

JACKFRUIT AND WILD HONEY

This is the story of Ebenezer Rajaratnam Sabhapathy who was the son of a Telugu doctor who worked in what was then the Wardlaw Thompson Hospital, Chikballapur, Mysore (now Karnataka) State. In his childhood and youth he grew up in a secure family environment within the predominantly Christian community of the hospital.

The first part is his story which he told me. It follows his childhood from his mother's death when he was eight years old, his father's remarriage and his time at boarding school in Mysore city, to the break up of the family after his father's death in 1942.

As a young College student in Bangalore he wasted his opportunity then felt rebellious when taken out of college and expected to enter the Public Service.

Some chapters deal with his time in the Public Service and his ever present desire to re-enter college and complete a medical course.

The premature death of his father left him bearing a burden of guilt and resulted in a quarrel with his stepmother leaving him with a great sense of disillusionment as he had loved her as his own mother.

I have added background to his account.

Part two consists of episodes from his life which were known or told to me personally. Most chapters are a story complete in themselves.

In 1967 he developed an Acoustic Neuroma and underwent surgery. He was no longer able to cycle from village to village but undeterred, he travelled by bus or on foot. Two of the local bus companies offered him free travel wherever he wanted to go.

His living example was Mahatma Gandhi who followed the teachings of Christ and it was his dream that a Christian congregation be established in the area. That dream was realised before his death in 1983. He never achieved his youthful ambition to follow in his father's footsteps and study medicine but he accomplished much more.

PART 1

Chapter 1

PROLOGUE

The conductor gave two resounding thumps to the back of the bus. "Raight!" It shuddered then moved off slowly.

There was little fear of falling to the floor of the vehicle for the thirty or so standing passengers were packed like corn on a cob, filling all the available floor space. In spite of this I clutched the green-brown parcel of sewn leaves in one hand and clung to a roof strap with the other, enveloped in the pungent aroma of sweaty bodies.

I was on a kind of pilgrimage. It was twelve years since I had been down the road to Gollahalli and a rush of memories flooded my mind creating a sad sweet blend: so much seemed the same but the man who for thirty years had been a driving force in the area was gone and the leaf-stitched parcel I held contained garlands to put on his grave.

The bus groaned up to the edge of the Southern Deccan and made the winding steep descent, past Dr. Thompson's rock, the temple and the huts in the foothills; past the Jakkalamadugu crossroad.

The bright morning sun dazzled me as I jumped down. Instead of the bare angle of dirt I had known, a well-grown Flame tree stood between the main road and the path to Gollahalli and under its shade a raised granite slab with a simple stone cross for a headstone. E. R. Sabhapathy 1917-1983.

I snapped the thin cotton wound around my parcel and took out two garlands of jasmine and roses - the heady perfume brought more memories flooding back - weddings, arrivals and farewells. One garland I laid on the slab, the other I draped over the cross.

As I stood for a moment and closed my eyes I could see his small wiry figure, pancha blown by the wind, his white handloom jubba to below his waist, one arm outstretched in typical stance to illustrate a point and I felt glad that Sabhapathy's last resting place was under one of the flowering trees grown from seeds he had planted as he travelled around the villages.

Ebenezer Rajaratnam Sabhapathy was the eldest son of Cuddapah Rajaratnam who was one of a group of four young men given medical training by Dr. Thompson at the London Mission Hospital, Jammalamadugu.

At the time of Sabhapathy's birth his father was a doctor in a rural hospital at Simhadripuram and sent his wife, Jane, to Chikballapur for confinement. The name Sabhapathy was chosen by her for she hoped he would indeed become a 'leader of the congregation.'

His mother Jane Sowbhagia became the first headmistress of the Girls' Middle School, Chikballapur.

Dr. Rajaratnam later came to work at Chikballapur in what was then Mysore State, (now Karnataka) first with Dr. Thompson and later with Dr. Cutting. He was a dedicated Doctor and much loved and respected by the local people.

Before we left India Sabhapathy told me his story as follows:-

Chapter 2

I was only eight years old when my mother died. I was asleep on the verandah, the sheet pulled over my head to avoid a mosquito which had somehow slipped into my net.

I was dreaming that I heard weeping, but slowly I rose from the depths of sleep to realise it was no dream. I pulled down the sheet and listened. Where was the sound coming from? From mother and father's bedroom? I crept out of bed, a sinking feeling in the pit of my stomach – that surely was my father weeping! I had never heard my father weep. Fear gripped my heart and almost paralysed my movement as I padded silently towards the door of their bedroom, which opened on to the verandah. I put my face to the glass pane of the french doors. Between the door frame and the curtain I could just see my mother lying on the bed very still and my father kneeling at the bedside weeping, with great racking sobs that tore at me, draining the strength from my legs.

I saw my elder sister, Kanya, appear at the other door of the bedroom – I must go to her – I ran along the verandah and into the main room of the house. Kanya had disappeared. As I approached the door of my parent's room I heard Kanya's voice added to father's weeping – "Mummy! Mummy!" she called, and began to sob. I froze where I stood in the doorway until my father turned and saw me. He came and put his arms around me and led me gently to my mother's bedside. I did not weep, I felt frozen inside as I saw my mother lying as though peacefully sleeping but with no flicker of movement.

It was many years before father told me the events of that night. He had been called to the hospital after the evening meal to help with a difficult delivery and was away several hours. He returned to find my mother sitting up in bed gasping. He went to his medical bag to prepare an injection but before he could assemble the syringe she gave a loud gasp which was followed by a horrifying quiet. He rushed to her side and tried to resuscitate her but the attack must have been too much for her heart and she had gone.

Father did not like leaving us alone so he went and called Krupa Danam, our cook, to stay with us while he went and informed the night staff and sent one of them to tell Dr. Thompson.

Kanya put her arms around me and we sat huddled on a mat in the dining hall. Even Kanya's embrace could not stop my shivering.

Father returned from the hospital but appeared oblivious of our presence as he went to the bed and knelt at mother's side, then he returned to the dining room and sat at the table looking stunned and bewildered, probably trying to come to terms with the fact that his beloved Jane had gone.

We older children sat quietly, afraid to move or break the silence. After what seemed an eternity, Dr. Thompson arrived. I observed over the years that there was complete understanding between Dr.Thompson and my father. He now took charge.

"Kanya! Thammu! You had better go to bed and get some sleep, Daddy is going to need your help tomorrow with Sampath and your sisters".

Danam reappeared in the doorway with a tray containing tumblers of hot sweet coffee

"Drink coffee Sir."

We all sat and sipped in silence then Kanya took me by the hand and led me to her bed where we lay, the warmth of her body soothing me until at last I fell asleep.

Dr. Thompson took over many of the tasks which had to be done. He helped my father word telegrams to relatives and friends and arranged to have the pastor informed and to send someone to the carpenter's shop to order a coffin to be made.

In India, burials must be arranged as soon as anyone dies as the warm climate and lack of refrigeration make it necessary to hold the funeral service on the day of death or early next day.

The service in the Church was to be at three o'clock. Anandamma Aunty came to help get us children ready. The women of the Church were busy making garlands of jasmine, chrysanthemum and marigold to adorn the coffin.

For me the whole experience was a kaleidoscope of blurred impressions - the coffin open in the front of the church for friends and relatives to look at my mother for the last time – the strong sweet smell of jasmine, tube rose and other flowers mingled with the scent of incense sticks to a perfume which even now evokes sad memories – the service, the singing and the tears, then the coffin closed and hoisted high on to the shoulders of some of the hospital staff and carried to the waiting ox cart.

My smaller brothers and sisters travelled in a jutka with my aunts while father, Kanya and I walked behind followed by Dr. and Mrs. Thompson, aunts, uncles, hospital staff and numerous friends from the town, singing as they walked the mile to the cemetery. Many Hindu and Muslim friends joined in the procession as my mother was held in high regard by the townsfolk.

The next year was a lonely one for my brother and sisters and me. We had been used to coming home from the London Mission Primary School in the Palya to find mother already home from her work as headmistress of the Government Middle School in Chikballapur. She saw that we had a drink of hot sweet milky coffee and a snack as she listened to the events of our day. She had begun to teach us English and I was also attending English classes held by Mrs. MacFarlane for a group of boys and girls.

My father cared for us lovingly when he was at home but the hospital took up most of his time and he often came in only after we were sleeping, when he would go to our beds, pull up the covers and kiss each one of us as we slept.

Prior to my mother's death we always had family prayers before the evening meal, now that did not happen unless father was able to be there.

My mother and father had been very close and our home had been a happy and harmonious one so my mother's death left a huge void in all our hearts.

Chapter 3

As the months went by my father realised he could not manage to bring up his family alone. Dr.Thompson and Miss Butler with the help of an old friend Sampamma, arranged a second marriage for my father with Victoriamma, my mother's younger sister, who was teaching in Kolar.

We children were five in number. Sukanya at almost ten was the eldest, I was next. Then Sarojini followed by my brother Sampath(Chichu). Mary Dharambha, known as Dathi, was only three years old at this time and was the youngest, for our baby brother Noel had died of Diphtheria a year earlier. As plans for the wedding went ahead we began to look forward with some unease, to having a new mother. We already knew her and called her Aunty.

I can remember the wedding quite well. Everyone was busy from early morning preparing food for the hundreds of guests.

I was sent to the bazaar several times to buy a little more of some spice, to collect the betel leaves and to ask the merchant to send some extra coconuts.

My brother Sampath and I sat with the other children on mats at the front of the church, the air heavy with the scent of jasmine, and watched with interest as father held the threads of the'tali'(Black cord equivalent to a western wedding ring) at the back of my aunty's neck while he made his vows. At the conclusion of the ceremony in the church our father and our new mother were garlanded by many friends. They then went off in the hospital Ford to our house, while my stepmother changed from her white bridal sari into her reception sari, a beautiful coloured silk with gold-threaded border which, according to custom, had been presented to her at the engagement ceremony by my father.

A pandal (open shed) had been erected in front of the house, each upright decorated with banana suckers and strings of jasmine flowers strung between the poles, the covering of coconut mats providing good shelter from the sun. By the time the bride and groom arrived for the reception the bhajana party, having tuned their drums and other instruments, were ready. Two chairs had been placed on a low dais at one end of the pandal for my father and his bride. As soon as they approached, the bhajana group began to play and I sat down in a corner to watch. Friends went up, one by one to garland them both and present their gifts. My stepmother's sister was there to remove the garlands from her neck as they threatened to submerge her and likewise a friend of my father's removed the strings of heavily scented tube rose and marigold from his neck. Father's male friends, after garlanding him, handed a second garland to my father who then placed it around the neck of his bride as she rose, head still bowed, eyes downcast, as becomes a young Indian bride.

Guests who were not staying for the meal were presented with a coconut and some betel nut and leaf as they left, but most were remaining to take food, and soon members of the hospital staff who were helping to serve the meal began to ask people to rise while they relaid the mats in rows for ease of serving. The tantalising smell of spicy meat in rice filled the air and I realised I was hungry. For a few moments there seemed to be chaos with servers hurrying to and fro, guests moving, the throbbing of the bhajana music a background to the heat and bustle. When everyone was seated, servers placed a leaf plate before each guest. They were closely followed by others carrying bowls of steaming pilau, a handful of which was served to each plate. More servers followed with fresh tomato and yoghurt chutney. There was a sudden diminuendo of sound then silence as the pastor stood to say grace. Behind the scenes the servers were being told not to serve too much initially as many more guests had come than were expected.

The children were some of the first to be fed as by this time it was late. The bride and groom and the servers ate last and I went and sat on a mat not far from the bhajana, which was a new group now, for the ones who had been playing were now eating. The facial contortions and head-jerking in rhythm seem to be an essential part of the drummer's role. His right hand was busy beating out the 'raga' on the skin-covered mouth of a brass pot. His left hand accompanied it on the taut skin of an earthenware pot which could be fine-tuned by altering the tension of leather thongs. He played on and on. Partly mesmerised by the rhythm, like many of the children I was overcome by sleep, but wakened at the touch of a sheet being put over me. I glanced up into the face of my new stepmother, and dropped off to sleep again content.

Chapter 4

Each year father took us all to the Travellers' Bungalow (T.B.) at Peresandra for holidays. We all enjoyed it. Mother was responsible for organising our packing and departure as father was usually busy in the hospital until we left.

Father arranged oxcarts to carry us and our belongings and made sure his guns were cleaned and greased and that there was enough ammunition.

In the bustle to get ready, mother would order us about, "Thammu-nayana, Lakshmamma has not brought the clothes back; she promised she would bring them last night. Take the list and check it and bring them back yourself."

I hopped on my bike and cycled down the road to the dhobi's house. I could see her through the doorway wielding the heavy charcoal-burning iron as she hurried to iron my father's last shirts. The smell of hot iron on damp starched clothes assailed my nostrils.

"Amma, mother is waiting for the clean clothes. Are they ready? Mother told me to bring them home."

"No, Chinna Babu, they are not ready, I have one more shirt to iron. I will finish and bring them myself immediately."

"Bring them quickly then because we are going camping".

I cycled home and mother sent me on another errand to the bazaar.

"Nayana, go and buy two seers of jasmine flowers and some Betel leaves to take for our friend the Reddy's family. I would feel embarrassed to go without taking flowers for the women. The girls will enjoy stringing them together."

My sisters were busy packing clothes and provisions.

The ox carts arrived, each with a pair of carefully matched oxen yoked to a crossbar at the end of a stout wooden shaft. One cart had a huge scoop-like basket lashed with the open end towards the rear. This was the one in which mother, the girls and the smaller children travelled.

Father, my brother and I travelled front and rear of the other 'bandi' with the trunks, baskets and bags packed in the middle.

As we grew older we often went by bus with our 'saaman' loaded on top but in the early days the buses were too infrequent.

Travel by cart is slow - not much more than walking pace - so it took us several hours to reach our destination. We children didn't mind. We were in a holiday mood and often sang as we went, sometimes Christian lyrics, sometimes cinema songs to the accompanying creak, creak of the huge wooden wheels.

The giant mango and fig trees lining the road cast a dappled shade in which we made leisurely progress, only occasionally being disturbed by the raucous blast on the horn of an approaching lorry as the driver squeezed the rubber bulb in plenty of time for the oxen to move us off the centre strip and on to the grassy verge to let the vehicle pass.

The sun was a glowing ball on our right and the shadows long, before we came over the last rise and saw the village of Peresandra with the T.B.nestling in a grove of trees just off the road.

The peon {servant} was expecting us and we could see him sitting cross-legged, a kerosene lamp beside him, on the raised stone floor of the front verandah.

"Namaskara Doctorgaru, Ammagaru" he saluted us, then helped the drivers of the carts unload the luggage and carry it into the two main rooms.

At the rear of each main room was a bathroom, part of which was separated off by a ten inch high wall. This area contained a huge earthenware 'bana' full of water which was cold on the hottest of days. The main part of the bathroom held a washstand, wooden towel rail and commode. The rudimentary plumbing was a hole through the outer wall. On hot days snakes sometimes came in through the hole in search of cool and damp.

Those buildings were built in the days when labour was cheap. The walls were of solid granite blocks ten inches thick, and the floors of slate slabs imported from Cuddapah district. Huge wooden beams supported a tiled roof and in each room was a fireplace. In the cooler winter months we enjoyed a log fire at night.

Mother handed some rice to the peon who also doubled as cook's assistant while we were there.

"As we are late we will eat some of our prepared vindaloo and pickle with the rice tonight. The children will be too tired to eat if we wait while you cook dhal(split peas)."

"Yes, Amma."

"Here is some coffee powder and 'jaggery'(raw sugar). Make coffee and bring it to us while the rice cooks."

The peon disappeared out of the door and across the yard to the kitchens.

"Kanya, see that Sarojini and the boys collect their bedding rolls and spread them in the next room."

Mother and father and the smaller children occupied the other room and Krupa Danam, our cook, helped mother unpack. Each room contained two wooden beds laced across with webbing. We boys bagged the one near the window and the girls shared the other. We were accustomed to sleeping on beds for father had come from Cuddapah District where most people sleep on beds to avoid scorpions which come out at night and are often deadly.

After arranging our bedding, Chichu and I walked out to the front verandah. Father was sitting in a squatter's chair smoking a cigarette as he read the paper.

Two white clad figures emerged from the darkness, towels wrapped around their heads turban style. They were good 'shikaris'(hunters) who usually accompanied us when shooting.

They greeted father. "Namaskaram, swami. Will you please go hunting tonight?"

"We will take rest tonight and go tomorrow" Father said.

"Last night one of the village goats was killed by a tiger. We knew you were coming to-day so have set up the kill and wish you to come and sit watch with us to-night."

I could see that father was interested. After a moment's consideration he said. "In that case I'll come tonight."

"Daddy, please let me go too." I asked.

I'd gone hunting with father many times but mainly in the early evening looking for hare or sambar. I'd never gone to wait for a tiger to appear at its kill.

Father was silent. I held my breath.

"Please Father." I begged again.

"All right, you may come."

Just then my mother appeared in the doorway. "Food is ready. Will you eat?"

My Father said he would take food and turned again to the men. "At what time do you wish to start?"

"You say, swami."

"We'll be ready in an hour. Come again then."

We went inside and seated ourselves. Mother and Father sat at a small table while we children sat on mats against one wall. Father led family prayers then our cook, Danam, helped the matey serve us.

I heard father telling mother what was planned.

Mother said. "Do you think he is old enough to go with you? It may be dangerous!"

I strained to hear father's reply as I continued to eat as though unconcerned.

"Yes, I think he's responsible enough and he can handle a gun."

I sighed with relief and felt a surge of pride. I mustn't let Father down.

Suddenly the excitement killed my hunger.

"May I go and get ready father?"

"No! You haven't eaten your food."

"I'm not hungry."

"You must eat for we may be out all night and you'll be hungry later."

I took a handful of rice and began eating as quickly as possible.

As we came from the lighted room on to the verandah the dark of the night was so intense it seemed to advance to engulf us.

Mother handed me a cloth bag containing a brass chembu of lime juice and a brass tiffin carrier full of savoury chakli.

"Take these, nayana, you may need them during the night. And be careful."

"I will Mummy."

Father handed me the single-barrelled gun and kept the double-barrelled himself. Three men were there waiting, the light from the room dimly reflected from their white clothes. Father carried his long-barrelled torch and without a word we set out.

I walked behind father, often stumbling over rocks or roots hidden from me by his shadow.

"We must reach our hide before the moon rises." Father said.

We hurried on through the night which was strangely silent except for the occasional "chee, chee" of a cicada or the rustle of some small animal as it fled from our path.

The men had chosen a very large rock as our perch. It towered above me. They used their hands as footsteps to heave Father upwards. He was quite heavily built and they began to sweat as he searched for a handhold to help himself.

I was pushed up next, an easier task, and then we helped the men.

The rough warm rock under us felt friendly to our touch while a cool breeze fanned our faces, welcome after the hot day.

A whispered conversation ensued as it was agreed father would have the first shot, then I could fire, followed by the men.

I peered into the darkness in the direction the men indicated but could see nothing.

After a few minutes wait the outline of trees began to grow clearer and I looked behind us to see the first glow of the moon as it rose above the horizon.

Gradually the clearing in front of us was filled with light and I could see the black and white hair of the dead goat lying on the track at the edge of the clearing.

We made our guns ready and waited there without a word or movement for the rock did not give much room. It seemed like hours. I must have nodded off into half sleep as I sat, to come suddenly wide awake in response to a tenseness in my companions.

I saw the tiger standing in the track in half shadow, swinging its tail from side to side, its head held proudly. As it took two paces forward father fired and I followed. It leapt forward and fell. The last two shots were not needed.

In my excitement I dropped the bag mother had given me and it fell with a clatter to the ground. We descended quickly from the rock and approached the still form. It looked very dead, but father had always impressed on us the need for caution. It was dead!

One man had a 'mattsu' and quickly cut a stout sapling while the other approached father. "Please give me your torchlight, Swami. I'll cut some vines."

In no time he was back and the men lashed the tiger's feet securely to the pole, then we sat down, drank the lime juice and ate the chakli before the men heaved the pole to their shoulders with some difficulty and we set off for the village feeling very pleased with ourselves.

Dawn was about to break as we approached. Cattle tethered near the first hut caught the scent of the tiger, swished their tails, rolled their eyes and swung their rumps in an attempt to face us but their heads were pulled up sharply by their nose ropes and they had to be content with breathing heavily to show their alarm.

Ahead of us the village street was quiet, even the cocks waiting for that first light. A 'pi' dog barked and along the street a door opened and a man stepped out, clasping his 'chembu'{small pot} on his way to the fields to squat.

When he saw us approaching he stopped.

"Praise the Lord, you've shot the tiger." He shouted. "The tiger is dead."

Doors began to open and sleepy figures emerged, re-tying their loincloths or re-pleating a sari to tuck in ready for a new day.

"Now we don't need to fear for our sheep or our cattle."

"That's a good job you've done, Swami."

Everyone felt elated.

"Please take breakfast with us." Several people invited us.

But Father said "Thank you, we are tired, we'll return to the T.B. and take rest."

The shikari said "Swami, we'll bring the tiger to the bungalow."

"No, you keep it and send me the skin." Father was only interested in the skin and knew the men would be able to sell parts of the body to the soothsayer and some for ayurvedic medicine.

The rest of the family were still sleeping when we reached the bungalow but Danam and the matey were in the kitchen, the matey blowing a hesitant flame in the fireplace while Danam kneaded dough for chapathi.

"Did you get the tiger, swami?"

"Yes, we did and the villagers are celebrating."

"Was it a big one?"

"A very big one." I said proudly.

"Quite big! The men will bring the skin here and then you can take it to the tanners in Chikka. It will make a good rug."

"Babu must be tired! I'll make hot milk and bring it to you."

I had been so elated at helping to shoot the tiger that I hadn't felt tired at all but now the feeling of excitement was replaced by a satisfied glow and I realised I was ready for sleep.

Danam soon produced the milk which Father and I drank in companionable silence. Then I crawled into bed and was soon asleep, not even disturbed by the talk of Chichu and the girls when they wakened.

I finally roused to the sound of voices on the verandah and went out to investigate.

The shikaris who had gone hunting with us had brought the skin. They unrolled it and held it up for us. It was beautifully marked and some six feet long without the tail.

Father examined it carefully. "You have made a good job of skinning it. There is no blemish!"

"No swami, your shot hit it in the centre of its chest and we cut it at that point."

"Thammu, go and ask Danam to bring salt."

Only one shot, I thought with disappointment as I went out to the back porch and called across to the kitchen.

"Anna".

Danam appeared in the kitchen doorway.

"The men have brought the skin and father wants you to come and bring salt."

Danam disappeared into the kitchen and reappeared with a newspaper poke of salt.

"I bought extra salt this morning when I went into the village."

We joined them on the verandah.

Father said "Put plenty of salt on the skin and roll it up or it will go bad in this heat."

We all watched Danam sprinkle the salt and rub it in. As he rubbed, the sweat formed glistening beads on his forehead which dropped with a splat on to the skin.

He rolled it up and secured it with a piece of twine.

"Take it down to the tanners and ask them to tan it well. I would like to give it as a gift to Mr. and Mrs. Cox when they go on furlough." The shikaris made their farewells and Danam disappeared down the road.

Mother had spread mats for the younger children while she and father sat in deck chairs.

No one felt like doing anything. The heat seemed to dominate our thoughts as we sat dangling our legs over the verandah which was partly shaded by trees. Not a whisper of breeze stirred the leaves and the midday hush was broken only by the mournful 'tonk,tonk' of a rainbird. I looked and there he was, a tiny figure high in a nearby fig tree.

"Do you think it's going to rain father?"

"The rainbird seems to think so!"

"Oh, I've heard the rainbird for days and it still hasn't rained." I felt sceptical.

Kanya said "Let's go down to the tank later and try to catch some crabs. Amma, are there any bones?"

"No, the only meat we have is what is left of the vindaloo and we can't buy meat here." Mother said.

"Crabs won't eat cooked meat." said Chichu.

Father said "Why don't you go fishing? You could dig some yabbies to use for bait. But you can't go in this heat."

"If we shoot a hare we can keep some for crab bait."

My younger sisters had some jack bones and were absorbed in their game, we watched them idly until the matey came to the door and said "Food is ready, Amma. Will you eat?"

"Yes." said Mother, and we all rose and went inside.

Chapter 5

By four o'clock the sun was lower and we could walk on the bare earth without burning our feet. We took our fishing lines and set out for the house of our friend, the Reddy's, to see if we could borrow a spade.

As we entered the courtyard of their house Reddy was sitting crosslegged on a stone slab bench under a drumstick tree reading the paper.

"Namaskaram, Anna."

"Namaskaram! How are your mother and father?"

"They are well, anna."

"Please come in and sit down."

He called to his wife "Amma, the doctor sahib's children are here."

His wife appeared and spread a mat.

"Mother asked me to give you these." I handed her the leaf-wrapped parcel of flowers. She made namaskaram.

"How are your mother and father?"

"They are well thank you."

We sat down. His two daughters appeared in the doorway and came to join us on the mat. We were anxious to go off to the tank but we knew that courtesy demanded we curb our impatience. While his wife supervised the preparation of coffee and opened a cupboard to take some rice, sesame and jaggery cakes from a jar, our friend enquired after the welfare of our family.

"Where are you going now?" our friend asked.

I seized the opportunity. "We are going fishing in the tank and would like to borrow a spade to dig yabbies."

"Good! I will give you one and you can use it while you are staying here. We won't be needing it until the rains come."

We finished our coffee and rice cakes and rose to our feet.

"Namaskaram ayya, we will go and come."

He called to a boy who was sitting in the courtyard. "Ganganna, bring a spade from the shed and give it to the young master. Here are the keys."

At last we were off. We took the track to the bank of the tank and walked along it, the bed of the tank stretched below us and as far as we could see was a huge expanse of cracked mud except for a deep hole near the outlet gate. We slithered down the steep bank and looked into the water. Small fish were swimming with an occasional larger fish moving among them, a swathe of silver opening out before them as the minnows fled from their path.

Kanya said "Look at those big ones, let's dig for yabbies quickly."

We chose a damp spot just above water level where some holes were visible in the sticky mud. I wielded the 'gadapara'.

"Dig quickly Thunnu or they'll get away."

"There's one," Chichu grabbed and dropped it into the empty coffee tin we'd brought for the purpose.

"Cover it with mud or it will jump out." Kanya said.

Too late, it was gone and we saw a fish make a dive as the yabbie tried to reach a muddy shelter.

I dug on and soon we had half a dozen yabbies and two small crabs.

"That will do" said Kanya "it will soon be dark."

We baited our hook and threw in the line. There was a tug and we landed a fair sized catfish. I stabbed it firmly to the ground with our knife while Chichu tried to remove the hook. We were cautious - the sharp points on either side of the head could inflict a nasty wound. No matter how hard Chichu tried he could not free the hook.

By this time the sun had sunk below the horizon.

"We must go back to the bungalow." said Kanya.

We did not argue. In our hearts none of us wanted to be caught by darkness still outside the village. I wound up the line and gingerly carried the fish dangling from the hook. It would provide a meal and we could use the skeleton to catch crabs next day,

We went crabbing, we swam in the muddy water of the tank, we rode Reddy's ponies and went hunting but the weather did not break.

The rainbird continued its maddening 'tonk, tonk' and we spent the heat of the day indoors.

"Bird, you don't know what you are talking about! There's not a sign of rain." I scolded it.

But one morning as we were returning from a hunting trip we saw black clouds gathering on the horizon and by the time we had eaten our midday meal the sky was obscured by billowing storm clouds. The mynahs began to quarrel noisily over perching places in the huge fig trees, perhaps thinking night was about to fall. The fallen leaves began to rise and whirl in little eddies as gusts of wind rose and fell.

We gathered on the verandah in excited anticipation. The sweat prickling under our shirts. The mali was on the roof making a last minute attempt to clean the leaves out of the guttering.

"Thunnu, Chichu, empty the leaves out of the banas, make sure they are under the downpipes" father said.

We struggled to move the big earthenware pots so that they would catch every drop. We could smell the pungent aroma of rain on dry earth, then we heard the roar of it approaching over the parched fields and hills. The first drops fell sounding single blows on the roof - a flash of lightning made us flinch, then a crack of thunder and the storm broke - the rain teemed down.

"Come on" Kanya said and danced out into it. We followed.

We climbed in turn into the bana and stood under the stream of water from the downpipe, luxuriating in the cold freshness on our hot skins. We were so intoxicated with delight that the thunder and lightning crashing and flashing about us only added to our excitement and we had no fear.

As the rain lost it's intensity we realised mother was calling us. "Come inside and take off those wet clothes."

We stopped dancing around and realised we were beginning to feel quite cold for the temperature had fallen dramatically.

Danam had had the presence of mind to bring our drums of bathwater in out of the sun and put them in the padded baskets in the bathrooms. We poured the hot water over one another, towelled ourselves and put on clean clothes.

The air was now soft and balmy and seemed to caress us as we went, once again, to sit on the verandah.

Already the dusk was filled with a cacophony of croaks as the frogs emerged from their summer entombment and began the urgent business of calling for mates.

That night as mother came to kiss us in our beds we curled up snugly under our blankets and listened to the screech owls calling as they too rejoiced in the surge of new life.

By the time we returned to Chikka a few days later we were moving through a different landscape. The villagers' holiday season was over. Farmers who owned their own oxen were out in the fields guiding the sharp wooden ploughs as they bit into the red earth. The caw-caw of the crows and noisy chatter of blue jays could be heard as they followed behind, gleaning worms and insects.

The red of the newly ploughed fields made a patchwork held together by the green of grassy banks interspersed with yellow-brown boulders.

It was almost time for the new school year to begin. As we travelled back to Chikka in our carts we passed groups of children hurling stones into the tall mango trees by the roadside to knock down the green fruit. They were very sour but good to eat in the eyes of children and not many of these roadside fruit reached maturity, for what the children didn't eat, the monkeys and parrots consumed.

Chapter 6

Kanya and I looked forward to the rainy season with mixed feelings for we were both asthmatic.

After the holidays we were eager for school. Kanya was already attending High School in the town but Chichu and I walked each morning, our cloth bags containing our books, slung over our shoulders. As we approached the tank which stretched between the Gauribidanur road and the Palya(outcaste quarters) I said "Look Chichu, they are trying to get the last of the bricks out of the tank before more rain falls."

We stopped to watch the men encouraging the oxen to pull the heavy brickladen carts out of the muddy tank bed.

Chichu and I stood watching as the men tugged and shouted to encourage the oxen straining to pull the heavy carts to firm ground. We forgot time until rudely reminded by the distant ringing of the school bell.

"Come on, we'll be late!"

We ran as fast as we could and slipped panting, and as unobtrusively as possible, into the ranks of children lined up and already singing "God save the King" as the Union Jack was raised.

The headmaster conducted prayers, and reminded us that we must buy our new text books by the end of the week then we marched into class.

First lesson was always arithmetic and we spent the first ten minutes reciting the multiplication tables from one to sixteen in unison. As our voices rose and fell our teacher tapped the desk in time with his ruler. I watched his tall well-built figure anxiously. Was he like our teacher last year whose short temper matched his stature and whose round form could easily be recognised at a sideways glance by his striped underknickers showing through his fine white pancha tied Telugu style? He had an unnerving habit of prowling around the room and tapping hard the legs of anyone whose attention wandered.

The tables finished "Take out your slates!"

There was a scuffling as thirty children reached into their bags for their slates and pencils.

Mental arithmetic was next, each small sum being rattled off fast and followed by "Pencils down, hands away!" Any laggard would be likely to feel the ruler across his knuckles.

I was always relieved when this was over and we could do some sums which Sir wrote on the board.

As I sat in class on the wooden bench which four of us shared, my mind wandered to the football which we would be commencing this term. What sort of team could we muster to play against the other schools in the town? I could move quickly but was rather small and light for football, maybe I would get a place on the wing.

My thoughts were rudely interrupted by the sarcastic voice of my teacher. "Mr.Sabhapathy - no doubt you have finished those sums!"

"No sir!" I realised I'd hardly begun.

"Get to work then or you can spend the lunch hour here until they are finished."

I put my head down and got to work.

The bell went and English lesson commenced.

"Take out your exercises and write the story of your holidays. Use your pens."

We looked in our inkwells. They were empty. "Please sir, the inkwells are empty."

"Very well then, use pencil today but we will elect monitors now and they can fill the inkwells at lunchtime."

I found myself elected with one of my friends. It did not really matter for most of us had a turn but I had been looking forward to talking to friends this first lunch hour.

When the bell went Danam was waiting outside with our food in a brass tiffin carrier and water in a chembu on the handlebars of his cycle.

Chichu went up to him.

"Where's Thammu?" Danam asked.

Just then I came across "I have to fill the inkwells. I won't be long."

That done we too were off, down to a tree near the tank where we usually ate our lunch.

Many of the children attending the school came from the outcaste quarters surrounding it. In most cases, if their parents had work, they ate their main meal of the day before coming to school. Now their parents were out doing labour in the fields or town, or cutting firewood in the hills, and the houses were locked. Groups of them were playing marbles in the street in front of the school.

We had early breakfast as father was at hospital by 7:30 am for morning prayers and did not have time to come home during the morning except for a quick glass of lime juice and a smoke.

Chichu had waited until we arrived. We opened the brass tiffin carrier and divided the contents between the four tiers. There were usually others to share our lunch which today was of rice and split pea curry with some lime pickle for extra flavour.

The tamarind trees at the edge of the tank gave good shade but we had to watch for monkeys. More than once in the past a large monkey had come down quickly and silently and snatched food from our hands. Today there were no tamarind fruit but the tree was a beautiful sight, covered with fresh light green leaves and pale honey-coloured flowers, the scent of nectar heavy on the air.

Prasad said "Anna, give me a leg up into the tree - Amma asked me to bring home some fresh flowers and shoots to put in our dhal curry this evening."

I leant against the massive trunk, my cheek and arm pressed to the rough bark while he used my shoulder as a foothold to reach the first branch. He had to climb high to pluck the tender leaves which he pushed into the pocket of his pants.

"The curry did not have much taste this morning, these will improve it." he said as he leapt down and landed at our feet.

Prasad lived with his parents and five brothers and sisters in the palya. His father was the Church peon, so received a regular salary, but it was barely enough to feed his family.

Just then Danam rode up. "Have you finished your food?"

"Yes, anna." We handed him the empty tiffin carrier and chembu, and he slipped them on to the handlebars of the cycle to join the cloth bags of provisions already hanging there.

"Amma said to come straight home from school."

"We will."we replied. Our idea of going straight home from school was not always the same as mother's.

I felt thirsty, for the day was hot. "Let's go and get a drink from the well."

We set off towards the school house. The peon was drawing water from the well and as he drew each brass pot a row of cupped hands were waiting. We took our places among the other children and held out our hands. When our turn came the water was cool and sweet.

"Anna, anna, a little more please." One drink was not enough to quench our thirst.

The peon, a tall, thin, slightly stooped man with hollow cheeks and a drooping moustache, was good natured and drew pot after pot of water, filling the hands in front of him.

There was the bell! Most of the boys hastily wiped their faces on the tails of their shirts. Mother always sent us to school supplied with clean handkerchiefs which we now used as we ran to line up.

Afternoon school was more enjoyable as we had either science, history or geography. I liked science best and hoped we would have science today. But no! It was geography so I settled myself to look interested and avoid undue attention until the bell rang.

Mother had given us each 10 paisa so we called at the 'petty' shop outside Gopal's temple and bought some puffed dhal.

We walked over to the huge arched doorway into the temple courtyard. Just then three women dressed in colourful saris came along. We smelt the flowers in their hair as they stopped near us to leave their sandals before entering the temple.

"Boys, look after our sandals for us while we are inside." The oldest woman told us.

"All right amma, we will".

Each woman carried a brass plate containing a coconut, some flowers and some coloured pigment.

They crossed the courtyard to the inner shrine and we peered in but could only see their shadowy forms in the dim light in contrast to the bright sunlight pouring into the courtyard.

We heard the sound of the gong as they summoned God to the shrine to listen to their prayers.

We sat on the ledge at the base of the pillars eating our puffed dhal.

They soon reappeared, their brass plates empty but for the pigment which had been blessed, put on their sandals then handed us each five paisa.

We put our hands together in namaskaram and watched them go.

"Shall we buy some peanuts?" said Chichu.

"No, let's keep it until tomorrow, and buy some on the way home then."

Just across from the towering Gopuram of the temple where pigeons fought for nesting places among the carvings, was a blacksmith's shop.

The blacksmith was working the bellows hard as we approached and we stopped to watch the piece of iron above the fire become red then white with heat. Even our faces glowed although we were several feet away.

At last the heat was right and the blacksmith pulled it out with his tongs, put it on a low anvil and beat it hard with a huge sledge hammer. The tail of the towel wrapped around his head turbanwise slapped his neck with each blow and his powerful muscles glistened with sweat. In no time the lump of iron was flattened.

"What's he making?" asked Chichu.

"It's a reaping hook."

A couple more bangs and on to the fire it went again, to become malleable enough to be shaped further.

"We'd better go or mother will be angry" I said.

Mother was angry.

"Where have you been? I told Danam to tell you to come straight home."

"We did mother, we just bought some 'pappulu' and watched the blacksmith for a few minutes." We did not mention the paisa we'd earned watching the sandals. Mother, we felt, would not have approved.

Mother was feeding the baby, Nani, some soft rice and dhal. We watched her mixing it, deftly forming it into a ball with her fingers and popping it into Nani's mouth.

"Go and do your homework, then you can go out to play." "Danam" she called, "the boys are home, make them some lime juice."

That night after I went to bed, it rained, and before long, as the temperature dropped, I found myself gasping for breath. It had happened before but I always found it frightening.

Mother came out to see whether we were warm enough. "Here, put this sweater on. I will call your father."

Father came and gave me a tablet but I didn't have much sleep until finally at dawn I dozed off.

Mother did not wake me and when I finally stirred and looked about the sun was high.

I ran into the dining hall "Mummy, why didn't you wake me?"

"You didn't have much sleep last night and it won't hurt you to miss a day's school."

I didn't really mind and settled down to read.

This seemed to happen too often and father was worried by it. He discussed it with Dr. Thompson.

"Why not send him to boarding school in Mysore next year?" Dr. Thompson said.

"That would be expensive" father said. "I doubt if we could afford it."

"The fees are not high, the main costs would be shoes and extra clothing."

One night as we sat on the front verandah after taking food, father, as was his custom, smoking a cigarette, said, as though talking to himself "Perhaps I should have gone to Hyderabad after all."

"What do you mean, father?" I asked.

"When your younger brother Noel was two years old I wrote to the Medical Department of the Nizam of Hyderabad applying for a position."

"Why did you do that, I thought you loved the hospital and the work here?"

"Yes, I do but the salary is very low and I'd heard from a number of people that the Nizam paid very good salaries. I had a family to support and thought we could do very well there."

"What happened then? Why didn't you go?"

"Before I received a reply to my application your brother Noel became ill and we realised he had diphtheria, we couldn't save him, he died within two days. I decided then that it was not the will of God for me to go to Hyderabad and when a letter came a few days later offering me a position, I wrote and said I had changed my mind."

"What did my mother say to that?" I asked.

Your mother was happy with the decision, she always said "I am relying on Jesus, my stay, to provide." She always hoped you would become a pastor. She chose the name Sabhapathy for you hoping that you would indeed become a 'leader of the congregation'.

I pondered father's words on more than one occasion.

Chapter 7

Some weeks later I was sitting at the table in the dining hall doing my homework when father came in from the hospital. He put his hand on my shoulder "Thammu, I have good news, you will be going to Hardwick High School in Mysore next year; I've had a letter today from the school manager accepting my application."

I looked up. "Where will I be living?"

"There is a boarding school residence not very far from the school where a lot of the students live. You'll stay there and walk to school each day. You'll need to pass Grade 7 this year to enter the high school but I'm sure you'll do that."

"Yes daddy."

Father went to bathe before taking his food and I sat, my mind a welter of conflicting emotions. I couldn't concentrate on my homework and finally went to bed after completing the bare essentials in a rather scrappy manner.

As the time for going to school in Mysore drew nearer, father came in one day and said "Dr. Thompson says the car must go into Bangalore for 'overoiling' next week and he suggested I take you in to buy a tin trunk, new school bag and shoes"

At 6am, a few days later, father and I were ready waiting. I thought how nice he looked in his white pancha, tied Telugu style, grey jacket and white silk turban threaded with gold. I felt proud to be his son."

Samuel, our hospital driver, drew up outside our gate in the Ford. I had the day off school and had wakened in time to hear the muezzin being called from the mosque down the road.

Miss Fear, the Nursing Superintendent, was already seated in the car, she was going into Bangalore to buy cloth and equipment for the hospital. It was cooler travelling at that time of day although the sun was already fairly high. Samanna was anxious to travel well ahead of the train for if we were held up at the first level crossing we would have to stop at each of the next six before reaching Bangalore.

As we approached the city the carts became more numerous and Samanna had to keep his hand on the rubber bulb of the horn. Some of the drivers were still asleep on the carts and rose hastily at the sound but the oxen were already pulling to the side of the road.

Miss Fear said "Samuel, drop me off at Mrs. Cox's bungalow in Mission road. When do you expect the car to be ready?"

"Four or five hours, amma."

"Then I'll wait for you at the bungalow to take me to pick up goods and make any purchases I haven't had time for."

"Yes, amma."

"Where would you like to be dropped off, Doctorgaru?"

"We'll get down at the bungalow with Sisteramma, it's only a short walk down to Chickpet from there."

"Right, Sir."

As we drove in through the gateway of the bungalow the brilliant crimson sprays of Bouganvillea spilled over the portico. We pulled up in its shade.

Mrs. Cox came out to greet us. "This is a pleasant surprise!" She kissed Miss Fear. "You must have left early - come in and take coffee."

Samuel opened the car door for Miss Fear. The gardener was watering, moving from plant to plant, lowering the pot from his shoulder and breaking the force of the stream with his hand. Samuel called to him.

"Josephanna, come and take Miss Fear's bags inside."

The gardener put his brass pot to the ground, came forward, put his hands together in greeting, gathered Miss Fear's numerous empty bags and followed the ladies into the house.

Father said to Samuel "Don't wait for us, we'll walk from here after taking coffee."

Samuel disappeared around the corner of the house, probably to take coffee with the cook and other house servants. We went inside.

I'd been to Mrs. Cox's house a few times. The teak and rosewood furniture always gleamed with polish and even the unglazed earthenware tiles on the floor were polished, unlike those in the bungalow at Chikka. The bookshelves full of books fascinated me, and I moved over to read some of the titles.

Mrs. Cox returned to the room. "I hear you are going to Boarding school in Mysore, Thammu? Are you looking forward to that?"

"Yes, amma" I said. I didn't feel like elaborating on any of my inner doubts.

After we'd had coffee father rose "We will take leave, amma. We are going down to Chickpet to do our shopping."

We both made Namaskaram.

As we walked down the driveway from the porch the petunias and zinnias in the flowerbeds were in marked contrast to the dried up brown of the lawn. Joseph, the gardener, was dipping his pot into the small granite slab water tank filled by the one tap on the compound.

We crossed Mission Road, dodging between oxcarts, jutkas and rickshaws. Cars were still a comparatively rare sight, especially down towards the old city where we were headed. They could be heard approaching some distance away as the drivers blew their horns to clear a path before them.

Father walked fast, he was a big man and I had no time to look around if I wanted to keep up with him. I would have liked to dawdle as there was so much to see. We passed a large shop stacked from floor to ceiling with aluminium ware - plates, small pots, cooking vessels - some large enough for me to hide in. By the time we reached the beginning of Chickpet I was out of breath.

The narrow street leading down to the main shopping centre in Chickpet was still relatively quiet as the shops were just beginning to take down their heavy wooden shutters to commence the day's trading.

A call of "Dowa! Dowa!" behind us made me jump to one side as a man straining at the crosspiece of a giant barrow struggled past.

Father said "Keep to the side, Thammu. It makes the work for a cart-puller much harder if he has to slow down - getting up speed again takes a lot of effort". He was a drink seller pushing his stall to its daily position. It was laden with large pots of water, a basket of limes, some bottles of brightly coloured liquid and a small container of seeds.

We turned down the main bazaar road. It was equally narrow and full of all kinds of traffic - handcarts, jutkas, oxcarts, rickshaws, cycles; with pedestrians dodging in and out.

As we passed a cloth shop a hand-drawn rickshaw pulled up. The puller, dressed in snow-white loincloth and shirt, with a turban on his head, lowered the shafts gently and stepped back to help the passenger out. She was a beautifully dressed lady in a green silk sari with wide gold border, carrying a green silk parasol to match. The rickshaw too was no ordinary one, but was painted in red and gold and upholstered in red and gold satin. The lady stepped out daintily and walked into the shop.

I was so busy staring at this unusual sight that when I looked for father he'd disappeared.

I ran on along the street trying to catch a glimpse of him and soon saw his white silk turban ahead among the crowd.

"Did you see that rickshaw daddy?"

"No!"

"It was brightly painted, and a beautiful lady stepped out of it."

"It was probably her own private rickshaw," father said "many wealthy people in Bangalore have their own rickshaws and men to pull them, then they can use them whenever they wish and have no fear of getting their clothes soiled or being bitten by bugs or lice."

We purchased a trunk and padlock then cloth for shirts and short pants but when we asked for shoes they were nowhere to be found. Even the Bata shoe store had adult men's shoes but none for boys.

"For shoes you must go to the Cantonment sir, there is no demand here."

"We will need to go to the Cantonment then, Thammu" father said.

"What's the Cantonment Daddy?"

"That's the shopping area near the Cantonment Army Barracks and parade ground. It's the part of the city which was built on by the British when they took over India. We'll go to Commercial Street, we're sure to be able to buy them there."

As we left the shop a rickshaw was passing slowly. "Rickshaw!" Father called. The rickshaw wallah did a swirling turn and pulled up in front of us, "Cantonment! Commercial Street! How much?" Father asked.

"One rupee, sir"

"You're joking! Four annas!"

The coolie laughed in disdain "Eight annas swami"

"Six annas" Father said.

The coolie waved his hand towards the canopy-covered seat and tucked the ends of his loin cloth more firmly into his waist. We climbed in and he picked up the shafts.

We turned the corner and the rickshaw wallah ran down the hill to gain some momentum for the uphill pull. As we climbed the rise he leant forward between the shafts and his neck and shoulder muscles bunched with the strain. As I watched him straining up the hill towards the corporation offices I felt some embarrassment sitting there, but soon we were on the level again, jogging along.

After we left the old city, the streets became broad and tree-lined. A row of huge "Pride of India" trees in full bloom lined one side of the road, with green grass and trees stretching as far as I could see. We turned right along South Parade with the parade ground on our left. I was fascinated by rows of mounted cavalry drilling in the sun. Their horses looked much larger than the ponies we rode at Peresandra. "Look at those beautiful horses, daddy, their coats shine almost as much as the brass buckles on the girths."

We went down hill to Commercial Street. By this time it was full of people. I'd never seen so many Europeans in my life before. "Daddy, why are there so many white people here?"

"This is where the Europeans do their shopping."

"But why are they here?"

"They are mostly wives of army officers, the people who run Binnys cotton mills and other big companies. They buy most of their clothes here and I think it becomes almost a social event."

"What does that mean?"

"They meet their friends, go and have coffee and cake together and probably gossip."

There were also a lot of poorly-dressed children. I saw them go up to the ladies, hold out their hands and say "Paisa, memsahib!" Down here they did not come to us. I noticed one of the women shook her head and said "Go away child!" but another felt in her handbag and put a small coin into the grimy outstretched hand. The boy ran off but the gift was not unnoticed, and as that lady moved up the street a crowd of little urchins dogged her heels.

After we'd made our purchases Father said "We'll walk to market square and have some lunch then go to the bungalow to catch Miss Fear."

When we reached the square we dodged across, avoiding jutkas and rickshaws and entered a restaurant over the door of which a crescent moon on a green background indicated that Muslim food would be served.

We sat at a small table. "What would you like Thammu? Biriyani or chicken curry with naan?"

"I'll have Biriyani." It was one of my favourite dishes.

Two steaming plates of Biriyani soon arrived each accompanied by a saucerful of chopped onion, tomato, and chilli. The delicious smell of chicken, cooked in spices with rice, filled the restaurant and I set to with enjoyment.

When we'd eaten father said "It's only twelve-thirty, we don't want to arrive at the bungalow while they are still at lunch. Come, we'll go and see what animals they have for sale."

We crossed the road to the meat market where large pieces of beef hung on hooks above huge chopping blocks. The Muslim butchers were calling out the merits of their cuts of beef to attract the attention of each approaching purchaser.

We walked down a narrow covered alley and came upon a number of stalls. We were greeted by cries from the stall-mongers.

"Lock, sahib, baby mynah, buy it for the babu and teach it to talk."

The young mynah hopped and flew, beating its wings against the bars of its small bamboo cage.

I had hardly seen it when my attention was drawn to the next stall where two tiny little animals sat huddled together on the floor of a cage, their arms around each other like small lost children.

"Oh, look at those baby monkeys, father!"

"They are not monkeys, Thammu, they're bush babies." (Slow Loris)

"Make lovely pet, sahib." The stall-monger said.

He reached into the cage, lifted one out and said "Come and hold it, Babu. Feel it's soft fur!"

I took it in my hand. Its small body was quivering with fear. "Daddy, can we buy them? I'll look after them."

"No, Thammu - you're off to boarding school - besides they need a big cage and special food. Rover and Rocket would soon kill them if we weren't very careful."

Another stall had a small black monkey which stared at us with bright inquisitive eyes.

"What about the Mynah, Daddy? The others would look after it and teach it to talk. Please! Dathi would love it!"

Father weakened "How much is the Mynah?"

My heart jumped with excitement and I examined the timid creature fluttering in its cage. I heard father say "How much is that larger cage?"

Soon a bargain was struck, the mynah transferred to the bigger cage and I took the handle, its proud owner.

"Don't let the bird free outside, swami, the wild birds will kill it."

We stopped at one of the butcher's tables. "Give us ten paisa worth of mince" father said. The butcher picked up a couple of meat scraps, chopped it into small pieces and wrapped it in a piece of paper.

"It's probably hungry - we can give it some meat on the way home. You'll all have to catch insects for it."

We walked out into the bright sunlight of the square and father hailed a rickshaw.

We climbed in and I held the cage tightly as we were pulled back to the bungalow. We were just in time, Miss Fear was just climbing into the Ford.

As I got out of the rickshaw with the cage Miss Fear said "What have you got there, Thammu?"

"It's a baby mynah, we're going to teach it to talk."

"Oh, your brothers and sisters will enjoy that!"

Samanna said "You'll need to catch grasshoppers and ants for it to eat."

"We'll do that. Don't you think Dathi will like it?" I was very fond of my baby sister.

As we drove down to the city to do more shopping I was oblivious of my surroundings as I said to the Mynah, over and over again, 'Good morning Dathi' and fed it small pieces of meat I managed to pull through a hole I'd made in the paper.

At last, as the shops began to light up, our purchases were complete, my blue trunk safely tied to the boot rack. We made our way slowly, with much blowing of the horn, through the busy streets, filled with people doing their evening shopping.

Once out on the north road the traffic was sparse, our headlights making a hole through the avenue of roadside trees which swished past, their limbs stretched across our heads like the arms of great spectres of the night.

Bird, I noticed, was asleep - and very soon I joined him, to awaken as we pulled up outside our gate.

Chapter 8

The day I was to leave for Mysore we were all up early. Mother called to me.

"Thammu, Danam is busy in the kitchen so you will need to pack your bedding."

"Yes Mother."

"Remember to take a blanket from the almirah, you may not need it now but you will as soon as the rains come. Spread your bed sheet, blanket and dzumkhana on your bedding roll and tuck your pillow in the end."

"Kanyakka, please come and help me roll my bedding tightly."

We took the end together and knelt on it as we rolled it up. Kanya balanced on top of it to keep it tight. I pulled the straps suddenly and Kanya rolled backwards on to the floor, the roll unwinding behind her. She grabbed a cushion from a chair and chased me around the room beating me on the head. Mother stood in the doorway. "The jutka will be here in a minute. If you aren't ready you'll miss the train."

Laughing and shouting at each other we pulled the two straps tight around the bundle.

Nani came running in "Amma the jutka is here."

I went to the door and looked out, the jutka wallah pulled some grass from beneath the dzumkhana covering the floor of the cart and gave it to the pony to munch.

Danam picked up my trunk and I took my bedding roll. Its awkward weight bumped against my leg at every step. I stopped on the verandah and went back to make namaskaram to mother. I felt very grown up. Mother and then my sisters kissed me.

"Hurry up, we will miss the train." father called.

Danam came back to take the bedding roll and speed my departure. Father was already seated at the back of the pony cart, his legs dangling.

"Come to the front for balance, Babu" the jutka wallah called me, so I climbed up beside him.

As the jutka wallah cracked his whip and told the pony to chirruk, chirruk, we set off looking back and waving to the assembled family.

This June morning the rains had not yet come but the trees were clothed in all their glory - bright red gul mohar (Delonix regia), mauve jacarandas, pink cassias and the creamy powder puff blossoms on the rain trees.

My father was known to everyone in the town and the station master asked "Where are you going Doctorgaru?"

"My son is going to high school in Mysore." father said.

I felt that a new page had been turned in my life.

The little train was at the station the engine blowing off a blast of steam. We travelled first class and had the compartment to ourselves. Bangalore was only thirty-five miles from Chikka by road but the journey took four and a half hours, so father had come prepared with some medical journals and a book to read. I was happy to look out the window - I had rarely travelled to Bangalore.

The Station Master rang the bell, then the guard blew his whistle and the train pulled slowly from the station. I put my head out the window. There was a man clinging to the side of the train, a tray of bananas balanced on his head.

"Father, look at that fellow, I hope he doesn't fall." Father, immersed in his medical journal, grunted in reply.

I watched the banana seller put his tray of bananas in through a window then climb in after it. A moment later the door to our compartment opened and a blind man led by a young girl, appeared. The girl began to sing a cinema song accompanying it with vigorous beating on a tambourine. Father felt in his pocket and gave them five paisa. They moved on.

Soon a boy with a tray containing peanuts and roasted peas appeared. He held a small tin measure.

"Five paisa sir" he said, indicating the measure.

"No, we don't want any." father said.

By this time the train had passed the first level crossing with a warning blast on its whistle. The gateman was beside the gates waiting to open them and let the traffic through as soon as we'd passed. Two oxcarts piled high with bags of potatoes or perhaps onions, waited. The drivers roused from a doze as we passed, for the gateman had probably shut the gates too soon.

By this time we had left behind the market gardens around Chikka and dry fields stretched on either side broken only by the line of trees which marked the Bangalore road and in the distance towering shapes of Kalawara and Nandi Hills rising two thousand feet from the plateau.

The train ambled along on the narrow gauge track,the engine puffing mightily to go up each rise then running on the down grade with a relieved che, che, che, che, che and occasional blast on the whistle to warn cattle or local herdsmen off the track.

As we approached Devanahalli the old walls of the little town loomed into view.

"Father, why does Devanahalli have such strong walls?" I asked.

"Surely you've been taught in your history lessons that this was the birthplace of the famous Muslim warrior, Tippu Sultan."

"No, we only learn English History but now I remember you showed us where he threw his prisoners from the top of Nandi Hill but I didn't know he was born here."

"His father Hyder Ali defended Devanahalli against the British soldiers. It was during that siege that his son Tippu was born."

I looked at the huge blocks of rock of which the walls were built. They were still as strong as ever in spite of some small trees struggling to gain a roothold in the crevices between the stones.

When we reached Bangalore father said "We'll check your 'saaman' into left luggage for the day, Thammu, I have some Hospital shopping to do and our train doesn't leave until 10-40 pm. Do you want to come with me or stay at one of the Bungalows - I'm sure Mrs. Cox or Miss Butler would not mind if you spent the day there."

"I'll come with you, Daddy." I wasn't in the city often enough to be bored with the sights.

When we reached the station after our day's shopping, it was a hive of activity and we went straight to the luggage office to reclaim our bags.

We had reserved intermediate class sleepers so did not need to fight for a place. We soon found our compartment, a six berth one, already occupied by a lady and gentleman whose box was labelled in bold letters, Brahmacharya. We identified our two sleeping berths.

"Can I sleep in the top one Daddy?"

"Yes, you may, but don't have a nightmare and fall off."

This train was rarely crowded, we discovered, as it took six hours to travel the 80 miles; delivering mail, parcels and picking up milk and fresh vegetables for Mysore city en route.

It suited us, for we spent a comfortable night on our bedding in the bunks and arrived in Mysore at 5:30 am with the day ahead of us.

Having settled our luggage and spread our bedding we sat on the lower bunk and exchanged greetings with our companions who were from Bombay travelling to Mysore for the wedding of one of the Maharaja's staff, a distant relative.

A man with a tray containing leaf-wrapped bundles of Biriyani stopped at the window. "Biriyani ,Sir?"

I realised I was hungry, we'd missed our evening meal.

"Please Daddy, may I have Biriyani?"

Father gave me a warning look as he glanced towards our companions. They were Jains, the very strictest of vegetarians who don't even eat after nightfall for fear of accidentally eating an insect. It would have been discourteous to eat meat in their presence.

"Go and wash your hands."

I went to the small toilet cubicle at the end of the compartment. When I returned father had bought two leaf packets of vegetarian pilau, spread the daily newspaper on the lower bunk and opened out the leaf plates. We excused ourselves to our travelling companions, turned away from them as far as possible, and enjoyed the spicy food.

Before we'd finished, the departure bell rang and the train moved slowly out of the station.

I lost no time in stretching out on my bedding in the upper berth. It had been a long day, and the sounds of Father conversing with our travelling companions soon drifted further and further away with the thump, thump, thump of the carriage wheels as sleep overcame me.

Chapter 9

"Wake up Thammu! Wake up!"

Where was I? It was father's voice. I sat up to the thud of wheels and rocking motion of the train.

"You'd better get up and wash. We are only 30 minutes out of Mysore."

A pale dawn had broken and the noise of the train wheels had become a low hollow sound. I looked out to see the boulder strewn bed of a river below us.

"What's that river, Daddy?"

"That's the Cauvery, it will become a raging torrent once the rains come. Look out to the left there and in a moment you'll see the Fort of Sri Ranga Patna(Seringapatan), another of Tippu's strongholds."

There it was, the massive walls surrounded by a moat - now grass-grown.

"I'd like to look inside those walls, Daddy. Do people still live there?"

"No, I don't think so. It's in ruins. We'll go and visit it one day when you have holidays. Now go and wash, we must roll up the bedding."

Our travelling companions were already seated, their bedding and baskets neatly arranged beside them. By the time I'd cleaned my teeth Father had the luggage strapped and we sat on the seat listening to the train crossing the points as it approached the station.

I remembered this was the day I'd been dreading. What was the High School going to be like and more important still, the boarding? I had a sinking sensation in the pit of my stomach.

When the train stopped, father engaged a coolie. "Restaurant!" he said.

"We'll go and have breakfast before going to the boarding."

The Indian style restaurant was not busy for most of the passengers had left for their various destinations in the city. A waiter came up with two glasses of water and wiped the marble-topped table with a damp and rather grubby cloth.

"What would you like sir?"

"How about iddli,Thammu?"

I nodded consent - somehow I didn't feel very hungry.

Within moments the waiter had returned with two plates each containing three steaming white iddli, some dhal sambar poured over them.

Father finished his iddli quickly.

"Come on Thammu, you usually eat more than three iddli. What's the matter?"

"I don't feel very hungry."

Father looked at me intently. "I'm sure you'll like the school. Everyone speaks well of it - you'll soon make friends."

A paper seller approached. "Deccan Herald sir?"

Father took 20 paisa from his pocket and gave it to the boy. The waiter brought two coffees and father became immersed in the paper as he drank.

I struggled to get my iddli past the lump in my throat. At last I wiped up the last of the sambar and poured water over my hand.

"Ready then?" Father put down the paper and signalled to the waiter for the chit. We rose and rejoined the coolie sitting with our luggage outside the door.

"Look at those jutkas, Father, they are quite different."

"They are called tongas here, Thammu, not jutkas."

A tonga-wallah, whip in hand, was eager for our custom and led us to his pony cart. These Mysore tongas were constructed on two levels with a capacious step each end to place our feet instead of leaving them dangling in mid air.

"Mission boarding!" Father said to the driver.

"They seem to go much faster too, Daddy" I said as we spun along the wide tree-lined streets, the bells on the pony's neck tinkling merrily. The city certainly looked attractive, lots of parks and flowering trees.

"Are those golden domes on the palace roof?"

"Yes, the Mysore Palace is a really beautiful one. The present Maharaja is also a very philanthropic man."

"What does that mean?"

"He's interested in supporting good causes. I believe he is the largest single subscriber to the London Symphony Orchestra. He's very fond of music."

The tonga slowed down as the driver pulled on the reins and turned in between whitewashed pillars marking the gateway in a long whitewashed wall. We came to a halt under the porch and I just managed to summon up enough strength to climb down from the cart. That sinking feeling was threatening to overwhelm me.

The tonga-wallah had lifted the luggage out and carried it to the top of the wide stairway. Another tonga was just driving away from the entrance, having deposited a boy and his father.

A tall, dark man was already greeting them at the top of the steps and turned towards us as we approached. "I am Samson, the warden," he said "perhaps you would all like to look around and then I will show the boys where to keep their 'saaman'."

We followed his white-clad form along a wide stone-paved hallway and into a very large bare room.

"This is the dining hall." Samson said.

At one end was a huge painting of Jesus Christ and a smaller one of King George V and Queen Mary. Underneath the portrayal of Christ was a wooden plaque with the words "Christ is the head of this house, the unseen guest at every meal and the unseen listener to every conversation."

The light from the tall windows along the outer wall formed a patchwork of light and shade on the grey slab floor. A number of narrow rolled mats were stacked neatly at one end. Two boys, each with bundles of millet stalks tied together as brooms, were just completing the sweeping of the floor after breakfast. They stopped as we entered, put down their brooms and made namaskaram.

As the warden was telling our fathers about the daily routine I could feel the boys intent stares summing us up.

Did I meet with their approval I wondered? Were my new shoes different from the other boys? They certainly felt conspicuous on my unaccustomed feet. I was relieved when we moved on through the next room, shelved to accommodate each student's cup and plate, with a washing-up area in one corner. As we entered the kitchen the cook and some more boys were busily preparing for the next meal. The boys were seated on the floor, boards in front of them, chopping vegetables, while the cook was washing rice in a huge saucepan, swishing the water from side to side and pouring it off, deftly catching in her hand any grains of rice which escaped over the rim.

We emerged from the kitchen into a courtyard where the feathery leaves of a drumstick tree provided some shade. Two boys were sitting by the stone water-filled 'torti', a small pot of ash beside them and a bundle of coconut fibre in their hands scrubbing vigorously at the huge brass pots which had been used to cook the breakfast. They too, paused in their task to look at us closely. I had heard Mr. Samson telling father that the boys took turns with the housework. I had never had to help in the kitchen or with housework, my sisters had always done any extra jobs if Danam had too much to do. It would be something new for me and I didn't really look forward to it. The warden led us into a long room on the other side of the courtyard. This was a dormitory and we were shown two vacant spots we could have. Each boy occupied a space on the floor where he kept his trunk against the wall and spread his mat and bedding, which were now rolled up in front of each trunk for the day. A number of boys dressed in long cotton trousers and coloured shirts were tidying up.

"Hurry up boys, it's time to leave for Church - Suresh, tie your shoe laces! David, button your shirt!"

The boys hastily melted from the room.

Mr. Samson led the party back to the front verandah. Father gripped my shoulder and gave it a squeeze. The two fathers took leave of the three of us and we returned their namaskaras. I felt like a pawn in some adult game.

The warden said, "Take your boxes and bedding to the dormitory, boys."

We both picked up our boxes and carried them down the hall and into the sleeping area, placing them against the wall.

"What's your name?" We turned to each other and asked.

"Christopher! What's your village?"

"I come from Chikballapur." I said.

"Where's that? I've heard of it."

"It's a market town near Nandi Hills, north of Bangalore."

"I come from Chamarajnagar. My father is an overseer on a coffee plantation."

We headed for the verandah again to collect our bedding rolls. I think we were both glad of one another's support. I know I didn't feel quite as alone as I had before.

Complete quiet had descended on the boarding home for the boys had left in crocodile file for Wesley Church. Mr. Samson came to the door of the dormitory as we stood looking at one another and wondering what to do next.

"Come with me boys, we'll join the others at church."

"Yes Sir."

We followed him and walked, or almost ran, to keep up with his long strides. The last bell was ringing and when we finally arrived in the Church grounds, out of breath, we were last on the porch. I stooped to untie my shoelaces.

Christopher nudged me, "There's no need to take off your shoes, no one else has."

I straightened and looked. Sure enough there were no rows of sandals outside as there would have been in Chikka.

Sir led the way in. Everyone was sitting on long wooden seats, unlike the mats on the floor in Chikka. Out in front, facing the congregation, were about twenty people on tiered seats. The pastor had just entered the pulpit which stood high in the front and instead of a Bhajana group with drums, accordion and clappers, a man was seated high up playing, what looked to me like a large piano. As the choir rose to sing I thought to myself, "Life is very different here."

Chapter 10

I found there was little time to indulge in homesickness - our days were full. Up at 6am when we all had our rostered duties - helping prepare breakfast, sweeping out the huge rooms, carrying water from the well in the courtyard to the kitchen and bathrooms - the only task we were spared was that of cleaning the latrines which, of course, was done by a woman from the outcaste quarters of the town.

Because I was reasonably good at sport the bullies tended to leave me alone and for that I was thankful.

From the age of eight I had been in the scouting movement, first as a cub, now as a scout. We had some good scout masters; Mr. H.S.Satyadas, headmaster of Hardwick Middle School, and Rev. Boote. To this day when I pick up a horseshoe from the road and put it out of harm's way I think of Rev. Boote. Mr. Sutton, our English teacher, was also rover scout master and between them they took us on a number of excursions - camping in the Mysore jungle, or by the Cauvery River, exploring the old Fort at Sri Ranga Patna (Seringapatan).

Rev. Grouse, one of our teachers, was a gifted Urdu scholar and piano player. His talent was much in demand by the Wesley Guild, an amateur group which performed plays and light opera. Nurses from the Holdsworth Hospital and scholars from Sawday and Hardwick schools were involved in this and I enjoyed it.

One day I sat absorbed watching a hornet return with another ball of soft mud and shape it expertly with its legs to complete the neat container it was building on the wall of the classroom. With a small part of my mind I was conscious of my history teacher telling us about Oliver Cromwell and King Charles. A new ring came into his voice as I heard him say "History is being made now!"

I forgot the hornet as I gave my full attention to what he was saying.

"What do you mean sir?"

"Mahatma Gandhi is leading a march of people to the sea."

"What for sir?"

"To make salt."

"But you can buy salt in all the shops."

"Yes but did you know that 'The Salt Act' forbids anyone to use salt not bought from the government. The Mahatma is marching to make salt as a protest."

It was 1930 and I was thirteen years old. As my teacher spoke I saw in my mind's eye the slim wiry form of the Mahatma with some hundreds of people, clad in white, walking behind him; reaching the shore at last; dipping a pot into the sea; gathering sticks and lighting a fire on the beach, then boiling the water until at last the salt began to spit and crackle in the bottom of the vessel.

"You know boys Mahatma Gandhi follows the teaching of Jesus Christ."

From that time I watched the Mahatma's role as a leader of the independence movement with great interest; in particular his belief in 'satyagraha' (non-violence), as the best means of achieving his aim.

During my last two years at Hardwick I became interested in the Oxford Group Movement and I believe the commitment I gave to Christ at that time has had the greatest influence on the rest of my life.

My life was full and although I missed my family I was too much involved with events around me to be homesick except for one occasion.

I wakened one morning feeling very hot and had no inclination to get up. When the rising bell went I pulled my bed sheet over my head and shut my eyes. Christopher gave me a poke.

"Time to get up, anna."

"I don't feel well, I'm not getting up."

"You'd better get up or you'll be in trouble."

"I don't care!" I said and lay there aching all over.

I must have dozed off for I was wakened by the master in charge pulling down my bedsheet.

"Come on! What's the matter with you?" He put his hand on my head.

"You've got fever, better stay there - I'll tell Christopher to bring you some breakfast."

"I don't want any breakfast!"

"You'd better have a drink then."

By evening I felt still worse, so next morning the warden called a tonga and took me to Holdsworth Hospital. As I sat in outpatients, waiting to be examined I thought of home with longing.

When the doctor examined me he looked at my back and said "How long have you had those blisters?"

"What blisters?"

"Show me your hands!"

I held them out. To my surprise there were three watery blisters on the palms.

The doctor turned to the warden. "This boy has smallpox. You should not have brought him here."

Smallpox! The word struck fear into my heart and I scarcely noticed what happened next but found myself once again in a tonga, this time the warden following in a second vehicle. I was admitted to the isolation hospital and Mr Samson said before leaving "I will send a telegram to your father."

I lay there feeling ill and frightened and very much alone.

I wakened to hear my father's voice and immediately felt better. He strode up to my bed and looked at me closely, then put his arms around me with a hand on my bare neck.

"Daddy, they say I've got smallpox."

"How do you feel?"

"Much better now you're here."

"You don't feel too hot now - let me look at those blisters, have you any more?"

He examined my hands - the same three blisters were there but no more.

"You've been vaccinated you know. See, there's the scar on your arm. You do have smallpox but because you've been vaccinated it's not serious."

I sighed with relief as father sat down on the bed beside me.

"Can I come home until I'm better?"

"No, you'll have to stay here because you are still infectious to other people. Do you feel like eating?"

I realised I did, I had scarcely eaten anything for three days.

"I'll go out and buy you some iddli." Father went off and I lay back in anticipation - all gloomy thoughts of funeral services and weeping family banished from my mind.

When father returned he sat on my bed while I ate.

"When you were a small child you were very ill with high fever. I was walking up and down with you in my arms and praying. I heard a voice say "Your son will be alright." As I travelled today and prayed I felt an inner peace and knew I did not need to be afraid."

Father returned home next day but I was content.

The culmination of our years at Hardwick were the Senior School Leaving Certificate examinations. As a group of us set out from Hardwick Boarding to the Examination Hall, not a breath of air stirred. This was the time we had been working towards over the last years but for most of us the real sweat had been put in during the few weeks before the exams.

Looking back I realise I enjoyed those boarding school years, the companionship, the sport, acting with the repertory group, scouting and even the study under, for the most part, good teachers.

Our walk to the hall was extraordinarily quiet. Maybe the others, as I was, were wishing they had spent more time studying and less time on the playing fields.

Our first exam was English. We filed into the hall and each took our seat behind a wooden desk. A number of stern looking supervisors were strategically placed around the room. I couldn't imagine anyone having the temerity to cheat under those eagle eyes.

"When there is complete silence I will distribute the examination books," the head supervisor announced in quelling tones.

The foot shuffling, chair scraping and coughing stopped and but for the beating of a hundred hearts the room could have been empty, it was so quiet.

We received our papers. It did not look too bad, I thought, glancing at the questions. I'll leave the essay until last, I thought, as I began 'correction of sentences'.

The breathing and heat of a hundred boys added to the temperature and I felt trickles of sweat making their way down my back and legs. I had filled a book. As I rose from my chair I heard a tearing sound as my knickers were pulled from the varnished chair to which my sweat had caused them to stick.

"Finish writing and sit quietly until your papers are collected."

We emerged from the hall and exchanged notes.

"How about stopping off for a coffee and khiru?" I said to Chris.

"We'll need to persuade the others to come too, if they go straight back without us questions will be asked."

We hurried to catch the rest of our group. "Let's go and have a coffee and some sweet. It's my shout!" I said. I had money father had sent for my train fare home.

We all entered our favourite hotel and spent half an hour relaxing. "We'd better go, they will wonder why we're so late back." Daniel said.

Prior to and during the exams we seniors were excused from boarding house chores - now we returned to study for next day's maths exam. Each day of that week was much the same until we completed the last paper - no loitering this time as we made for the boarding house, eager to be off to our homes.

Chapter 11

I travelled back from Mysore to Bangalore on the night train. It was surprisingly difficult saying goodbye to everyone - Rev. Boote, Perstan Sutton and Mr. Satyadas who had been my scout masters as well as teachers. Rev. Grouse, whose expertise on the piano had helped make many of our Wesley Guild repertory performances so successful. I would also miss my classmates, most of whom would continue their education in Mysore. But I was looking forward to seeing my brothers and sisters again, especially Chichu who was already taller than I was last time I was home.

On reaching Bangalore I engaged a coolie and hurried across to the narrow gauge platform. I had only just enough time to catch the train and would have to travel third class having spent the upper class fare shouting my classmates in the hotel. As usual it was crowded and most of the passengers had already settled themselves. I hurried along the train looking for a space, the coolie jogging behind me. Having come to the end of the third class carriages I had to turn my back regretfully on the empty first class and retrace my steps - the bell rang.

"Come on ."I said to the coolie "I'll have to get in somewhere," and I tried the door of the nearest compartment. It wouldn't budge - a man was standing just inside - "Please open the door."

"There are baskets against it" he said.

"Well, move them!"

He spoke to someone further in and a village man, a red-checked towel tied around his head, began tugging at the baskets.

Meanwhile the coolie had taken the initiative and was putting my luggage through the window.

"Get in Babu." he said and indicated the open window.

The second bell rang and without more ado I climbed through the open window as the train moved off.

I sat on my trunk in the aisle then realised I had not paid the coolie who was jogging along beside the train. I hastily felt in my pocket - found twenty paisa and pressed it into his hand as the train gathered speed. He touched his brow and dropped back and I turned to survey my travelling companions. Poultry, looking cowed by the whole proceeding, huddled in a basket crate to my right.

"You nearly put your trunk on my fowls."the owner said.

"Forgive me, we couldn't see them from outside."

"That's all right."

The baskets which had prevented the opening of the door were full of aluminium pots and pans. On the rack opposite me was a bundle of home spun black and brown woollen blankets, tied up in an old bed sheet.

Suddenly realisation dawned - it was Saturday! Market day in Chikka - no wonder the train was packed.

The man sitting opposite had a cage full of green parrots. He was the man who sat under a tree in the main street and used the parrots to tell fortunes. He had a small square bundle tied in a cloth. I presumed it was his box of paper slips each printed with a fortune. The parrots were very tame, quite unworried by the crowd around them. He was giving them pieces of puffed dhal through the cane slats and each bird took its portion as daintily as a lady eating cake at a tea party.

The compartment had seemed to me crowded to its limit, but I was mistaken, at each station more baskets were pushed through the windows, their owners following. The last straw was at Avati where lidded baskets of tuberoses were pushed in. The smell was overpoweringly sweet but each basket dripped muddy water - having been recently dunked in the water of the tank to keep them fresh.

"Please remove your basket from my bedding."I said.

The unfortunate owner looked around helplessly. I had a brainwave. "Lift your basket and I will put my bedding roll across it." The basket and bedding roll having been exchanged we settled down for the last four miles to Chikka.

I saw Samanna's well-built form waiting on the platform as the train pulled in and waved to attract his attention. He made a dignified approach through the crowd to the compartment window.

"Take these, Anna." I handed out my bedding roll and then my trunk.

Samanna called a coolie and I waited while the rush to get baskets, gunny sacks and bundles out the narrow carriage door subsided.

"It's good that you're here, Anna!"

"Your father told me you were coming and I also have parcels to collect from the station master."

"Good, I'll go to the car."

Samanna appeared with two large parcels for the hospital and we drove off.

When Samanna stopped the car outside our gate, Nani, Philip and Rava came running down the path to meet me. The two little girls both had their hair tied up on top with large pink bows. I lifted Rava on to my shoulder while Nani and Philip clung to my other arm and made progress slow. I disengaged myself at the top step and put Rava down, the strong smell of Sampangi flowers invaded my nostrils, Dathi and Sarojini were there. I noticed that Dathi too was now in a half sari and both had Sampangi flowers tucked into the base of their long shining plaits.

Chichu appeared in the doorway, he had grown even in the last six months, was now a head taller than me and looked fit and well. Mother's short round figure appeared next, baby Thomas Prasanna on her hip. Chichu and Sarojini grabbed my luggage and I went to greet her. We embraced.

Danam greeted me from the kitchen doorway, to appear a few minutes later with cups of coffee and some muruku. the crisp ghee-laden push biscuits, made especially for me.

"Where's Kanya?"

"Kanya won't be back from Bangalore until next week when her training finishes and she has been given a position teaching in the Nursery School here. Mrs. Cutting will be pleased to have her working with her."

"How were the exams, Anna?" Chichu asked.

"Not too bad - I hope I've passed!"

Chapter 12

Father was pleased to see me home and arranged for us to go shooting down the ghat road on Wednesday evening. "We'll go down to Dr.Thompson's rock by bus and ask Samanna to pick us up in the car later. Jacobanna may like to go with us."

"I'll go and ask him father. Will he be at home now?"

"He was on duty this morning so should be off."

I walked along the road around to the hospital quarters and knocked on Jacob's door. Jacob was one of the senior staff nurses who had trained as a dispenser at Jammalamadugu Hospital when father did his medical training there.

Leelamma appeared at the door of the next house.

"I am looking for Jacobanna."

"He has gone to the Bazaar."

"Never mind I'll see him tomorrow."

On Wednesday we walked to the bus stand with our guns and knapsacks. The bus came in and there was the usual scramble for seats.

The conductor called out to father. "You sit in the front seat, swami."

We climbed up into the front seat to sit next to the driver in glorious isolation from the crowded passengers in the back of the bus. Father said to me in an undertone. "The seats of honour for the passengers who will be killed first if we crash."

"We want to get down at the big rock halfway down the ghat road."

The conductor, with barely a foothold, swinging on the back step, thumped the back of the bus twice and we were off. It was a long steady grade up to the top of the pass and we advanced with the shadows of the avenue trees as the sun sank towards the horizon behind us. Before we reached the top the engine between us and the driver was boiling. To my mind that was the main disadvantage of the front seat, the engine fumes heavy on the warm air around us.

At last we came to the top and commenced the winding descent, slowly, in low gear.

"The brakes aren't good." The driver leant across to tell us.

The huge granite rock, as large as a house, came into sight as we rounded a bend and the driver pulled on the hand brake. The conductor leapt down and put a big stone, kept under the back seat for the purpose, in front of the rear wheel.

We opened the door, climbed down and the bus moved off.

It was not easy climbing on to the rock but with some scrambling and heaving we got there. Once on top there was plenty of room and we sat and talked, for it was a bit too early for animal movement. Father always enjoyed recounting to us incidents from his younger days when he and Dr.Thompson had waited on this rock for game. The rock overlooked a long gully, the sides of which were covered with small trees, lantana and wait-a-while. In wet weather a stream trickled down between rocks in the bottom but now only a small pool remained near an open grassy patch some hundred yards below us.

"Did you hear about the tiger?" Jacobanna asked.

"Dathi mentioned it when she wrote. What happened exactly?"

"A tiger was seen near the hospital mortuary, then one of the night nurses saw it just outside the back entrance to the maternity block. Everyone was frightened, especially the night nurses. They were afraid to move from ward to ward alone so they asked me to shoot it. The ward boys rigged up a mat shelter for me near the big fig tree and I sat down to wait. At 2am the night nurse brought me some coffee . The moon was just slipping below the horizon and it was difficult to see even a few yards. I had almost given up hope when I saw two eyes gleaming out of the darkness. I took aim and fired then shone my torch to make sure it was dead. There it was lying on the ground but as I approached through the darkness it didn't look right and I realised with dismay that it was the dhobi's donkey. I'll never live that down."

"What happened to the tiger?"

"We never saw it again, but one was shot shortly afterwards near Sushepalya so it was probably the same one."

As the sun sank we were still. The next hour would be crucial - we would have enough light to see by.

The next bus went rattling down the road, a lorry came groaning up. A little owl swooped down in front of us and reappeared with a small animal, probably a mouse, in its talons. A movement on the patch and the white on the chest of a hare as it hopped into view.

We were after bigger game - tiger, panther, samba or jinka. My eyes fixed on the clearing began to see imaginary objects. I blinked to clear my vision. There was something! Two small deer had moved into the clearing and were cropping the short grass. More joined them.

We sat watching them. After what seemed like hours Father said softly "They are too quiet - I don't think we are going to get bigger game tonight. When I give the signal we'll shoot."

A few moments later we fired and two jinka lay dead as the others fled in terror.

Samanna was to bring the car to the temple near the bridge at the foot of the hill. We slid and slipped down off the road and looked for an animal track through the thorn bushes. By this time we needed our torches.

"Jacobanna, you stay by the road until Samanna comes, then bring the men down to the clearing. Thammu and I will go down and sling the animals on poles, ready to be carried".

As father and I stumbled down an animal track, the thorny creepers clutching at our hair and our clothes, my heart was in my mouth. I felt as though a tiger was just behind me; my scramble was one of urgency - getting away from whatever lurked in the darkness - although commonsense told me our shots had probably frightened off anything nearby. At last we emerged into the lighter clearing and saw the two dead deer. One had two bullets in it and the other was shot through the head. Father was pleased. He took out his knife and cut the throat of each animal.

"Thammu, we must look for some small saplings - I noticed some up to the right of here as we sat waiting on the rock."

I shone my torch up the hillside to the right - sure enough there were some cassia trees. We looked for a track leading towards them but could find none.

"The cane knife is in your bag Thammu. We'll have to cut through the lantana. Choose a spot where there are more trees and less lantana - we can push through them and won't have so much to cut."

I ducked under a small custard apple tree. "I hope I don't meet a cobra or a krait."

"Make a noise and they will move out of your way."

"I hope so." I said.

The cassias were ideal, long straight branches of regrowth - the pendulous blooms beginning to open.

"What a shame to cut them."

"They grow quickly and we only need two poles ."Father said.

A couple of blows with the 'mattsu' felled each one. I chopped off the small branches and we dragged them back the way we'd come.

"Samanna is a long time coming. I don't think Jacobanna will be too happy alone up there in the dark."

"No!"

"Anna" father shouted "are you alright?" We heard a shout in reply.

I began searching the undergrowth around the clearing for vines. "These creepers are all thorny."

"Look at the edge of the stream you may find some wild grape."

Sure enough there were some and I cut off some long lengths. My years of scouting came in handy when it came to tying the feet of the jinkas to the poles.

"That sounds like the car!" We heard voices then a torch began bobbing above us.

"Here we are" we called, and flashed our own torch back in reply.

The bobbing light came nearer, the silence punctuated now by the low curses of the ward boys as the thorns tore at their bare legs. The headlights of the car moved slowly down the winding road as Samanna drove down to the temple to wait for us.

"What thorns!" exclaimed David as the three came into the clearing.

They examined the jinkas -"You've tied them well, Swami." I was pleased with the praise.

The tread of woodcutters had made a well-worn track from the clearing down to the bridge. "You'll need to make two trips." Father said. "Jacobanna you go down to the car with the boys and we'll wait here until they come back."

We helped them hoist one jinka to their shoulders and Jacob led the way down the track with the torch. We squatted down and waited quietly - father lit a cigarette and its dull glow was all that could be seen in the enclosing darkness. Complete silence descended - I think neither of us felt like breaking it as we gazed into the sky filled with a million twinkling stars. Some small animal scurried in the bushes and broke the spell.

"These are the moments which make hunting special" father said.

"Mmm" I murmered, still half entranced by the magnitude of the heavens above us.

"How wonderful it would be to spread wings and fly off into space."

A noise of undergrowth being displaced and the bobbing torch approached. Krishnappa and David reappeared. They shouldered the animal and we shone the light on the path as we all walked back to the car.

"Here's some rag, don't get blood in the car!" Samanna said.

There was scarcely room for all of us and the car complained with many groans as we wound our way back up the steep ghat road.

The boys carried the deer through to our back courtyard behind the house where they'd be safe from dogs.

"Which of you are on afternoon duty tomorrow?"

"Daniel and Dastagiri."

"Ask them to come here early and help cut up the Jinkas. No! Don't ask Dastagiri Sahib, he and his family won't be able to eat the meat. Is there anyone else?" father asked.

"My son is home on holiday, he will help." Krishna said.

"Good!"

"We'll go and come, Doctorgaru."

Father and I went into the kitchen. "Would you like a cup of coffee?"

"I'll light the stove." We had a little kerosene stove for such occasions and I filled a small saucepan and lit the wick.

We sat at the small table in the dining hall.

"Thammu, you'll need to supervise the cutting of the jinkas tomorrow. Make sure the larger families on the staff receive more meat. Send some to the Pastor and the Church peon also."

"Will we wrap it in leaf plates?"

"Yes, there may be some left over from the dinner we gave on my birthday."

"Send Danam to the bazaar for thin twine to tie around the bundles. If you run out of leaf plates mother may have an old sari you can tear up."

The water was boiling - I threw in some coffee and lumps of raw sugar then looked in our small flyproof 'dooli' for milk.

"There's no milk, father, it has all been set for tomorrow's curds."

"Your mother keeps a tin of powdered milk in the store. I'll get her keys." Father went into the bedroom and came back with mother's bunch of keys and we found the milk powder. We sipped in silence.

Then father said "How many chickens do we have?"

"The little black hen hatched twelve but I can remember Nani writing to tell me a crow got one, the rest are almost full grown."

"Then give Dastagiri, Karim and Pir Sahib's families a chicken each - they can read the passages from the Koran and kill their own. It's a pity they should miss out, they are all good members of staff. I've got early surgery tomorrow so we'd better get to bed" said father as he stubbed out his cigarette and rose.

Chapter 13

The day the S.S.L.C. results were due to be published we were all at Peresandra. I was up at first light and decided to ride in to Chikka for the paper. I scribbled a note for mother, went out and put the bridle on my pony, Eve, and set off. Even at 4-30 am it was warm, though pleasant enough, before the sun rose high above the horizon. We did the thirteen miles at a leisurely pace and reached Chikka just after 6am but the papers would reach the town on the train at 10-30 so I went to Ananda aunty's and knocked.

"Thammu, what are you doing here - is everything alright?"

"Yes aunty - my results come out today so I rode in before it becomes too hot."

"Come in and sit down! Do you want to take a bath?"

"No thank you, I'll wait until I return to Peresandra."

Ananda aunty was busy in the kitchen making chapathies for breakfast. I could see her squatting as she rolled them deftly on a small piece of polished slab and heard the flap as she turned each one. She had not expected me but I knew a cooked breakfast would be put before me within a short time.

Our voices had wakened her youngest daughter, Charla and she emerged from the bedroom and stood in the door way, still half asleep, staring at me with wide eyes. I patted the mat beside me and she came and sat half reclining on my knee. A few minutes later her elder sisters Prilla and Padma appeared and went to the bathroom to wash and get ready for high school.

Ananda aunty heaved her stout form up from its squatting position and moved to the stove where she had placed a pot of water as soon as I entered. A lump of jaggery, some coffee powder and then the milk, were added, then aunty poured it into a silver tumbler and brought it to me. I sipped and read the previous day's Deccan Herald as she finished preparing breakfast.

I had unhobbled Eve and made my way down to the station by ten-fifteen.

The post peon was already on the station waiting to collect the mail. At last I heard the distant whistle as the train came through the level crossing and set out on the last easy run to the station. Soon the plume of smoke from the engine could be seen and she puffed in.

The guard handed the post bag to the peon.

"Please give me my father's paper" I asked him.

"I'm sorry swami - I can't give you any mail here - you'll have to come to the post office."

"I just want our paper."

"I can't give you even that. I don't have the key to the bag - you'll have to come to the post office and collect it there."

I felt a bit miffed but as he didn't have the key there wasn't much I could do, so I mounted Eve and we plodded across the town.

Samanna was at the P.O. when we arrived. "I'll take father's mail with me anna, I'm going back to Peresandra."

The postal clerk handed the hospital mail across the counter and Samanna separated ours. I took it from him, jumped on Eve and trotted out to the Bagepalle road. I wanted to read the paper in private; I was not sure enough of my results to desire an audience.

Under a huge tamarind tree I pulled on the reins and dismounted. My hands were clumsy as I tried to tear the thick brown wrapper with my fingernail. At last I had it open and found the page. My name was there - not only had I matriculated but also obtained eligibility for public service. I'll be able to go to college and then on to study medicine! I pushed the paper back into my bag, leapt on to Eve and shouted "Come on" as I gave her a slap on the rump. It wasn't until Eve slowed to a trot and then a walk that I realised how hot it was and felt the sweat on her neck.

"You poor lady - you need a drink and so do I."

We were already several miles outside the town - the avenue trees stretching ahead of us a welcomimg green in contrast to the hot bare fields shimmering in the heat.

"We'll get you a drink at Chitravati tank" I told Eve. The bund of the tank showed as a raised earth bank to our right just beyond an ancient temple which we often visited during the big cattle fair held in conjunction with the annual parade and bathing ceremony of the temple deity.

I gave Eve an encouraging slap and she scrambled up the bank. At first glance the tank looked dry, the cracked mud giving the bed a tessellated appearance but along to the right, near the outlet, I could see a small expanse of water passing me signals from the sun.

As we walked along the bund I saw, splashing in the water, three small boys cooling off. Beside their discarded clothing on the bank were three mukkeries [wide-mouthed shallow baskets] with the flat wide trowels used for scraping off the meagre grass. They scrambled up the bank and began putting on their clothes. I watched one taking care to put his arm into the sleeve which was difficult to distinguish amongst the tatters that hung from the collar.

"What is your village, swami?"

"I'm from Chikballapur. Where are you from?

They pointed further west.

I led Eve down the bank carefully, that sticky mud at the edge of the water could be treacherous. Eve drank her fill.

As we climbed back up the bank the boys were busy scraping grass off the surface and putting it in their baskets. They were young. It is hot work for them in the sun filling those baskets to take home for the cattle but they shouldn't be scraping the tank bund bare, I thought.

"You shouldn't scrape grass off the bank, it will wash away when the rains come."

The eldest of the three boys stopped and looked me up and down.

"You, who eats 'til your belly is full, are telling us what to do! Get lost, son of a jackal!"

They gave me a withering stare and bent again to their task.

I felt angry but also ashamed, mounted Eve and rode off. I was so busy thinking about what he had said, I was back on the road before I remembered my thirst. I must have a drink! I pulled Eve around and headed back to the temple - surely the 'poojari' would have good water.

Outside the arched stone gateway into the temple courtyard I tied Eve to a Neem tree, left my sandals and entered. The large pool in the middle did not seem to mitigate the heat thrown up from the stone surrounds. I began to walk across the pavement to look down the terraced sides of the pool but had to retreat in haste, the slabs were baking hot on my bare feet. I stood in the shadow cast by the doorway and looked around the courtyard. Across to my left was the doorway into the courtyard proper - I went back to Eve and retrieved my sandals - the priests quarters would be within those inner walls. When I reached the second doorway the heat was not so forbidding, an arched colonnade provided shade to the poojari's doorway and a large neem tree shaded the paved area.

The poojari's wife was sitting on a low stool outside the door cleaning grain.

"Amma - do you have good water - I'm thirsty."

She looked at me closely. "What village are you from? What caste are you?"

"I am a Christian from Chikballapur, my father is a doctor in the Mission hospital." Surely she won't refuse me, I thought.

She rose and entered the house - I knew better than to approach any closer - and reappeared carrying a small brass pot of water. I held out my cupped hands and she poured water into them as I drank thirstily.

"Thank you, amma."

"Go and come, young brother."

It was hot on the road in spite of the avenue of trees and I had to ask for water again but this time I entered a village and asked at one of the poorer houses.

When I reached the traveller's bungalow at Peresandra the sun was still high and mother and father were resting. Chichu, Kanya and Saroja were on the verandah reading and Philip was riding his tricycle up and down. "How did you go?" Chichu called as I came in the gateway.

"I passed!"

"How wonderful, Thammu, I knew you would!" Kanya said.

Philip pedalled into the room where mother and father were resting while Prasanna, the baby, slept.

"Mummy! Daddy! Thammu is back - he's passed!"

Prasanna wakened with a yell. Their peace was shattered but it didn't matter. Father came out on to the verandah and gripped me affectionately on the shoulder. "Good work, Thammu - now we will have to make arrangements for you to go to college".

I heard mother calling to Danam and a few minutes later he appeared with large drinks of cool fresh lime juice for all of us.

Father and I sat in deck chairs and soon mother joined us, putting Prasanna on a mat at our feet.

When I told father about asking at the temple for water he said "You should have had more sense than to ride out in the heat of the day. It's not good to have to ask for water, especially in the hot weather when Cholera and Typhoid outbreaks are common."

I did not tell anyone of the small boy's remarks - somehow I felt inwardly ashamed.

As we sipped our drinks father said "Well Thammu, what now?"

"I'd like to do a pre-university course which would lead on to study medicine then perhaps I can work on in the hospital after you retire."

We sat in companionable silence then father said "Last week I made a few enquiries in Bangalore about accommodation for you. Our finances are tight with all the younger children to be educated but Mr. Cox said you could mess with the boys in the United Mission High School Boarding and now that the Cox children are studying in England he has offered to let you live in one of the rooms in their bungalow."

"Thank you father, I didn't think you would make any plans until you knew whether I had passed or not."

Father put out his hand and gripped my arm . "I had faith in you."

A warm glow spread through me.

Chapter 14

I managed to secure a place in the Bangalore Intermediate College and chose Botany, Zoology and Chemistry as my subjects as these were suitable to lead on to a medical course.

A few days before I was to leave Chikka I came home to find mother and Kanya in the kitchen, a pan of hot oil on the stove.

"What are you doing?"

"We're making some 'tindi' for you to take to Bangalore."

Piled up on newspaper beside them were deep-fried sweet jaggery rice cakes and savoury 'chakli'.

"These will all keep for weeks. You'll probably get hungry studying in the evenings."

"Don't eat them all now, Thammu!" Kanya said as I took one from the pile.

Philip and Rava were standing looking longingly at the goodies.

"Go away all of you." mother said.

"Mummy let them all have one - I don't need all those for myself."

"They have already had one each, that will do." mother said firmly.

Father had said he would go into Bangalore with me and make final arrangements with Mrs. Cox and the boarding house manager.

We went in on Friday's train and took a jutka straight to the bungalow. Mrs. Cox came to the door as the jutka wallah carried my trunk up the steps to the low verandah.

"Namaskaram doctor - you've brought Thammu."

"Yes, amma - it's very good of you to have him here, I hope he won't cause you any trouble."

"Congratulations, Thammu, on matriculating. I hope you'll be happy here. I'll show you your room."

Mrs. Cox led the way down the hall to a small room on the ground floor at the back of the house. It contained a bed, a chair and a table I could use as a desk. Also a large teak chest of drawers. A window, partly shaded by a tree tomato (Tamarillo) opened out to the back garden.

"You should be comfortable here but if there's anything else you need just ask me. Leave your outer bathroom door unlocked so that the sweeper and the water boy can come in."

Father said "Unpack your trunk, Thammu, while I speak to Mrs. Cox then we'll go and see the boarding manager."

They left me and I began to explore. The bed was already made up with clean sheets and a brightly woven cotton bedspread. I opened the door leading off the bedroom - the bathroom was huge; a marble-topped washstand held china bowl, jug and soap dish. A cotton-padded basket was now empty but would no doubt be filled each evening with a can of hot water for bathing. A large tin tub lay upside down in the bathing place. I won't be using the tub I thought to myself. I had always enjoyed my 'pour' bath. A commode completed the scene - I looked at that with some distaste - I had been used to an outdoor bore-hole latrine at home and at school but I knew commodes were the usual practice in European bungalows and, in fact, we had used them at Peresandra. I will just need to get used to it I suppose.

I finally began to unpack my few clothes and put them in the drawers. Father reappeared at the door.

"Come, Thammu, we'll go to the boarding home. You'd better lock the bathroom door, we're not in Chikka now!"

As we walked across to the boarding I said to father. "Do you have to pay Mrs. Cox much for my room?"

"Mrs. Cox refuses to take anything, she says you won't cost any extra as the servants have a lot less to do now that her family are not here."

"That's very good of her."

"You must be careful not to cause her any worry. She said you could come and go as you please but they lock up about 10pm when they go to bed so you must be sure to be in by then."

"Oh, I'll be studying at night father."

"You will need to pay for your own washing - the dhobi charges 2 pice an article so just count the articles you put in and give that amount to Mrs. Cox each week.

We entered the front door of the boarding house and went down the hall into the back courtyard. The cook was squatting in front of a steaming pot busy shaping the red millet balls for the boys' lunch. She looked up.

"We would like to see the manager." father said

"He's in his office." She pointed to a doorway across the courtyard.

The manager looked up from his accounts as our shadows fell across the doorway.

"Mr. Cox has made arrangements for my son, Sabhapathy, to eat here while attending college."

"Yes swami - he mentioned it to me."

"I will pay you one month's board now." Father handed him five rupees.

The manager turned to me "Morning prayers are at 7am, breakfast follows. Lunch is at twelve and the evening meal at 6pm. Please be punctual."

"Yes sir!" We made namaskara and left.

Chapter 15

That year 1936 in Bangalore was an exciting one for me - I had meals in the boarding home but apart from that I was free to come and go as I pleased.

Two of my friends from Mysore and three from Chikka were at college with me and I made new friends. During our first week we had trials for the cricket team and I was selected. We practised twice weekly and played matches on Wednesday afternoons or Saturday.

Although Chikka was only 35 miles from Bangalore I did not go home at the weekend - transport was difficult and impossible if we were playing Saturday matches.

I attended Hudson Memorial Church on Sunday morning and was asked to join the Choir. We had choir practice every Thursday night. We also did some acting, putting on a play for harvest festival.

Our youth group had various projects, one of which was visiting a squatter's village at Hessaraghatta on the outskirts of Bangalore. During times of drought in rural areas the people there had come into Bangalore looking for work. Unskilled labouring is hard to find, especially if you are raw from the country and many of these people found themselves caught. People from drought-stricken areas of Cuddapah and Godavari had squatted on vacant land, built walls of mud, collected empty drums and hammered them flat as roofing. Their only water supply was the tank, their sanitation was non-existent.

One Sunday on arrival at their cluster of huts the children greeted us as usual. One bright little boy was missing. "Where's Chinna?" we asked.

"He has fever, he is very sick - come and see him, anna."

They took us to his home which was a low mud hut about ten feet square, without windows. The flat tin roof only six feet high made the hut like an oven. Chinna was lying on a mat in one corner - his mother was sitting on the earthen floor pinning leaves together with grass stalks - she would be able to sell the plates she made to the merchants for a small amount.

"Chinna, how are you?"

I bent over him - his eyes were sunken and he did not answer but managed a weak smile. I felt his forehead, it was very hot. I turned to his mother.

"How long has he been ill?"

"He's had fever and headache for a week."

"Has he had diarrhoea?"

"Yes swami."

"He should be in hospital."

She held out her hands helplessly then wiped tears from her eyes with the corner of her sari.

"What can I do?"

We went outside and held a conference.

"Let's take him to hospital, we can all give something towards a jutka." I turned back towards his mother.

"Amma, we'll take him to the mission hospital - you'd better come too so that you know where he is."

She looked frightened "Wait until his father comes!"

"When will his father come?"

"Tonight."

"He's very ill - it's dangerous to wait."

She looked at us and looked at Chinna "Do as you wish, swami. It's God's will."

Some of the group had already gone to call a jutka, it pulled up and we lifted Chinna in. His clothes were soiled and smelt.

His mother ran next door to tell her neighbour and ask her to keep an eye on their few possessions and tell his father when he returned.

Two of us went with them in the Jutka and left the rest of our party to tell stories to the children and anyone else who cared to listen.

A ward boy put Chinna on a stretcher and we carried him into the examination room. Within minutes a slight middle-aged English lady appeared, stethoscope in hand. After examining Chinna carefully she said "I suspect typhoid, we'll admit him, he may need a drip. We'll treat him free."

She turned to the mother and spoke in Urdu. The mother looked blank. We translated into Telugu.

"Doctoramma says your little boy is very ill, but don't fear they will give him the best treatment."

"Tell the mother to go home and come back tomorrow. Does she have other children?"

"Yes"

"Then tell her to bring them too and we'll give them all needle medicine to prevent them getting this illness."

Chinna's mother was frightened and confused. "I'll stay here and look after him."

We explained that this was a city hospital and they did not have room to accommodate relatives, then led her back to the jutka, managed to find the return fare and a little extra between us and sent her off home.

As we walked back to the city area the streets were beginning to empty, pedestrians were few and the heavy lorries, not allowed on the streets during daylight hours, were on the move.

We passed the huge statue of Queen Victoria at the corner of Cubbon Park and a soft breeze fanned our faces - giving promise of a cooler night.

"If Chinna recovers let's see if we can get him admitted to the mission boarding as a charity student."

"He's a bright little boy - perhaps the youth group could raise money to sponsor him."

When we reached the mission compound I took leave of Daniel who still had a mile to walk.

Next day, after classes finished, I cycled across to the hospital. Chinna was lying in bed very weak and still very subdued but he was no longer dehydrated.

"He's doing well but he's still very ill and it's a matter of watching his condition carefully and nursing him as best we can. There is no drug effective against typhoid."

"Did his mother bring his brothers and sisters for inoculation?"

"Yes, they all came this morning, the father as well, visited Chinna and had inoculations."

I felt relieved as I did not have much time during the day to bring them and would have had to miss classes.

When I visited him on Friday afternoon he was sitting propped up in bed and greeted me with a wide smile. I decided then and there to go and visit the headmaster of the London Mission Primary School and try to have him admitted as a charity student.

Next day as soon as I'd finished breakfast I went over to the school which was in the same compound. The headmaster was in the staffroom.

"Good morning Sir."

"Good morning." He looked at me enquiringly. I explained the situation.

"It may be possible but you'll need to see the Manager."

"Who is the manager?"

"Cox Dorra."

"Oh, I live in Mr. Cox's bungalow. I will go and speak to him now."

Mr. Cox was in his office, busy with accounts.

"Our classes are officially full but I think we could squeeze in one more. What about books? We couldn't supply those. He'd need to start in grade 1 and the cost there would not be much."

"We'll manage the books somehow. Thank you very much, Sir." I took leave and went to my classes feeling very happy.

A few days later when I visited Chinna he was looking much better and sat up in bed to greet me.

"Would you like to go to school?"

"Yes sir, but we are poor people."

"I'll speak to your father and mother about it."

The following Sunday when our group went down to the squatters village his father and mother were both there. His father was a dark, well-built man in his late thirties I guessed. He looked as though he would be a good worker.

They greeted us warmly and had prepared coffee for us.

"Chinna won't be strong enough to come home for a week or two but I was wondering if you'd be willing to let him go to school?"

"Look at us, sir, we are poor people."

"Yes, but we can get him into school for you, he can live there during the week and come home at weekends and you won't have to pay fees. We will buy books for him."

"Let him study, then my grandchildren will not have to sweat to live as I do."

As we discussed the matter further we realised he would need clothes and a bed sheet. I had not thought about that and felt a bit non-plussed. We had already committed ourselves to books. To my relief his father said, "We can have a shirt and pants stitched and buy a sheet. I get 'coolie' most days and we will manage."

Chinna did well at school and completed carpentry training after Grade 7. He could have gone further but he himself was eager to earn and help support his brothers and sisters.

Chapter 16

After our cricket matches a group of us went to our favourite hotel for coffee. We often sat there for several hours discussing politics. British rule was a popular and often heated topic on which our views differed. One of our group believed that if the British left, our country would fragment into states which would be at one another's throats and chaos would result. Some of us were very anti British, uttering wild statements which if overheard in some quarters could have got them into trouble. Most of us were against British rule but argued that it had brought benefits such as a democratic system of government, trial by jury, and a good railway system. I was of this latter view but having seen the work of the mission hospitals and schools and the opportunities they had provided for education and training I was not anti British. I had a very high personal regard for many of my teachers who were British and appreciated their dedication. Father used to say 'the Christians here must show more responsibility to their own people as the missionaries may not be able to stay. They have come a long way to serve God here and we must play our part.'

Mahatma Gandhi had been my hero ever since my first year in high school.

When at the Coffee shop I kept an eye on the time to make sure I was able to reach the Bungalow before 10 pm. Mrs. Cox was good to me, often bringing me a cup of coffee and biscuits if I was studying in my room at night.

With a shock I realised the exams were only a month away. I cut out my coffee shop excursions and began to study in earnest; some of my hastily scribbled lecture notes I found unintelligible; I realised I should have transcribed them on the day of the lecture. As the day of the first exam drew near I realised I had no hope of covering all the work, much less remembering it. I went to bed with a sick feeling in the pit of my stomach and when I got up, as realisation again dawned, the feeling returned.

Two nights before the exams when Mrs. Cox came with hot cocoa she asked me "How are you getting on, Thammu?"

"There is an awful lot of work to cover, amma - I should not have done so many other things."

Lying in bed next night I made a decision. I would not sit for the exams this year but take an extra year, study hard and try for honours and a scholarship to university. Having made the decision I slept and was wakened by a knock on the door.

"Are you alright, Thammu?"

I leapt out of bed and opened the door "Yes, Amma."

"I wondered because I heard no movement. It's almost time for you to go to the examination hall."

"I've decided not to sit but to repeat the year."

"Is that wise, what will your father think about that?"

"I'll explain the situation to him."

Mrs. Cox looked doubtful but retreated. Most of that day I slept; after the midnight oil I'd burnt during the last few weeks I needed it.

After returning from the evening meal in the Hostel I sat down to read. There was a sharp knock on the door.

"Yes? Come in."

Father entered. I had never seen him look so angry. I leapt to my feet.

"I hear you didn't sit for your exam today!"

"No, father."

"Why not?"

"I felt if I repeated the year I could do better."

"What do you mean by spending your time and our slender resources and then not appearing for the exams. I find your behaviour inexcusable. How can we support you here for an extra year when you have simply wasted your time?"

"Father, if I study harder I may win a scholarship next year." I was angry now and raised my voice to a shout.

"Haven't you studied hard this year? If not, why not?"

"I have studied!"

"Then you sit for the next two exams! Do you hear me!"

I certainly did hear him.

"If you can't pass them you have not got the ability to do further study and had better go out to work."

"I'm sorry father I didn't mean to let you down."

"You'd better start studying now for tomorrow's exam. I will go and take food and see you in the morning."

I was shaking with a mixture of anger and shame. I pulled out a chemistry book and sat looking at it - the page blurring before my eyes. If I had found it difficult to remember facts before, it was now an impossibility and I finally went to bed, where I tossed until sleep finally blotted out my misery.

Next morning, as I left the house to have breakfast in the hostel, father was breakfasting with Rev. and Mrs. Cox.

"I will drop you off at the examination hall on my way back to Chikka."

"Yes father."

Chapter 17

I duly sat for the exams and returned home to receive the news a few weeks later that I had failed in both papers. I was not surprised and after what had happened, neither was the family.

After my return from Bangalore relations between father and me were strained. The evening after the results came out Father came in from the hospital and called to me as I sat on the verandah reading. "Come, Thammu, we'll take the dogs for a walk."

As soon as father appeared with his stick, Rover and Rocket began running round in circles and jumping up at us eager to be off. We headed out along the Mushtur road, then across the fields, now dry and hard waiting for the summer rains. We walked for a few minutes then I said what had been waiting in my mind for this opportunity.

"Father, I'm sorry I let you down - I didn't realise that I was spending too much time on other things and not enough on study."

"Well Thammu, it's done now and I feel it's best that you should work for a few years then perhaps try again."

"But father I feel that if I repeated this year I could gain first class and a scholarship to study medicine."

"I've discussed it with Dr. Cutting and he says you are not bright enough and would be better working for a few years."

Anger surged within me but I held my tongue. I knew I had only myself to blame.

As we approached the stream the excited barking of the dogs drew our attention. They were digging in the sandy bank at the root of an oleander bush as they tried to unearth a bandicoot. To this day the heady perfume of oleander mixed with the scent of kanuga (Pongamia) blossom brings a feeling of deep disappointment.

"I think it is best if you study for the Central Government exam and seek an appointment with the Central Recruitment Board."

"Yes, father."

"The best way to do that would be to enrol at the high school and do the exam at the end of the year. I've made some enquiries about it."

I turned away, jumped down the bank and walked over to a date palm to look for fruit. My disappointment was so great I could not meet father's eyes. The palm was only just coming into flower and some weaver birds with nests on the fronds rose excitedly in protest.

I called the dogs and, having regained my composure, climbed the bank. The sun dipped below the horizon and we stepped out briskly. As we entered the hospital gate the sound of the mynahs fighting for nesting places in the huge weeping figs, was deafening and I stood for a moment allowing it to blot out my thoughts.

Having swallowed my pride, I found myself enjoying the year's study. Although I had done an extra year, many of my classmates were as old as I was. Some had even completed their twentieth year. I was elected Cricket captain and we played regular matches against teams from other towns, the hospital team and the town team. I played football in the town team and competed for them in field sports.

Chichu, now sixteen, was only a year behind me in high school and already taller than me. As he excelled in all sports I felt proud to be his brother on the playing fields.

When we returned from our Saturday matches Danam always had a kerosene tin of piping hot water sitting over embers in the back courtyard. Chichu and I took either end of the piece of wood hammered across the top and carried it into the bathroom. Chichu poured the water for me while I soaped and rinsed then I did the same for him.

"What are you going to do next year Thammu?"

"Get a job in the public service I hope.

"Are you very disappointed?"

"Yes." I answered somewhat shortly - the subject was still too painful to discuss.

"I would like to do Med. when I matriculate."

"Well don't make a mess of things the way I have. You're good at sport, you'll need to watch you leave enough time for study.!"

"I will, anna - don't worry."

We towelled ourselves down, tied our panchas and put on our shirts.

Kanya was studying at Kolar this year. We missed her, as being the eldest, she tended to spoil us a bit, as well as order us around.

We sat on mats in the dining room waiting for Danam to serve food. Three year old Rava, her head on a cushion had already fallen asleep on a mat. Philip, then five, crawled on to my lap. "Tell me a story, anna!"

"What about?"

"About the time the Maharaja's son came to tea."

That was a story he loved. He settled his small slim body comfortably on my crossed legs and I began.

"When the nursery school was very new the Municipal Council invited the Maharaja's son, Prince Jayachamarajendra to come and open it.

He said he would come, so everyone got very excited. The council sent out men to paint red and white bands on all the avenue trees between here and Bangalore".

"Why did they do that?"

"To show him respect."

Then the Municipal President came and asked Mrs. Cutting to provide afternoon tea for the Prince and his friends.

She said she would. She went and told her cook, Yesudas, to make special tea, sandwiches and cakes for the tea party.

The bungalow was all scrubbed and polished and the nursery school was decorated with flying flags.

"Did he come on his elephant, anna?"

"No, he came in a Rolls Royce."

"What's that?"

"That's a very special car!"

"I'd rather he'd come on an elephant!"

"It's a long way for an elephant to walk all the way from Mysore, it would take a long, long time."

Cutting ammagaru's cook made the cakes and the sandwiches and decorated the room very beautifully. Mrs. Cutting said "That's beautiful, Yesudas" and went across to the Nursery School to greet the Prince.

Yesudas sat on the back verandah for a while then he went out to the drive and looked at all the people under the Pandal in front of the nursery school. All the men in their best white shirts and dhotis, wearing their best gold-threaded turbans and the women in their beautiful saris with sweet-smelling flowers in their hair.

Then the Prince and his friends came in three shining cars.

Yesudas ran back to the house and shut all the doors.

"What did he do that for?"

"To keep thieves out."

Then he ran across the road and worked his way through the crowd standing in the street until he could see the prince quite clearly.

"Was the prince wearing gold and diamonds?"

"Yes, he had beautifully embroidered clothes and sparkling gold and diamond rings on his fingers."

"Where were the monkeys?"

Anjan and his tribe of monkeys were in the big mango tree. They ate a few small green fruit then Ganga, the curious one, climbed on to the roof of the bungalow and peered in the fanlight.

What a sight met his eyes - all those colourful cakes and sweets and flowers. He chattered in excitement and his uncles and his aunts and cousins and brothers all came jumping across."

"What about his mother and father?"

"Yes, they were there."

It was easy, the fanlights were open, they all climbed down the ropes.

They tried some of everything.

"Did they eat the flowers?"

"Yes, even the flowers, they had a real feast."

Then, suddenly, the door opened. Yesudas stood there, stick in hand. "Swami! What a disaster!"

The monkeys looked at his face and decided they weren't welcome. Some scaled up the ropes, others dodged out the door past Yesudas' flailing waddy, and all were gone in a flash.

"Did he hit any?"

"No, they were too quick for him."

Cake crumbs, icing, banana skins and flower petals covered the room in a sticky mess. The table cloth was ruined.

Yesudas' shouts had brought his wife and children running. He began giving orders. You clean up the mess while I go to the bazaar and buy some food. Son, go over to the function and tell Mrs. Cutting secretly, what has happened. Ask her to try to delay the Prince's arrival here by a few minutes.

Mother and children all began cleaning up - all that beautiful food in the rubbish basket - no time for a cloth - a quick polish to the table, rearrange the undamaged flowers.

Yesudas was back again, paper pokes of wadda, chakli, Mysore pak, and Bombay mixture in bags on the handlebars - just time to put them on the table as the Prince and Mrs. Cutting arrived at the front door.

I looked down at Philip, he was asleep. "Chikka Thammu, wake up - you haven't had food yet." It was no use trying to rouse him and I carried him off to his bed as Danam appeared in the doorway with the dinner plates.

Chapter 18

At the end of the year I sat for the Central Recruitment Board examinations and missed first class by two marks.

Apart from my disappointment, the year had been a good one - it was many years since I had lived at home and I enjoyed being with my family.

Father, Chichu and I went hunting together every Wednesday evening. Jacobanna often accompanied us -sometimes we went by jutka, sometimes in the hospital Ford.

Since that night in Bangalore there was a sensitive area between father and me - it was there until his death, but we loved one another and he would tease me about my broad view because I loved my stepmother as though she were my own mother and often sang cinema songs as well as Christian lyrics while taking my bath.

In 1937, because I was able to type, I received a temporary appointment as clerk in the Assistant Commissioner's Office in Chikka. Under the Indian system the States are divided into districts and each district has a Collector or Commissioner in charge who also acts as civil judge to settle disputes. Each district is further sub-divided into Taluqs and an assistant commissioner is appointed to see to the administration of a number of these.

In 1938 I received a permanent appointment as Taluq Office clerk and from there was transferred to the Magistrate's court. In 1939 I was transferred to the Magistrate's court in Kolar Gold Fields. I rented a small room and for the first time seriously tried my hand at cooking.

Before taking up this new post I had once again asked father to send me for further study - he did not give me a reply.

Some days before receiving my first pay I went down to one of the jewellers' shops. The jeweller beckoned me in and waved me to a mat.

"Please sit down. Will you take coffee?"

"Yes please." I was not used to ordering jewellery; sipping coffee would give me time to think.

The jeweller called a small boy from the street, pressed some pice into his hand and told him to bring coffee from a nearby hotel.

"What is it you desire?"

"I would like you to make a gold chain."

"For a marriage?"

"No, for my mother. I can afford to pay fifty rupees on receipt of this month's salary."

"Let me show you some designs!" The jeweller unlocked a glass-fronted display cabinet and took out a number of gold chains of traditional patterns. Some very fine and delicate, some much heavier.

"Which designs are more expensive?"

"It doesn't matter how intricate the design you choose, you pay by weight for the quantity of gold. Of course it is all 18carat gold.

The small boy had reappeared with the coffee and been rewarded with a few pice for his errand. I sipped thoughtfully as I wavered between a fairly solid mango design and a lacy threadwork.

"I would like the threadwork."

The jeweller weighed the chain and made some calculations on his abacus. "I can give you a suitable length made into a necklace for forty-eight rupees, sir."

"Thank you. Do you want a deposit?"

"Give me five rupees deposit. When will you collect it?"

"On the afternoon of September 2nd."

I walked back towards my room singing the latest cinema song under my breath. I must order a special garland I thought and turned right towards the bus stand. The road was lined with petty shops, most of them large wooden boxes on spindly wooden legs, the shop-keeper with just enough room to sit cross-legged amongst his goods.

Wide-mouthed baskets of marigold and jasmine sat within his reach so that he could splash water on them from an earthenware pot at his side. As he sat with a length of twine in his right hand he selected flowers from the baskets and deftly strung them together to form a garland, "What do you want, swami."

"I would like to order a special garland."

"Which flowers would you like?"

"Do you have roses available now?"

"Yes, but they are more costly!"

"I would like a garland of roses and jasmine. How much would that cost?"

"That would be two rupees."

"One rupee is surely enough."

"I'll make it for you, sir, for one rupee eight anna."

"Right, I would like it on Tuesday afternoon."

"I will have it ready without fail, sir."

After signing for my salary on Tuesday afternoon I went to the jewellers to collect the chain. It looked very beautiful nestling on tissue paper in a small blue box.

The garland was also ready and I caught a bus for home.

Mother was in the kitchen organising the evening meal. I put my purchases on the small table and untied the thread from the garland which was wrapped in a package of sewn leaves. It was beautiful, the scent of the flowers mingled and the red roses showed up in sharp contrast against the white jasmine.

"Amma, come here for a moment please."

Mother appeared in the doorway a look of surprise on her face. I stepped forward, placed the garland around her neck and kissed her on both cheeks then I presented her with the jewel box and watched with anxious anticipation as she opened it.

Her face lit up with surprise and pleasure, it was all the thanks I needed.

Chapter 19

Before taking up this new post at Kolar Gold Fields {KGF} I had again asked father to send me for further study - he did not give me an answer and I was harbouring resentment against him for not giving me a second chance to study . Because of this after returning to KGF I did not write to father or mother.

Each day, after work, I went to the bazaar to make my purchases of fresh vegetables. If I met an acquaintance we sometimes went to an hotel and drank coffee. One evening, a few minutes after my return home a shadow fell across the doorway. I looked up expecting to see a woodcutter with his load but was surprised to see mother, Philip, Rava and Prasanna. My heart jumped for a moment in fear that something had happened to father or my sisters and I said "Mother, what brings you here, is everyone well at home?"

"Yes, we are all well. I came to see how you are managing."

Ravi and Prasanna ran to me and I lifted one on each arm. How good it was to see them! A flood of warmth swept over me and I realised how much I had been missing them all.

Taking my mat from the corner I spread it on the floor.

"Amma, please sit down." Mother sat down and Philip curled up beside her.

I dipped my small aluminium pot into the earthenware water jar and threw in some lumps of raw sugar; then with a few blows through a piece of tin pipe my infant fire roared to a blaze.

I drew up my peeta (low wooden stool) in front of mother.

"How are Chichu and my sisters ?"

"They are well and studying hard?"

"And father?"

"Your father is well and very busy while Dr. Cutting is away on furlough. Do you remember Pillappagaru?"

"Which Pillappa?"

"A friend of your father's who has land near Sushepalya. He was brought in the other day very serious. He was trying to irrigate his fields and the pump was not running smoothly so he bent over to adjust it - his turban caught on the belt and his scalp was pulled off. His brother and a friend put him on a cart and brought him in bleeding badly - they did not bring the scalp. Your father was very upset and tried to graft the skin of a goat on to his head but it went bad after a day."

"Did Pillappa die?"

"No, he is doing well - the wound is healing but his head looks dreadful. He will need to conceal it always with his turban."

Rava and Prasanna were wandering around the room examining everything. Rava stood still "Mummy, I want to go to the bathroom?"

"For number one?" I asked "Just go down the lane beside the next house."

"Philip, you come with me." Rava grabbed Philip by the hand and they went out together.

Mother got up and went to the door. "That's very inconvenient for you Thammu."

"I can manage mother - the Reddy owns this room and allows me to bathe there and use his toilet."

"Why don't you rent a larger place?"

"To rent a house would take nearly all my salary - I want to save all I can." A pity father doesn't save some of that money he spends on cigarettes, I thought.

Mother broke in "Philip had another bad fit two days ago the tablets don't seem to control them entirely. He came home from school and was riding his tricycle on the verandah. When he fell he hit his head on a post and made it bleed - fortunately I was home and Prasanna called out "Mummy, Philip's sick!" I went running. That's why I brought him with me."

The water was boiling and I made coffee with the little bit of milk I kept for curds.

While Mother and the children sipped coffee I put dhal (split peas) on the stove and turned to the coconut and other spices I had put on my new curry stone ready to grind.

I felt angry with father. I was sure he had sent mother because I hadn't written, but I would wait for mother to tell me herself.

That day I had bought some small brinjals to stuff - it was one of my favourite dishes.

"Mother, you've come just at the right moment to tell me the right ingredients for masala eggplant. I've never made them, How does that look?" I waved towards the spices on the curry stone.

"Where are the egg plant?" Mother got up and went to my spice shelf - a pinch more of one, a spoonful of another, some cinnamon and cloves. Mother was in her element.

I made a mental picture of the ingredients.

"Give me the peeta Thammu - I don't like to see you grinding masala, that is woman's work."

"I don't mind, in fact, I rather enjoy it." Mother squatted down in front of the curry stone - sprinkled a little water and began to grind.

I sat back and finished my coffee in some amusement. Mother never ground masala at home, that was Danam's job.

Soon the rice was cooked - I served us all and we ate. I was still waiting for mother to tell me why she had come. At last the silence was broken.

"Why haven't you written, Thammu?"

"I have been busy." I hedged.

"Your father and I have been worrying about you."

"There is no need to worry."

"Your father sent me to see how you were."

"When is father going to send me to study? I live very frugally and have managed to save some money but it wouldn't be enough without father's support. He did promise to send me after two years."

"There are all the younger children to consider, Thammu."

"But if I obtained a medical degree I would be able to help put them through college."

"I'll speak to your father about it."

Mother spent a week with me but we did not mention the matter again.

Chapter 20

Because I knew typing next year I was transferred to Kolar as clerk in the Assistant Commissioner's office. One Saturday our Kolar office cricket team played the Chikka team and beat them. At this time Mr. Shafi Dharasha who captained their team was sub-collector in Chikka, and was also a member of the Mysore cricket XI. After the match he came up to me. "I hear you are from Chikka, we could do with a good batsman. Why don't you put in for transfer back to our office."

"I haven't been in Kolar very long sir."

"That doesn't matter, there will be a lot of transfers taking place in June, I think you'd have a good chance."

In bed that night, the more I thought about it the more the idea of being with the family again appealed to me. Next day I filed an application for transfer.

So in June 1940 I returned to Chikka as clerk in the sub divisional office. It was good to be home again. Chichu had just completed his matriculation and to our delight did very well. Two days after his results came out Kanya, Chichu and I were sitting waiting for the B.B.C. news, as was our custom. Kanya had completed her College course and was home again teaching under Mrs. Cutting in the Municipal Nursery School.

Chichu broke the silence "I've decided to look for a job."

"Why, Chichu? You did very well in your exams, you should continue with your studies."

"I had a talk with father - finances are very tight - all the younger children have to be educated."

"That is mother's influence" Kanya chipped in, "it will be interesting to see what happens when the younger children are ready to study."

I looked at Kanya in surprise "Surely that is an unfair remark, Kanya!"

"You don't know what goes on, Thammu. Father won't let mother favour her own children but mother has ways of getting around it. She gives Krupa aunty money when she goes to Bangalore to buy new clothes for the young ones, then Krupa aunty brings them back as gifts."

I kept quiet. I knew Mother sometimes seemed a bit unconcerned about Kanya's asthma.

Chichu looked annoyed. "Never mind about that Kanya. I hear they are looking for workers for the new aircraft factory that is being built in Bangalore. If I worked there I would also feel I was doing something towards the war effort."

"I hear it's easier to obtain work in Bangalore now with so many troops stationed there."

"You know the army is cutting down trees on the hills around here by the truckload and taking them in for firewood".

"They are doing the same around Kolar. The other day I had to go into Bangalore on the last bus - we were passing cartloads of wood all the way. They travel all night to reach the city before dawn. It made our journey very slow and our driver had his hand on the bulb of the horn most of the way."

At this stage the war in Europe had not affected us greatly. We had food shortages, mainly because the army paid a good price and bought up the best fruit and vegetables. Grain was rationed for the same reason.

Many school - leavers joined the Indian Army to train as officers, able people who were unemployed also joined up.

Each night we older ones listened to the news then had family prayers before taking food.

Chichu had made up his mind and on Monday morning took the train into Bangalore. When I returned that night he was excited.

"I've got a job on the assembly line at Hindustan Aircraft and will join next month when the factory opens. The pay is not bad either - I should be able to save something."

"Where will you live?"

"Seschu went with me - we'll go in next week and look for a room, if we share it will keep costs down! Do you know they have a Canteen and also want to organise sporting teams! When I was interviewed they asked me what sports I played. I think I might even enjoy it."

"I expect you will." I looked at my younger brother fondly. His light-hearted optimism and zest for life made him very attractive. Did I also feel a slight twinge of envy? No, just some regret that my more serious nature did not allow me to fly to the same heights as he did.

It was a pleasure playing cricket under the captaincy of Mr. Shafi Dharashi, but we had only played two matches, which we won, when he became ill and had to be hospitalised in Bangalore.

He was replaced by Mr. Ananta Ramaiah, a self-made man. I found him good to work for. He was very honest and liked me because I was honest and sincere. He later appointed me bench clerk.

Now that I was back in Chikka I bought myself a pony and often rode two or three miles into the country in the cool of the evening. Sometimes, if father was free, we went walking across the fields. We were good friends again and enjoyed talking about world events or events nearer home.

Father had purchased a building site in the Chikballapur extension. One day when we were walking Father said, "I won't be going shooting with you this Wednesday, I am going to Avati to organise slabs for the foundations of the house. It will be good to have a place of our own - we need more room."

"Do you intend to live there after you retire father?"

"That's a long way off but I would not want to retire here. I've seen it happen too often that someone who has worked in a hospital retires and sets up practice just down the road. It is very damaging to the hospital and I would not want to do that."

"Will you go to Gollahalli then?"

"Yes, that's what I had in mind when I bought the land there. I could move about the villages in that area - it would fill a need. I'd be able to grow some crops as well to supplement what I earned. By that time the younger ones will be old enough to fend for themselves."

"Will you go to Gollahalli then?"

"What about my studies? It is three years now since I began work - I have saved some money but not enough to support myself for several years."

"I will ask Mr. Ananta Ramaiah whether he thinks you could manage a medical course."

"Please father, do that" I felt angry but I kept quiet.

A few days later one of the clerks came into the office.

"Have you heard the news, anna? Two people from Sidlaghtta were just taken to the hospital in a jutka, one died before they reached outpatients and the other is very serious with vomiting and diarrhoea. Dr. Cutting suspects Cholera - they are checking now. They had both been on pilgrimage to Tirupati."

"How did you hear all this?"

"I was at the hospital getting some gripe water for our new baby. My wife can't leave the house yet."

This was bad news. I hurried through my afternoon's work, my mind whirling with thoughts of my younger brothers and sister. The children were told not to drink or eat away from home but children don't always do what they're told.

When I reached home mother had the children with her.

"You've heard the news?"

"Dr. Cutting has already sent Mahomed Pir Sahib in to the Government Hospital in Bangalore to see if vaccine is available. We'll all be vaccinated as soon as it arrives. I've warned the older children not to eat anything outside the house."

"You'd better keep the little ones with you - they are too young to be trusted and the other staff families love to feed them when they visit."

Pir Sahib arrived back too late to vaccinate that night. After I had gone to bed I remembered the S.D.O was in Bangalore. He had a young wife and children. I resolved to go to their house early next day.

Next morning, dressing quickly and without eating, I walked across to Mr. Ananta Ramaiah's Bungalow. As I approached the gateway a troop of monkeys was walking along the garden wall jumping from one pillar to the next across the gap then moving on towards the Cutting's Bungalow. After the mangoes no doubt! I hurled a stone, the leader drew back his teeth in a snarl but the troop only hastened its pace towards the mission compound. No time to pursue that diversion. As I walked up the driveway, the green parrots eating the flowers on the rain tree hushed their screeching, then took off with a whirr of wings.

I went up the broad stone stairway to the heavy wooden door and knocked. Their houseboy opened it, he looked surprised.

"I would like to speak to the ammagaru."

"Ammagaru is making her devotions."

"Don't disturb her, I will wait."

"Please come in, sir and sit down."

"It is cool and pleasant here on verandah, I will wait here."

A few minutes later the S.D.O.'s wife appeared, her pink voile sari tied immaculately, the pigment fresh on her forehead from her recent 'puja'.

"Amma, there is Cholera in the town and as ayyagaru is away I thought you might be unaware of it."

"I hadn't heard."

"We have managed to obtain vaccine from Bangalore. Perhaps I can escort you and the children to the hospital to be vaccinated. Two cases have been reported near here."

"That is very kind of you. We will come at once."

"Krishnappa, give Sabhapathygaru coffee while I get the children ready."

Krishnappa stood and watched me from the doorway as I drank.

"Has ammagaru taken food?" I asked him.

"Today is Ammagaru's fast day but the children have eaten sir."

"I knew Mrs. Ananta Ramaiah was a devout Hindu. Is it possible for you and the cook to accompany amma to the hospital? It is better if the whole household is vaccinated before the vaccine runs out."

"I will ask amma."

We all walked across to the hospital and were vaccinated. Isaiah told me three more cases had come in during the night. One had died half an hour after admission.

I returned home to find mother on the verandah. "Wherever were you Thammu? We've all been vaccinated you'd better go and have yours now."

"It's all right mother, I've been done!"

The car drove out the hospital gate, with Dr. Cutting and some of the nurses on board.

"They are going down to Kandawara to vaccinate people in that area. There were new cases in the night, it looks as if it is spreading."

One night I came in late after attending a meeting in the town. Father had just returned home looking haggard with exhaustion. Mother always waited up to serve him his food.

I joined them in the dining hall.

"Have there been many new cases today father?"

"Yes the small shed the Government lady doctor put at our disposal is full. I think it was once a mortuary, it only holds three beds."

"I hear they have decided to close the nursery school until the epidemic is over."

"Yes, Dr. Cutting has requested permission to use it as an isolation ward. Very few of the patients we've visited in the town will consent to admission, only the very poor or homeless and their condition is often already so bad that their chances of survival are slim.

The trouble is that most of them have no idea of the way it spreads and simply throw the excreta in the gutter and wash the dirty clothes in the tank. By the time we see them it's already been spread around.

"David was telling me we had run out of saline because our still is the only one in town and both the Government hospital and private doctors are coming for supplies."

"Fortunately we had some saline in stock and now we are running the still continuously. Saline is often the life saver. People who are brought in suffering severe loss of fluid and salt from the diarrhoea and vomiting usually look quite different after a drip has run for a few minutes."

The epidemic lasted a month. There were 40 cases in all and of those eighteen died. We all breathed a sigh of relief when it was over and life returned to normal.

Chapter 21

Shortly after the Cholera outbreak in 1941 Dathi was home from teacher's college for the summer holidays and had been busy stitching herself a jacket when I came in from work. I sat down to read the paper.

"Anna, wouldn't you like to get married?"

"What makes you say that?"

"Nothing in particular, but you're getting old, you're twenty-four next birthday."

"That's not old, even if it seems so to a 17 year old child like you."

"Have you ever been in love?"

"Not seriously!"

"Wouldn't you like a beautiful wife to look after you?"

"My greatest wish is to go back to college to study medicine. If I get married I'll have added responsibilities and it will be even more difficult to return to study."

That night in bed I pondered her question, it had come so suddenly and unexpectedly.

A few days later I had the answer. My father's sister and her daughter who had just passed her Senior School Leaving Certificate, were visiting Ananda Aunty.

I walked into our house after work to find mother entertaining them to coffee and 'tindi'.

"Thammu, meet your aunt and cousin from Nidubrolu."

I greeted them. Dathi's remarks fell into place as I saw her combing and plaiting Shantamma's hair while obviously treating her in a very sisterly fashion. Shanta looked an attractive and intelligent girl but I felt a surge of anger. I did not want to have a marriage arranged for me now. I picked up the Deccan Herald from the small table near the door, excused myself and went out to the verandah to lie on my bed until they were gone but my feelings were mixed as I lay there, and the paper had little of my attention.

I heard my mother, Kanya and Dathi escorting them to the gate. A few moments later Dathi appeared.

"Anna, how could you be so rude!"

"I wasn't rude, it looked like a ladies' party."

"Shanta thinks you are handsome and inscrutable,"

"I don't care what she thinks." I said rather too vehemently, secretly savouring the thought of being handsome - no one had ever before said I was handsome; and inscrutable - that gave me a feeling of superiority.

"Did she know what inscrutable meant?"

"Yes, she did! I asked her what it meant."

"Well, go away, Dathi, and leave me in peace."

"Oh, you are disappointing! I would like her for a sister-in-law, she's nice!"

Dathi left me, but not in peace, my mind was awhirl with conflicting emotions.

Father was very late coming home and no one else remarked on the visit. It was several days before father and I were alone together. I had been to the Cinema with some friends and came home late - Father had just come in and had sat down with the paper before taking his bath.

"You're late, Thammu!"

"I went to the late session to see 'Sattee Savitri'."

"Was it good?"

"Yes, you and mother should go. You are very late yourself."

"We had to do emergency surgery on a woman with a ruptured uterus - it was her eleventh pregnancy - she had lost a lot of blood."

"Did you manage to get blood for her?"

"Yes, fortunately Satya's blood was compatible - the transfusion is still running and I think she will pull through."

"That's good!"

"Thammu, I haven't had a chance to talk to you about your aunt's visit. She would like to arrange a marriage for her daughter who has just passed S.S.L.C. You are the obvious choice."

"I've told you father, I want to do more study."

"Don't get angry. I have told her you are asthmatic. It will be better if she completes nursing training before marrying you. She has consented."

"And are you going to give me a chance to study while she does that?"

"I'll see what I can do."

When I arrived home from work a few days later Father was reclining on the verandah, smoking a cigarette, his stick beside him. The two dogs rose excitedly and ran around me wagging their tails.

You're home early, father!"

"There seems to be a lull now. This afternoon we had quite a small outpatients."

"Perhaps that's because it's Tuesday," I said sitting down beside him. (Tuesday is regarded as an inauspicious day to travel or do anything new.)

"Possibly" father replied, "or since the rains, everyone is too busy in the fields to come to hospital."

Danam brought us each a tall glass of lime juice and we sat and sipped.

'Now that the rains have come the weather is quite pleasant,' I was thinking but within minutes the tiny eyeflies were hovering around my eyes and crawling in unless I kept them at bay with regular waves of my hand.

"Let's go walking," father said, "the flies aren't so troublesome when we're moving."

At the word 'walking' the two dogs, which had been sprawled by our deck chairs apparently oblivious, leapt to their feet and ran to the gate and back, urging us on.

We walked out along the Mushtur road worn down by the passing to and fro for centuries of cattle, carts and people. The freshly ploughed fields, spread out at shoulder height on either side, were bright red against the green backdrop of Harihareshware rising two thousand feet beyond them. The familiar smell of damp, freshly turned earth, was good. Even at this hour several farmers were walking behind their wooden ploughs which the yoked oxen strained to pull through the soft earth. A woman walked behind one, a small basket on her hip, throwing sorghum seed into the furrow.

When it rained enough to plough, the good farmers lost no time in sowing for they might not have a second chance.

Father broke the silence "I spoke to Mr. Ananta Ramaiah. He says you are a bright boy and I should have sent you to college long ago. But I discussed it with Dr. Cutting and he says you are not bright enough."

"And you will take his word for it, father?"

Father was silent.

"That's grossly unfair. He's not in a position to know." I was furious! I turned, whistled Rocket and without a word set off for home. I could not trust myself to speak to father again. Tears of anger and hurt stung my eyes and I scarcely noticed where I was going until a shout of "Hey! Dowa! Are you out of your mind!" roused me in time to jump out of the path of a laden oxcart.

"Are you trying to die, mad dog?" The irate driver yelled as he went past.

I didn't even apologise but hurried on. As I neared the house I realised I couldn't go in and face the family, much less father when he returned. I walked around to the back of the house and into the hall, picked up Queenie's bridle and set out for the other compound. Queenie saw me coming and came over, her nose nuzzling my hand for the fresh leaves I usually brought. I put the bit between her teeth, grabbed her mane and was up. We trotted out the lower gate, then once onto the Bagepalli road I let her head go.

"Dear God, why are you letting this happen to me? Surely I could be a more useful person if I studied medicine. It's all I really want to do. When are you going to give me a chance?"

The cool evening air, fanning my face, had a soothing effect and by the time Queenie slowed to a walk my emotions had simmered down. I rode on into the night, hardly noticing the occasional cart and moving aside automatically to give way to a lorry or two. Finally we came to a tank and I led Queenie down for a drink then set out for home. The lights were out and everyone in bed. I crept in noiselessly along the verandah, past the others sleeping under their nets, and went to bed but it was a long time before I slept.

From that time relations between father and me were strained and our former friendship was never restored.

Chapter 22

Father's fiftieth birthday fell on a Saturday and he expressed a wish to have a family dinner so I asked Mr. Ananta Ramaiah for permission to hold a family meal for him around the courthouse table. We had no large table at home and our small dining hall was cramped even if we all ate together seated on mats spread around the walls.

Ward boy, Chinnappa, came to our house early to help Danam with the cooking. At 7am I was ready to go down to the meat market on my bicycle.

"Make sure you buy good leg meat anna! The meat is not good just now, the rains have come but the sheep have not had time to put on any condition yet."

"I'll go down later and get banana leaf plates and betel leaves when I collect the garlands."

Mother and the girls were peeling garlic and chopping onions. Mother measured out the Masala ingredients for Danam to grind on the stone.

We had arranged for the hospital car to take all the food to the courthouse but at four o'clock Samanna came to the house. "Amma, some men have arrived requesting the car to bring in a boy who has fallen out of a tree while cutting leaves for his goats."

"Oh,dear, what a shame! Is he badly hurt?"

"He is unconscious."

"You go and come Samanna, we'll manage."

I was just leaving to pick up the betel nut and the special garland I had ordered. "Anna, you'd better bring a jutka back with you."

"Isn't it a bit early?"

"Ask one to come at 6 o'clock then."

The girls went across to the court early and decorated the table with fresh roses and jasmine. Danam and Chinnappa had borrowed some of Mrs. Cutting's pot plants and placed them around the room. When I arrived from the bazaar the courthouse was transformed.

"What a difference those plants and flowers make, father will be pleased!"

Danam arrived with the jutka, the food and the plates. The court peon (servant) had volunteered his services and helped with the unloading.

We were all there. Kanya, now twenty-six years old, headmistress of the nursery school; myself, 24 years; then Sarojini home for the weekend from her teaching post in Bangalore.

Chichu too had managed to get leave from the aircraft factory.

"Are you trying to keep a fair complexion." I teased him. He was pale from working long hours indoors.

Dathi, home from teachers college, her hair braided around her head, making her look very grown up, was as lively as usual.

Nani, just into a half sari and beginning to blossom into a beautiful young lady. Too old now to be riding my pony.

As I looked at Philip I felt a twinge of anguish. How much sadder must mother feel at the evident effect of the repeated epileptic seizures he experienced!

Ravi and Prasanna were still primary school students and as I watched, arguing over how we should sit.

Everything was ready and we awaited mother and father's arrival.

Prasanna dashed out the door and was back in a flash. "Here they come! Get ready!"

We hastily took our places around the table. Kanya had unwrapped the garland and as soon as mother and father appeared in the doorway, went forward, garlanded father and kissed him. Kanya was very fond of father and although father showed no favouritism I believe he had a special place in his heart for her.

We all burst into song "Happy Birthday to you" and Kanya led father to his decorated chair at the head of the table. Mother went to the opposite end and looked fondly at father. There was complete understanding between them.

Father was moved by his reception. He stood in silence for a moment and looked at us all before asking the blessing.

Danam and Chinnappa served us while the court peon hurried to and fro fetching more food from the larger vessels.

Father chose morsels from his plate or one of the main dishes and offered them to us one by one.

"I may not live to see my next birthday. If I die Kanya will cry a lot, I don't want that."

At this time I was rebelling against father and against God. I felt angry with father but was pricked in my conscience when I saw his love. When he arrived home from the hospital late at night, he would come to my bed and in my half sleep I was conscious of him pulling up the covers and buttoning my shirt. I thought, if father loves me like this, what about God? But when father offered me a piece of chicken a few minutes later rebellion welled within me and I refused to take it.

"When are you going to send me for study?"

"I will ask the magistrate's opinion tomorrow."

Chapter 23

A few weeks later father had a large table made but when the carpenter brought it to the house it wouldn't fit into the dining hall unless we removed the large steel safe which was concreted into one corner. Father called the hospital cleaners and it took four of them to move it.

Over the next weeks father preached three times and on the last occasion spoke in Telugu using the text 'Fear not little flock' and personally invited all the male nurses who were Telugu speaking.

One evening I was standing outside under the huge rain tree near the outpatient department. Father was talking with Jacob near the private wards while waiting to take a meal being given to all the hospital staff by a grateful osteomyelitis patient. Jacobanna told me later that Father said to him "Look at the way Thammu is standing, he is behaving just like me, go over and invite him to the meal."

Jacobanna came over to me.

"Anna, your father would like you to come and eat with us."

I went over and joined them.

That Friday afternoon father came to my office and said "Come on, we'll go for a walk."

"No, not until you give me a definite reply about my studies."

When I reached home at 5-30 father was waiting at the gate, stick in hand. "Come on, we'll go Thammu!"

"No, father." I walked inside. Kanya was there.

"Have you no shame? Fancy refusing to walk with father."

I felt embarrassed. "All right then, I'll go." I looked out the door but father was no longer there.

We were accustomed to having family prayers at 7-30 followed by the evening meal. As often happened, father had not returned home, so mother conducted prayers and we began to eat together around the new table.

Father returned before we were finished and took his seat at the head of the table. Mother rose to serve him.

"I don't want food."

Mother looked at him sharply.

"It's been a hot day, you should eat something, you look very tired."

"Perhaps some buttermilk,"

Mother called to Danam - "Anna, please prepare buttermilk for the doctor."

Danam appeared a few minutes later with a tall glass of buttermilk containing chopped chillies and coriander leaves and set it in front of father.

If my refusal to go walking had upset him, perhaps he would think a little of my situation. I rose from the table, washed my hands, rinsed my mouth and went out to the verandah to read. At 9 o'clock Kanya came and said "Father wants you."

"I'm not going." I snapped.

"Go,Thammu, you've upset Father - he's just been sitting there for over an hour, looking so sad."

"It won't hurt him to be upset - perhaps he'll take me more seriously."

"You should be ashamed - you know how father loves you!"

"Oh, leave me alone! I'll go then!"

I got up and went into the dining room, father was still sitting as I had last seen him, the half-empty glass of buttermilk in front of him.

"You called me father?"

"Take my hand, nayana, I feel a numbness."

I stood in front of him. He reached out his hand and forcibly took mine. His face seemed strained, altered somehow and as I stood looking at him I felt fear clutch at me even before he said " I think I'm going to have a stroke."

"Father!" No! You'll be alright! I'll call Dr.Cutting."

"Don't want." and with those words his face changed and he slumped sideways.

"Father!' Kanya had come to the doorway, she rushed forward, her voice a cry of fear.

Mother came out of the bedroom.

Father's hand still gripped mine and seemed to reach my very soul. I stood frozen until mother began to weep.

"I'll get Dr. Cutting!" Without waiting to ride my bicycle I ran out the door, down the steps, through the hospital gate and along the road. As I looked into the lighted room, through the glass of the front door of the bungalow, time seemed to stand still and my brain recorded an indelible picture of Mrs. Cutting in her armchair knitting, while Dr. sat reading close by; then I rapped on the glass. Dr. Cutting opened the door.

"Come quickly, it's father. He's had a stroke!"

"Oh no!" He went back for his stethoscope; then, as we hurried down the road, I told him what had happened.

When we reached the house it was a blaze of lights. Father was still lying slumped over the table, the family around him weeping. Dr. Cutting examined him.

"We'll have him admitted in the morning. Thammu, help me carry him to his bed." Together we managed to lift father .

As I looked at his changed countenance I wanted to weep but could not. I felt crushed by my own sense of guilt. Kanya put her arms around me - I think she understood how I felt.

The others went back to bed. Mother knelt by father's side. Kanya and I sat at the table each of us sending up silent prayers, mine filled with remorse.

At 1 o'clock Kanya went out to the kitchen and made us all a cup of coffee. Mother had just returned to father's side when he stirred, opened his eyes and looked at her. He did not, or could not, speak. Then he became limp - mother felt for his pulse.

"Nayana, call Dr. Cutting!"

I ran again to the bungalow, this time to the side verandah where they slept. Dr. Cutting came at once. When he examined father he prepared and gave an injection of Coramine.

"He is sinking!"

Dr. Cutting stood with his stethoscope over father's heart, listening intently, a moment later he lifted one of father's eyelids, I noticed the pupil was very large.

"He has gone!" Dr. Cutting turned away to hide his emotion. A moment of silence followed, then mother and Kanya began to weep. I felt stunned and went and sat down at the table, then I felt Dr. Cutting's hand on my shoulder.

"I will send one of the night staff over."

I rose and shook my head in assent then went with Dr. Cutting to the door. Words would not come. I returned to the bedroom, put my arms around mother and Kanya and looked down at father, he looked very peaceful.

Mother looked up. "Go to bed Nayana, there will be a lot to do in the morning."

I suddenly realised I was now the male head of the family and would be responsible for a lot of the arrangements.

I went to bed but did not sleep - I lay there making mental lists of relatives and friends to whom we must send telegrams. Could we delay the funeral until the following day? The nights are cool. I dozed off as the first light appeared, to awaken shortly afterwards to the sound of movement in the kitchen. I went out to find mother trying to light the fire. With her hair uncombed and her face swollen with weeping she seemed to have aged ten years. I put my arms around her.

"Did you sleep mother?"

"No Nayana! How could I sleep?"

"Here, give me those sticks!" I took them from her and set them in the stove then lit a match. We squatted on our heels in front of the flickering flame - my arms around her. As the fire took hold, its warmth seemed to reach out to our numbed hearts.

After a cup of coffee I went to the pastor's house. He was shocked when I told him the news.

"This is a sad day for all of you and for the hospital and the whole district! Your father will be greatly missed."

"We wonder if 11 am tomorrow will be a suitable time for you to conduct the service?"

"Yes, I'm free then."

"Please go to see my mother to make arrangements."

I went on to the carpenter's house and called him.

"My father has died."

"Ah Yo! that is bad news - what happened?"

"He had a stroke. Can you make a coffin today?"

"Yes, swami. What height was the Doctorgaru?"

I felt at a loss - I had not thought of those practical details.

"Would you like me to come and take measurements?"

"No, of course, father is 5ft 10 ins." I had remembered father remarking that Chichu at 5 ft 11 ins had overtaken him by one inch.

"He was a big man!"

"Yes."

"Don't worry swami, I'll bring the coffin around by 3pm."

When I remounted my cycle I could scarcely see for my tears as I pedalled towards the post office. Mother had checked my list and I spent a few minutes outside reading it through meaninglessly as I composed myself.

The telegrams were sent, a visit to the flower sellers and the grave diggers. Was that all?

As I cycled home again a great weariness came over me - my mind seemed numb, I would have liked to be alone but the house was full of people.

Father was lying on the bed in his best clothes. Mother and the girls had threaded flowers and placed them over and around him.

My feelings were very mixed. All those years of resentment fell away. Why had I wasted them in bitterness? If only I had known father's time was to be so short. I remembered all the good times we had spent together, walking the dogs, hunting, even just sitting on the verandah in companionable silence - I went to my bed, lay down and wept.

Chapter 24

By evening many relatives as well as all the immediate family had arrived. We made arrangements, for those we could not accommodate, to sleep with friends or in the travellers' bungalow. Mother and the girls were kept busy helping Danam cook for the large numbers. I was so busy looking after our guests that I had no time to think, and my mind seemed dead.

We had set the time for the funeral at 11am to give time for father's sisters and other relatives to arrive from the north on the night train.

I had made arrangements for an ox-cart to carry the coffin, first to the church, where friends could look upon him for the last time, and afterwards to the cemetery. The many people who came to the funeral not only filled the Church but the church grounds as well and included many Hindu and Muslim friends. The girls had made fresh garlands of Jasmine and roses and draped them around father. We also lit incense sticks to ensure that the air was sweet.

Chichu and I and some members of staff acted as pall bearers to carry the coffin in and out of the Church then we walked behind the ox-cart to the cemetery while mother and the girls were driven in the hospital Ford. A large procession followed with many people singing hymns through their tears. Father's grave had been dug next to my own mother's. As I stood with my stepmother, who had been as dear to me as my own mother, with my brothers and sisters around me and listened to the words of the burial service many of father's actions before he died flashed into my mind: the preaching of three sermons, his remarks at his birthday dinner, the commissioning of the large table and his attempt to make peace with me: it seemed clear that father had been preparing us. I decided then that I would like to work in the hospital which had meant so much to him and to us all. As we began to throw earth on to the coffin each thud seemed to stiffen my resolve and I left the graveside with a feeling of peace in that decision.

Some of the hospital staff had volunteered their help with cooking for our relatives and guests so that after returning from the funeral service we were able to spend some time talking with them as we passed around coffee and mixture.

When the meal was ready we served some seventy people, then were kept busy escorting some to catch buses or trains while a number remained with us for a few days, having come long distances.

When everyone had finally settled for the night, mother, Kanya and I, had a cup of coffee. We were all exhausted and sat for a few minutes without speaking, wrapped in our own thoughts. My remorse was threatening to overwhelm me. I craved father's forgiveness which I had refused when offered. Now perhaps I could please him by working in the hospital.

"Did father ever say anything to you about making a will?"

Mother's voice roused me from my reverie, I saw Kanya glance sharply at her. Had he said anything? My mind would not focus! Her words were a shock. I had been so immersed in my own feelings that the matter of a will had not entered my mind.

"No, he never mentioned it. If he had Mr. Partasarthaiah would probably have prepared it for him."

"Yes, that's likely! Perhaps you would ask him Thammu?"

"I'll see him tomorrow! Have you looked through father's papers?"

"Not really, I did glance through a file in his desk - there was nothing there."

"Mother, I've decided I would like to work in the hospital. I will speak to Dr. Cutting about it tomorrow. Perhaps there is some administrative work I could do."

"Why Thammu! You have a good position! The hospital would not be able to offer you the same security."

"But I would be happier serving here, it meant such a lot to father."

"Well, it's your decision, Nayana."

"We'd better take rest now, tomorrow will be another busy day.."

With so many decisions to be made it was a wonder I slept but I lay down and knew nothing until the first light wakened me.

I had taken two weeks' leave so next morning at nine o'clock I walked down the road to Mr. Partasarthaiah's house. I knew it was his custom to take food at 9-30 before leaving for the court.

He greeted me warmly. Father had been perhaps his closest friend.

"Come and sit down, Thammu."

"Have you taken food?"

"Not yet. How is your mother?"

"She is still very distressed but a little calmer since the funeral."

Mrs. Partasarthaiah appeared in the doorway and made namaskaram. "Please convey my good wishes to your mother."

"I will, amma."

She disappeared and returned a few minutes later with two tumblers of coffee on a tray, then left the room.

I felt I had better say why I had come at this time of day. It was not the usual hour for visiting.

"Mother wonders if you know whether father made a will?"

"No, he never mentioned the matter to me."

"Oh, we thought perhaps you would know if he had."

"I'm sorry Thammu, I know nothing about it. Perhaps Dr. Cutting would know."

"It's possible, I'll ask him."

We sipped our coffee in silence.

"Your father will be much missed by the townspeople, in fact by the whole area. He was a very caring person."

"I know, I'll miss him."

"Yes, it's a great shock to us all."

I felt a large lump obstructing my throat. "Father and I were such good friends and I spoilt it all by being full of resentment over my studies. Now it is finished and I can't restore our relationship or say I'm sorry. I hope father can feel my remorse and forgive me wherever he is now."

Mr. Partasarthaiah reached out his hand and gripped my arm. "Thammu, your father loved you dearly. He always said of you 'my son has a very kind heart and caring nature', I'm sure he understood and forgave you."

That was too much for me, a loud sob escaped me and I felt in my pocket for my handkerchief.

Mr. Partasarthaiah rose from his chair and put his hand on my shoulder.

"Namaskarayya! Thank you." I had to go before I made more of a fool of myself.

"Namaste! I will see you at the public meeting on Wednesday."

I returned home. We still had relatives with us so it was some time before I could speak to mother alone.

"Partasarthaiahgaru knows nothing about a will - he suggests we ask Dr. Cutting."

"Will you ask him nayana?"

"I think it will be better if you ask him yourself, mother."

Mother was silent but I left her to think about it.

Chapter 25

Sampamma had been an old friend of the family since before my own mother's death. She had, in fact, been partly responsible for arranging father's remarriage and over the years had visited us all frequently. If she thought our stepmother was not looking after us as well as she should be, she would mention it to my father who would give some hints to our stepmother.

Now that it was necessary for us to move from the hospital quarters she searched for a suitable house to accommodate the family and found one just three doors down from the hospital gate. I paid the rent of nineteen rupees each month through her.

Father, before his death, had been considering the purchase of some land at Udumalode so we decided to proceed with this. Chichu and I accompanied father's old friend Mr. Gundu Rao to look at it but on talking to the people in Udumalode discovered there was some dispute about it so decided not to proceed.

On the way home we halted for the night in Mr. Gundu Rao's home at Posettihalli and, after taking food, Mr. Gundu Rao said.

"There is talk that they are going to sell Jodi Chikkanahalli (Jodi means Brahmin hereditary village). We'll go and see."

We went and saw the land and Mr. Gundu Rao said "Sampamma has connections with this village and will know whether they are selling or not."

On our return to Chikka I went to see Sampamma.

"Yes, they are going to sell it. Tell Mr. Gundu Rao to come and see me about it."

Mr. Gundu Rao, who was a teacher, often came to Chikka to see the school inspector and took food in our house.

"Sampamma would like to see you about the Jodi Chikkanahalli land."

"I will go now. You come with me."

On arriving at Sampamma's house she beckoned us into a small room adjoining the hall and spoke slowly and quietly.

"Some merchants of Chikka are trying to purchase that land. Go now and bring the owner here."

Sampamma, Mr. Gundu Rao and the owner were all Brahmins of the same caste and probably connected.

Then Sampamma said "If you purchase the land in whose name will you register it?"

"In the name of the mother."

"Put it in son's and mother's names."

When I heard that I felt Sampamma ought not to have said it.

While this matter was still being argued about, the land was sold to a merchant in the town.

Sampamma said afterwards that Mr. Gundu Rao had purposely delayed proceedings.

Shortly after this mother tackled me one evening. "Why did you tell Mr. Gundu Rao to register the land in both yours and my name? Don't you trust me?"

"I didn't mother, that was Sampamma's idea. Of course I trust you."

But I don't think mother believed me.

At this time we were still trying to collect money and materials for completion of the house in the extension. Mr. Gundu Rao had said he would collect and asked me to approach the Inspector of schools on his behalf to obtain leave. I did this and on three occasions obtained one month's leave for him. He came and took food in our house but did not collect. When he approached me a fourth time I quarrelled with him.

"On three occasions I got leave for you and you did nothing."

"But this time I will collect."

"No, I'm not asking the inspector again."

On my return home I mentioned the matter to Sukanya.

"Oh, I know why he doesn't collect."

"What do you mean?"

"Mother is not in favour of building the house."

"But why not?"

"Because by Indian law the property goes to the eldest son ana that would make it yours."

"But Kanya, it would be for the whole family. Mother surely knows the whole family could live there."

"Mother is only willing if it is registered in her name."

I sat silent. I had loved my stepmother and trusted her implicitly.

"But I took out all my insurance policies in mother's name."

"You shouldn't have done that, anna!"

I looked at Kanya, I felt shocked and there was a sick feeling in the pit of my stomach. Surely what Kanya said wasn't true. I felt as though the ground beneath my feet had become quicksand leaving me groping.

I went to the door, put my feet in my sandals and whistled the dogs. After walking for hours through the night I finally returned home to find the house in darkness and the door locked. I beat upon it until Dathi came and let me in.

Shortly after moving from the hospital quarters mother received an appointment as a teacher in the middle school. We were all pleased as it gave her a new interest and independence. But not long after this mother invited the headmistress of the middle school to come and live with us.

At first life went on smoothly enough but then mother's friend began to make snide remarks and mother always supported her.

When Chichu came home from Bangalore on leave she said. "What gifts have you brought for your mother and sisters?"

Chichu looked at her in surprise. He brought birthday gifts and always brought flowers and something for the house.

"Whose birthday is it?"

"Not a birthday but surely earning big money in Bangalore you bring jewellery or fine clothes for your sisters."

Chichu was embarrassed. He flushed and continued to eat his dinner.

Mother joined in. "That would be nice, Chichu."

"Mother, you know I am trying to save up to do a medical course."

On other occasions she criticised my sister's dress and accused us of eating too much and not taking our share of household tasks.

One evening when I returned from the office Kanya had been home from work with asthma and was still breathing very badly. Mother was cooking. Suwaranamma said to Kanya.

"You are good at making excuses to avoid cooking."

I suddenly felt very angry.

"What right have you to move in here, be waited on by us and then criticise? You are a woman of low breed."

"Thammu! How dare you speak to Suwaranakka like that, you ought to be ashamed of yourself!"

"It's true mother, since she moved in, happiness has moved out, we are always being criticised and needled and you don't look after Kanya properly."

I went to my room and slammed the door.

An hour later Kanya came to say there was a policeman to see me. I went out to the hall.

"What is it?"

"Sir, Mrs. Suwaranamma has laid charges against you."

"What do you mean?"

"Abusive language! Will you please come to the station."

I was shocked, I turned to Kanya.

"Where's mother?"

"Mother went out with Suwaranamma."

"Your mother is also at the police station, sir."

"I'll come."

"No! Wait Thammu! You'd better take someone with you."

I thought quickly and decided to call Narayana Swamy Chetty who worked as a village level worker in Nandi Hubli and was a friend of mine.

When we reached the station on our cycles Mother and Suvaranamma were both there. I looked at mother, she looked away.

The officer said "Mrs. Suwaranamma has charged you with abusive language and Mrs. Rajaratnam signed as a witness."

Mother a witness against me! I found it hard to take in and listened in a daze as the officer read the charge.

"What do you have to say?"

Anger rose within me. "I have no quarrel with my mother but her friend has come in and disrupted the peace of our home."

Mother said angrily "You are trying to drive me out of the house so that you can take all the property."

"That's not true! I'm sure father wanted the family to stay together and we could all live together comfortably without outside interference." I shouted.

"The property should come to me and I will go to court if necessary." Mother said.

I looked at her in disgust. "You are not fit to be my father's wife!" I turned on my heel and began to walk out.

"One moment sir." The officer sat and reread the statement.

"This charge is not sufficient to warrant further action. You may go!"

I felt unable to accompany the others back to the house and went to Narayanaswamy Chetty's, returning home some hours later.

When Kanya heard what had happened at the police station she said "You should not have said that to mother."

I felt very miserable and was unable to talk about it to anyone. All these things were carried back to the ears of Dr. Cutting and I could not defend myself.

Mother moved into quarters in the town which she rented with Suwaranamma and refused to feed us.

It was then decided that a Panchayat should be held to decide the distribution of fathers estate. The five members of the Panchayat were all Christians and related by marriage except for Dr. Cutting and Mr. Partasarthaiah, father's old friend. It was necessary for the members of the family to sign consent for the Panchayat. My sisters were for it as they did not get on with mother but I was against it. They arranged a common meal and when they called me to sign were seated around the large table father had had made before his death.

I said "This table is a witness that the family should remain together. I won't sign!"

Dr. Cutting said "You can trust us Thammu."

So I signed.

PART 2

Chapter 1

CASUAL LEAVE

In 1954, I had been working for some years as a Revenue Inspector for half of Kolar District, and spent a good part of each year moving from one travellers' bungalow to the next, spending a week or more assessing the tax payable by farmers and landowners in that area.

For the convenience of officials, Travellers' Bungalows had been built during the British Raj, and although we spoke about going to camp, in fact the travellers' bungalows were very comfortable, being similar to the one at Peresandra in which we spent our family holidays. Most had a cook and water boy attached, the larger ones even having a 'matey' to assist the cook.

In Taluq headquarters the T.B.s usually had two or three self-contained guest rooms, the common kitchen block being separate. Frequently all three rooms were occupied, so that it was necessary to make bookings in advance for myself and the clerk who usually accompanied me.

By now I had come to know the circumstances of many of the people well, and had also had considerable experience in character assessment. This was a job which gave plenty of opportunity for dishonest practices and the people had come to trust me, because I made honest assessments and refused to take bribes.

It had been a hot day and I was sitting in a deck chair on the verandah of the T.B. at Melekota after taking food. A slight breeze was beginning to rustle the leaves of the Peepul tree in the compound, when I saw a group of men approaching, the man in front holding a brightly burning torch to light the way.

I wondered idly where they were going at this time of night, there was no fair on as far as I knew.

When they reached the compound gateway they stopped and their silhouettes drew together under the torch as if conferring, then they came through the gateway and crossed the compound.

"Swami, are you there?"

The voice sounded familiar.

"Who is it?"

"Narayanappa of Kallehalli."

"What brings you here so late?"

"You must help us, Swami!"

"What's wrong?"

"The Reddy (Village landowner) is trying to take my daughter!"

"Why?"

"He desires her and says he will forgive me my debt if I give her to him but he is not a good man and his wife also is bad tempered. My daughter doesn't stop weeping!"

"How much do you owe?"

"Fifty rupees."

"That's not a large sum."

"But I can't repay him sir. Because my cow died I was unable to plough in time, then the last rain was too early to fill the ears of grain. What I did harvest is scarcely enough to feed my family - I have none to sell. I have told him I will repay him when the rains come and I can do 'coolie' (day labour)"

"Why have you come to me?"

"Because I fear he may have me killed then he can do as he pleases."

"But what can I do?"

"Please come to the village, he will be afraid to do anything if you are there."

"Where's your daughter now?"

"She's safe in the village with some of the women."

I felt very angry, I knew this particular Reddy, he was an unscrupulous man who thought his wealth and position gave him the right to do anything, but I inwardly doubted the power of my presence. How easy it would be for him to have someone kill Narayanappa and make it look like an accident.

"I will come." The decision was not difficult. The thought of that man laying his hands on Narayanappa's young daughter filled me with revulsion.

I went inside, picked up my torch, slipped my feet into my sandals and came out again - but I would need to apply for a day's casual leave tomorrow. My mind was clouded with anger. I re-entered the bedroom, wrote a note to the sub-divisional officer, folded it and put it in an envelope then slipped it into my pocket. My Gandhi cap was on the dresser, I donned that. Walking through the night even at this time of year could be cool.

I walked around to the servants' quarters and knocked loudly on the door.

"Who is it?" a sleepy voice answered.

"It is I, Sabapathyayya."

The noise of the bolt being drawn was followed by the cook's head, blinking in the light of the torch.

"I have urgent business to attend to, so I will take leave tomorrow - I will return the following day."

"Right Sir - I will prepare midday food."

The men from Kallehalli were huddled at the gate - I joined them and we set out, the flickering flame of the torch held by the leading man cast dancing shadows among the trees on either side. We had an eight mile walk through the foothills with the huge granite mass of Nandi hill looming darkly two thousand feet above us on our right.

Part of the route led along rough cart tracks then we went on to a foot-track which wound up over thorny ridges and down into the scrubby jungle of stony gullies. The torch bobbing ahead served a dual purpose, to light our way and frighten off panther and wild bear or boar. Now we had to travel single file and even at night the exertion caused the sweat to trickle down between my shoulder blades. I used my torch on the path for the one in front was little help to me in avoiding rocks or rough patches on the track, which was not much used. Frequently a long branch of lantana snatched at my clothing or my skin as we hurried on.

I followed the men automatically, my mind sending up prayers for wisdom to grapple with the problem before us. How best could we ensure the safety of Narayanappa and his family?

The moon was behind us bathing jungle-clad hills in a cold light. When we came to a stream one of the men said "Douse the torch, it is better if we enter the village quietly."

We made a detour around the village to enter near Narayanappa's house.

A 'pi' dog barked, then another. The pre-dawn chill,(or was it the tension?) made me shiver, and I looked towards the east where a scarcely perceptible lightening of the sky made me realise there would not be much sleep that night.

Narayanappa went ahead of me to his house, our companions melting into the darkness. He stood at his doorway and waved me in.

"Take rest sir, we will call you."

I bent my head and entered under the thatch and through the door. The hut was empty, a mat and bed sheet laid ready for me. I dipped a small brass pot into a water jar and drank then lay down to sleep but I realised no sleep would come until I had reached a solution to the problem. As I lay there quietly it came to me - a 'patramu' - I would draw up a legal document ensuring payment of Narayanappa's debt and security for his wife and daughter. I could stand as guardian, and perhaps my lawyer friend with me. That being clear in my mind, I knew no more until Narayanappa called at the door.

"Hot water sir!" He took me to a small bathroom adjoining another house and I made my ablutions.

When I returned to his house his wife was there ready for us and immediately threw herself prostrate at my feet.

"Get up, amma, don't be afraid, I have a plan."

She rose to her feet, her face swollen with weeping - her hair uncombed. She looked little more than a child herself. I felt like putting my arms around her to comfort her. What a hard life these village women lived - married at fourteen, drawing water, cleaning grain, cooking, working in the fields and bearing children - they had a very short childhood.

"Swami, you are our father, please help us!"

"I will. Stop weeping, we will make plans."

"Give coffee to the ayyagaru - please sit down."

I sat down cross-legged on the mat and Narayanappa squatted, with his back to the doorpost, while his wife served coffee she had, no doubt, borrowed and prepared.

I outlined my plan and they nodded assent.

"It is good, Sir."

"We will start immediately as I must present my leave letter."

As we walked the nine miles to Chikka I said to Narayanappa, "Has your daughter become a woman?"

"Yes, swami, a few months ago."

"Then it might be wise for you to arrange a marriage for her."

"How can I afford to have her married in these hard times?"

"Discuss it with your wife. Does she have a younger brother who would be a correct match and not demand any dowry? It will be better still if he lives at a distance but make sure he is a good man."

"I will see swami."

"I will give any help I can."

Most village girls are married as soon as they mature and traditionally the wife's younger brother, if unmarried, would be given first opportunity, otherwise another partner would have to be found, then she would be safe.

We went to my lawyer friend's house and drew up a legal document. He was about to take food, so invited us to eat. He had known me for many years, so knew that he must be content to have Narayanappa eat with us, although he was of lower caste.

Next we went to the Tahsildar's office to have our signatures witnessed and the official seal applied.

Narayanappa and I both thanked my friend and decided to take a bus back down the Gauribidanur road.

"Now we must show this document to the Reddy."

"He will be very angry."

"Yes but we will do it calmly," I said, and tried to look confident, but I was inwardly quaking.

On our return, Narayanappa's wife served us coffee, then we waited until the men returned from the fields or the forest with the cattle. We needed witnesses!

When the men had gathered, we approached the Reddy's house and entered the courtyard. I prayed silently and went up to the door of the house.

"Reddygaru, we would like to speak to you." I managed to keep my voice bold and steady.

"Please come in and sit down."

"I have friends with me -it is better we talk in the courtyard."

He looked out the door at my companions and a muscle in his jaw began to twitch.

"What brings you here?"

"I have a document I would like you to see." I handed him the patramu, shone my torch and he began to read.

His face seemed to swell with fury as he unrolled the paper and read down the sheet.

"What is this to me?" he said angrily.

"It is an important document and we wish you to read it."

"This is none of your business!"

"I have made it my business, and it concerns all of us."

I thought for a minute he would strike me and had to make a conscious effort to stand firm, but he clenched his fist, handed the document back, swung on his heel and went inside.

We felt we had won the round, my tension eased, but the villagers were still very fearful, so next day I returned to Melekota, put my papers in order and applied for one month's casual leave. When I returned to Kallehalli, Narayanappa brought his daughter to see me. As she began to throw herself at my feet, I said, "Don't do that!"took her by the hand and pulled her upright. She was an attractive child, and my mind seethed as I thought of the Reddy. What a beast he must be to want a child like that, half the age of his own daughter!

Chapter 2
HUNTING

I realised that to be readily available when the villagers needed my help, I must live among them. I already had connections with Gollahalli, and owned two acres of dry land between the village and the road.

After Father's death, when mother refused to feed us, I felt embarrassed to eat elsewhere in Chikka unless I had to, and often went down to Gollahalli and took food in the house of our former cook Krupadanam, who had bought land and retired there. He had come to the hospital many years before as an orphan boy, suffering severe malnutrition, and father had taken him into our home where he had remained until father died. I now took up residence nearby in the home of an old friend Premadasappa.

Next morning when I rose and went out to the fields with my water pot to squat, the clouds were so close I felt I could almost touch them. The air was still and oppressive the bare fields baked hard. It was June and the rains would surely come soon.

I felt content about Narayanappa's daughter; the Reddy would be risking too much if he pursued the matter.

Now that I had taken leave, perhaps we could organise a hunt. Several of the men in the village were keen shikaris(hunters) and the panchayat which sat to distribute my father's estate had given me his single-barrelled gun. Returning to the hut I lifted it down from the rafters, where it reposed safe from Premadasappa's grandchildren, and sat down on the mat to clean and oil it in readiness.

I heard running feet approaching.

"Sir! Sir! Come quickly, my son is dying."

Avalappa, one of the Shikaris (hunters) was at the door.

"What's wrong?"

"My son Narasimhudu is having a fit."

I leapt up and ran after him. His ten-year-old son was on the floor, convulsed. Experience with my brother Philip had taught me what to do. I grabbed a wooden spoon and prised his teeth open pushing the end of the handle between them. Then fanned him with a winnowing tray.

Within a minute the spasms became less and he lay limp and exhausted.

"Now that he is better give him a drink!"

His mother dipped a small brass pot into the 'bana'.

"Just a few drops at a time - make sure he is swallowing properly."

She poured the water into his mouth as he looked up at her, fear and confusion in his eyes.

"What is it, swami?"

"He had a fit, you should take him to the hospital to find out what caused it. They will give you medicine for it."

"You take him, Swami!"

"You take him yourselves, and I will go with you. Will you go today?"

Avalappa and Akkayamma looked at one another

"Not today swami - we will make arrangements."

"Does he have a fever?" I put my hand on his forehead - it was cool. The fit had not been caused by a fever but it would be better to have a diagnosis.

"It is better to go soon."

"We will, swami, but not today."

I knew what was in their minds - they must first consult the soothsayer. If she said it was auspicious to go to hospital, they would go.

I returned to the hut, finished cleaning my gun, then set out for a village three miles away to help settle a land dispute.

Three weeks later on returning one evening I was met by Akkayamma weeping.

"Swami, our son had another fit today, you weren't here and we thought he was going to die."

"Is he alright now?"

"Yes."

"Don't weep then, we'll take him to the hospital tomorrow."

We approached her house to see Narasimhudu sitting outside. He put his hands together "Namaskara swami."

"How do you feel?"

"I'm better now but I feel a bit tired."

He was usually an energetic boy, always ready to help with any communal task.

"We'll go to the hospital tomorrow."

Next morning, after taking food, we caught the bus to Chikka. Akkayamma, five-year-old Krishna, Narasimhudu and I.

The doctor in the outpatient department had newly arrived from Vellore Christian Medical College and Hospital, where he had graduated and completed his residency. In conversation he asked me what I did, and I explained that I had taken one month's leave from my work as revenue inspector.

"Don't you find it boring in the village?"

"Oh, no, I'm kept very busy, and I have been hoping to have a chance to do some hunting."

"Hunting! That sounds good - I am very fond of hunting."

"Why don't you join us, doctor?"

"I would like that."

"We will arrange a time suitable to you. When will you be free?"

"This week on Saturday afternoon and Sunday."

"I will meet you here on Saturday then, and we will take the bus to Gollahalli. We can walk into the hills from there.

"Good."

Dr. Williams finished examining Narasimhudu, said the symptoms were consistent with epilepsy and prescribed some

Phenobarbitol tablets which we picked up from Jacobanna at the dispensary.

When I returned to the village and told Premadasappa's wife, Gangamma, that Dr. Williams was to spend Saturday night with us, she said "You will need to buy some meat, Maistrulu!"

"I'm sure he will be happy with dhal {split pea} curry."

"It will be good to buy meat, swami."

Actually we hadn't eaten meat for a long time so I went into Chikka on Saturday, purchased some meat, gave it to Chikkahanumanthudu to take back to the village and went to meet Dr. Williams.

As the overloaded bus groaned up to the edge of the Deccan I pointed out landmarks.

"Doctor, look at that group of rocks - as we come abreast tell me what you see."

As he watched in puzzlement I saw his face change.

"Mary bent over the crib, the angels above - that is remarkable!"

A few more yards and the impression was lost; then we drove over the edge and began a noisy descent, above which I had to shout as I pointed out Dr. Thompson's rock, on which we planned to sit in wait for panther during the evening.

During the short walk from the road to the house I pointed out local landmarks: the temple on an eminence to the right of the track; Nandi and Kalawara Hills rising 2000 ft some miles away to our left; Srinivasasagara dam shimmering beyond the village, with irrigated rice and sugarcane beyond.

When we reached the hut, Gangamma had a mat laid ready, and her daughter-in-law busied herself warming hot milk for us to drink.

"We will need to eat early, akka, we want to be in position before the light fades, and it is an hour's walk from here to the rock." I could smell the meat cooking so knew it had arrived safely.

Many of the village men and children came to the house and sat inside the doorway anxious to see the visitor. Gangamma handed them some freshly roasted peanuts which they shelled for us to eat. Gangamma's grandchildren settled themselves comfortably on convenient laps, while her daughter-in-law carried the baby on her hip as she prepared the food.

At last Gangamma waved everyone away.

"Doctorgaru will take food now." One by one the visitors left and Gangamma put fresh banana leaves in front of us and poured water on our hands. She then came and put two large handfuls of rice on Dr. Williams's leaf. Disappearing into the kitchen she reappeared with my two Ragi balls and put them on my plate. Dr. Williams looked at the heavy red cricket-ball-sized lumps of millet in surprise.

"What's that?"

"Ragi ball, it's the food of the village people in this area - made out of red millet. Ragi is the Telugu word for copper, and the grain is copper-coloured."

"I've never seen that before. May I try some?"

"You probably won't like it. Gangakka, give doctorugaru a small ragi ball."

Gangamma put two coconut shell ladles of meat and potato curry on our plates, and I saw Dr.Williams watch as I pulled off a glutinous lump of ragi ball, dipped it in the gravy and swallowed it. He followed suit. I watched him as he began to chew it.

"Don't chew it, sir, just swallow it whole!"

He finished the small portion Gangamma had given him.

"Would you like some more?"

"No thank you - I rather think it is an acquired taste! That glutinous texture is strange to me."

"They say if you throw a good ragi ball at the wall it should bounce off."

"I'll believe you!"

The meat curry was a treat for me, and I savoured every mouthful as I ate.

That night was uneventful - four of us went and sat on the rock but apart from a hare shot while we were walking home, we got nothing.

We were up early, took coffee, and set off along the well-worn cattle track out of the village and into the hills. Twenty men and six dogs accompanied us to take turns as beaters. We walked for an hour into the forest until we came to more heavily wooded country, then the beaters went ahead with the dogs and three of us waited at the edge of the clearing.

After an hour we heard the beaters approaching and there was a noise in the undergrowth ahead as two boar emerged, heads down. Our shots rang out - one boar fell but the other kept moving towards us. As we tried to reload Singalappa's dog, Nugget, flew out of the bushes behind it and made a dive at it, but the boar was quicker and grabbed the dog by the ear, swinging its head. Nugget flew sideways, bleeding profusely, but was in again before we had time to shoot. He got it by the throat and hung on. Dr. Williams moved forward and put a well-aimed shot into the boar's heart. It fell, and Singalappa ran to Nugget, who was lying panting, blood pouring from the stump of his ear.

I went into the undergrowth to find some leaves and vines, Gangappa came with me, 'mattsu' in hand and we hurried back with a bundle. Singalappa packed the leaves around Nugget's ear and tied his head with vines then cradled him in his arms and set out for home. The boars were big ones with tusks fully six inches long. Some of the men had gone off to cut poles and vines to carry them back to the village. As I looked at the huge black hairy bodies I thought, "We will all eat meat tonight!"

It was early afternoon by the time we reached Gollahalli. Gangamma had two large earthenware pots of bath water simmering over a fire and Doctor went to Nanjamma's bathroom to bathe while I bathed by the well.

As we sat on the mat in the house, feeling clean and relaxed, while Gangamma poured coffee, Doctor turned to me.

"I have noticed that several of the people I have met here look as though they have leprosy,"

"Oh, which were they?"

He described three of the men who had been in the house the previous day.

"The one sitting to the left of the doorway had lost most of his eyebrows and I noticed a paler patch on one arm."

"I know who you mean."

"Another chap had a rather puffy red face and swollen ears - he could be highly infectious."

I nodded.

"Then there was one man who had some bent fingers. Do you know of other people in this area with similar symptoms?"

"I know there is a man in Guyelahalli who has quite severe symptoms - he came to my father years ago for injections, then my father died, and I don't know what happened after that."

"I've done quite a bit of work with the Leprosy patients at Karigiri. If you have people like this in the area they should be having treatment."

"Can it be cured?"

"Yes, there are effective tablets, but it's a long course of treatment - five years. Of course it doesn't reverse deformities caused by destruction of nerve endings, but it does stop further damage."

"I will keep a look out for others, and get these three to go to hospital."

"I'll speak to Dr. Graham about it. Perhaps we can open a leprosy clinic."

The men had collected some wood and built a huge fire. Now that it was burning well they put the boars whole on the coals, turning them frequently so that each part of the skin was thoroughly scorched. The evening air was filled with the acrid stench of burning hair and flesh.

Taking them from the fire, they began scraping the skin to remove the hair. It was hard work and by the time they had finished, the men were nearly as black as the pigs.

The women had collected some pieces of old sari and bedsheets, and tore them into metre squares ready for the pieces of cut meat.

Now the men began cutting the carcasses, the village dogs hovering just out of reach in hopes of a mouthful or two.

I went and brought two leaf plates to put inside the cloth to hold Doctor's meat, as he would travel back to Chikka by bus and would not want to carry a blood soaked bundle.

Word had got around. A number of people from nearby villages just happened to be passing through, and were happy to carry off a bundle of pork.

A piece of offal was tossed to the dogs and a sharp and noisy scuffle ensued until the top dog asserted his dominance and the others slunk to a distance, tails between their legs, while he munched hungrily, still eyeing his rivals steadily.

The sun was beginning to sink before I accompanied Doctor up to the road.

It was the usual story - the bus was already overloaded and went flying past, but we heard a lorry coming and waved it down.

"The doctor needs to return to the hospital in Chikka."

The driver was agreeable.

"Get in, sir," he said, after telling one of the men in the cabin to climb into the back.

The lorry moved off, a number of villagers clinging precariously to the piled up bags of grain.

Chapter 3
RECONCILIATION

That week I persuaded the three men Dr. Williams had mentioned to go to the hospital. Dr. Graham was in outpatients. As he examined them he said, "These men are from your village, that suggests there are many more people suffering from Hansen's Disease in the area. You know we now call Leprosy 'Hansen's disease' after the man who identified the bacillus. It's a bit of a mouthful, so here we refer to them as H.D.patients."

"I hadn't heard that term before, doctor."

"Dr. Williams mentioned those men to me. A few weeks ago after seeing a patient here, I approached the Government about the incidence. They said there was practically no H.D. in this area, but after seeing these three I feel sure that can't be so."

"I've been thinking about it, Doctor, and know of at least one patient in many of the villages. There must be many more I wouldn't have identified."

"Will they come to the Rural dispensary?"

"I think it would be difficult to persuade them. They are very fearful. Some believe the hospitals give medicine to kill them off, in order to get rid of the disease!"

"Then we must go to the villages, but we need someone like you, that they trust, to persuade them we won't harm them. You could be of great help to us."

The hospital then began not only treating Hansenites but also looking for them. I used to search for them every time I was away from Gollahalli, and record names of suspected cases and their villages in my little black notebook. When I had a number of suspects in an area, I went and reported to Dr. Graham, and he arranged for us to go out on bicycles to check them out.

However the time came when I felt I was being used by the hospital. When I considered the harsh action of the Panchayat, elected to settle father's estate of which the former Medical Superintendent of the hospital, Dr. Cutting, had been a member, resentment rose afresh within me. The panchayat members knew that my brothers and sisters were not interested in shikari(hunting), whereas I was, but in spite of that they gave me only one of my father's guns, I stopped looking for new leprosy patients.

Dr. Cutting had been held in high regard by the people of Chikka and surrounding villages. Since he and father had been good friends I don't think he thought much of me because of the mess I had made of my opportunity to study in Bangalore and my quarrel with father over his refusal to send me for further study. One morning when the sun was barely above the horizon and I was returning from the fields with my 'chembu'(small brass pot), I happened to glance up the hill towards the track from the road and saw a cyclist riding cautiously down. As he drew closer I was even more surprised to recognise Dr. Graham. I hurried towards the village, put my chembu inside the door and said to Gangamma, "Dr. Graham has come!" Then I walked up the path between the houses to greet him.

"Namaskaram Doctor," I wondered what could have brought him here so early.

"Good morning Sabhapathy. I'm glad to see you here. I came hoping to have a talk with you."

"Please come to the house, doctor, and take coffee."

By the time we reached the house Gangamma was coaxing a fire to life and we sat down on the mat she had spread for us.

Dr. Graham sat and looked as though he did not know quite what to say.

"I am disturbed at your apparent anger against the hospital, and felt I should try to find the cause, because from what I hear of the work you are doing in the villages, we should be working together."

"Doctor, when father died he did not leave a will, so five people were chosen to sit as a Panchayat to distribute father's estate. Dr.

Cutting was one of them. I realise my anger is not really against the hospital but against those people who sat on the Panchayat and decided how Father's estate should be divided. Because of their decisions, the family split up; my younger sisters had to have marriages arranged; Sowbhagia lived for six months with Sister Morch and I took food in Mr. Partasarthaiah's house. We were not able to build on father's house site nor were we able to sell it. I was not able to go for further study. Chichu also continued to work at H.A.L. trying to earn money to do medicine, then caught T.B.and died. I blame the Panchayat for all that."

"Why have you taken leave from a good Government position to live so simply and help the village people?"

"Because when I read my Bible I see how Christ loved the people. I also admired Mahatma Gandhi very much, for he followed Christ's teaching. When the Mahatma died I fasted for three days; I hoped he might rise again as Christ did."

"We are both trying to do the same thing then, and the people trust and respect you, whereas I am new here, and could do a lot more to help them, if I had your support."

We sat in silence and Christ's words came to my mind 'Forgive not seven times but seventy times seven' I felt ashamed and offered a silent prayer for forgiveness.

Doctor pulled his watch out of his pocket "I must go, hospital prayers are at 7-30 and it is almost 6-30 now. Please think about it."

I was able to answer without hesitation. "I will give you all the help I can. Thank you for coming, Doctor."

I walked with him up to the road, and watched as he mounted his cycle and rode off. It was as though a great burden had been lifted from me and I resolved to visit mother next time I was in town.

Chapter 4

ADULT EDUCATION

A shout went up from the assembled villagers as the long sticks clashed and one of the men lost his balance on the greasy pole. Within a second he was hanging upside down, his crossed legs still gripping the slippery wood while the victor held his stick aloft.

It was May, the wedding season and one of our village sons was being married. As part of the entertainment offered to visiting friends and relatives, a well waxed pole had been set up in a horizontal position near the well for the evening's entertainment.

Most of us sat under the wedding pandal which almost covered the open area. It consisted of a frame of casuarina poles covered with palm leaf matting, the uprights decorated with banana suckers and mango branches. We sat on mats or borrowed benches, watching the young men and some of the older ones testing their balancing skills on the pole. Each man was armed with a hefty six foot stick, his aim being to unseat his opponent without using body blows.

The air was heavy with the mingled scent of flowers in the women's hair and burning Kanuga oil as the wicks of village lamps set around the area sputtered and glowed in their small earthenware saucers, illuminating the scene with a soft light. A faint stirring of cooler air across the tank gave slight relief from the oppressive midsummer heat.

The bride was from a village a few miles to the east and, as is the custom, many relatives and friends from that village had spent the last few days with us, watching the ceremonies, and feasting.

The bride belonged of course to the shepherd caste and to the same sub-caste as the people of Gollahalli. Discrimination against caste has been illegal since independence but most village marriages are still arranged within these limits.

As we applauded the winner and watched in relaxed mood as another man took up the stick to challenge him, the man sitting next to me said, "Swami, I hear you are teaching the men here to read."

"Yes, they read each evening and we teach each other - not only the men but the women as well."

"Please come to our village and teach us to read."

"It takes two hours to walk to your village. Do you have people in the village who can read?"

"Yes swami, Bhima Reddy and Venkatappa."

"Perhaps they would teach you."

"You ask them, swami."

We settled to watch the next two contestants, but my mind was busy exploring possibilities. What if we set up night schools in the villages? The people wanted to learn. They needed to learn, to protect themselves from unscrupulous rascals who took advantage of them. I decided I would go to see Bhima Reddy. He was well known to me as a good landlord who treated his workers fairly. Now was the season to visit him - no work could be done in the fields until the rains came and unless he too was off to a wedding he would have the leisure to talk to me.

I rose before the sun was up, made my ablutions and set out. As I cycled down towards the tank I disturbed a bandicoot which scurried back to its hole. The sun-baked mud had split into tesselated squares and triangles under which frogs and fish alike were entombed, well away from the summer heat. At this time of year we should all be nocturnal, I thought, as I watched the rising sun already causing shimmering fantasies of mist to form, dissolve and reform before my eyes.

When I reached the village and approached Bhima Reddy's house, the only large flat-roofed house in the village, Bhima Reddy was sitting cross-legged on a rock slab under a Neem tree. He was a tall well-built man and rose to greet me with a welcoming smile.

"Namaskaram ayya, are you well?"

"Namaskaram ayya, I'm well. And you?"

"I'm well. You're out early today."

"Yes, I wished to avoid the heat and meet with you."

"Please come in and sit down."

"It's cooler here in the shade, may I join you."

"Yes, sit down. I'll tell my wife you are here."

He disappeared inside, and I sat and watched the village fowls scratching and pecking in the dappled shade.

When he returned he sat down beside me.

"Some of the farmers in this village are interested in learning to read and write I wondered if you would be able to help them."

"In what way, anna?"

"By organising them into groups to teach one another and building a place for them to gather. You are their leader here and so in a position to help them most."

"Tell me what you would like me to do."

"In Gollahalli, most of the villagers were keen to learn, so, between us, we built a shed on a piece of land I own and we are gathering there at night. Those of us who can read teach the others. Some learn more quickly, then they are able to help with the teaching."

"It is good! If the people are keen they will build a hut, if I encourage them."

A young boy came out of the house and began chasing the chickens until he finally caught one and took it, flapping its wings and squawking lustily, into the house. I knew then that they would expect me to take food with them.

Ammagaru appeared carrying two steel tumblers of steaming coffee on a brass plate.

"You must take food with us swami."

"Thank you." They would have been hurt had I refused. We sat and sipped, discussing the merits of the last harvest, recent politics and offering solutions to world problems.

When we were finally called in to eat the heat inside the house was stifling, for although the house was comparatively large it did not boast a single window.

Bhima Reddy apologised for the discomfort.

"Why don't you put in a window so that the air can come and go?"

"That is a good idea, anna. I will see a carpenter about doing it."

During the next few weeks I spent much time travelling from village to village on my cycle, speaking to the village leaders and organising night schools. Some were enthusiastic, but others were only luke warm. In spite of this we opened many centres and I talked to the villagers, encouraging them to study. In most cases they were only too eager to learn. I thought the scheme was going well and visited the centres turn and turn about to give encouragement. Then I noticed that numbers began to fall off and on visiting one found only two people there, one a potter and the other a carpenter.

"Where are all the others?"

"They aren't coming, maistrulu."

"Why not? Are they too tired at night?" In Gollahalli we had changed our classes to early morning for that reason.

The men looked at me but were silent. I sensed a problem but had no idea what it could be.

"Tell me why the men aren't coming. There must be some reason."

"The Reddygaru doesn't like them to come."

I was puzzled "Why not?"

"He says if they learn to read and write, they will become too proud and won't work well.

"But that's ridiculous. They shouldn't listen to what he says."

"He says if they keep coming here he won't employ them."

"Oh!"

"What can they do, swami? They have to eat, and their families have to eat. Not only that but many of the Reddys and other land owners have talked to one another and they are all saying the same thing, so that those who come to classes won't get coolie (day labour) anywhere near here."

"We won't consent to that kind of treatment." I felt very angry. How dare they threaten them like that.

As I cycled back to Gollahalli, my mind searched for a way to overcome this new obstacle. I decided to go next morning to talk the matter over with Bhima Reddy, perhaps he would have a suggestion.

When I reached the house, Ammagaru greeted me.

"My master's away buying a pair of bullocks, he may not be back today. Please come in anna."

"Thank you." As I entered the house the heat hit me with an almost physical impact and the interior was so dark I could not at first see the women of the house who were sitting busy with their household tasks, one grinding grain between two stones, another shaking and tossing paddy in a winnowing tray to separate the grit and twigs. Bhima Reddy's wife told the younger of the two to make coffee, and she disappeared into the kitchen area where I heard her blowing on the coals to bring them to life and add more heat and smoke to the situation.

I sat down on the mat spread for me

"Your master hasn't called the carpenter to make that window yet?"

"No sir, he is always busy, and he doesn't spend time here during the heat of the day."

"It is so dark in here I can hardly see, it must be bad for your eyes."

"Yes sir, they are always burning."

I made a sudden decision.

"Do you have a crowbar, Amma?"

"A crowbar?" She thought her ears had deceived her.

"Yes, I want a crowbar."

She disappeared into a small store room at the front of the house, came back with a small 'gaddapara' and held it out to me. I took it from her.

"Amma do you give me permission to knock a hole in the wall of the house?"

She put her hand up to her mouth and looked at me then I saw her eyes twinkle with suppressed laughter.

"I don't give you permission but perhaps you'll do it anyway."

I took the crowbar firmly in my two hands, went over to the northern wall of the house and drove it into the wall with all my strength again and again, until the shattered mud finally showed a circle of light the size of a rupee. I worked on for nearly an hour, for the wall was a foot thick, until I had made an opening eighteen inches square. As I worked I had some moments of trepidation as I wondered whether I had perhaps misjudged the sort of response Bhima Reddy would make.

What a difference that small opening made to the atmosphere inside the room!

The women were all smiles. I felt that was a good omen. They surely knew him even better than I did.

"Tell your master that I have saved him some wages, and if I were a carpenter would save him even more, but this will have to do. Now I will go and come."

"Go and come swami."

As I was already halfway to Melekota I continued in that direction. As I cycled along the narrow tracks, dodging exposed roots and stones, my mind was working on the problem of the night schools. I had been acting as mediator in a boundary dispute near Melekota and was anxious to find out whether the verbal agreement which they had made had been kept. I visited both parties and they took me to see the survey stones in position. Satisfied with that outcome I decided to cycle on into Chikka and consult my lawyer friend. He might have some advice to offer.

His house was of stone, burnt granite from Avati no doubt, with a flat mud roof supported by heavy beams across which bamboo poles were laid side by side to support the thick layer of mud. The house was surrounded by a low compound wall. Just inside the gate and to the left was a small shed made of mats. I went up to the door of the house and knocked but there was no reply. As I turned to go back to the gate my friend's wife appeared in the doorway of the shed and called to me.

"My master's in Bangalore at court, ayya, he won't be home until late, and my servant has gone to the bazaar so I can't even offer you coffee, please forgive me."

"Never mind amma, I will call another day. I just wanted to ask his advice." It was evidently that time of the month for her when she was unclean and banished to the outhouse.

It was not my day, first Bhima Reddy was away and now Ananda Rao.

During the wedding season just past, some of our Gollahalli folk had been guests in a village northwest of Chikka and had told me on their return that there were many people in that village with pale anaesthetic patches. I decided to go and see for myself. I cycled west out along the Sidlaghatta road. The rains had come and water shimmered in the tank, the moist mud at its edge green with the growth of weeds making the most of the short wet season. A duck herd had placed his long pole at a slant in the ground and settled down under a thorn bush for a snooze while his feathered charges shovelled in the soft mud with their bills giving quacks of delight as they came upon a juicy worm or concealed snail. I wondered again at the intelligence of ducks, or lack of it, which allowed them to be kept in check simply by a pole stuck into the ground.

I took a cart track off to the left and cycled on, my head level with the fields on either side, which were now seas of waving green, Here and there women were weeding busily with their small weeding trowels, the weeds thrown into their mukkeris to take home for the cattle.

The village Karnam (hereditary surveyor for a group of villages) was known to me so I went first to his house. I saw him through the doorway busy at a table with his abacus.

"Namaskaram swami, are you well?"

"I'm well, and you?"

"I'm sorry to disturb you."

"That's all right, I'm just doing the measurements for a land sale which is being negotiated so that we can go out and put in the stone markers."

As we sat sipping coffee I considered the best way of approaching the point of my visit. People don't like to be told there may be leprosy patients in their village. Finally I said,

"The new doctor in the mission hospital is doing a survey to find out the number of leprosy patients in the surrounding villages and would like to come here and hold a clinic."

"There is no leprosy here as far as I know."

"Did you know there are now tablets which will cure the disease?"

"That's good, anna, but we haven't any here."

"Good, then perhaps we can come and examine the people for pale patches, and if there are none we can put this area down as clear."

We sat in silence for a while as he appeared to be wrestling with some unwelcome thoughts. Then he said,

"There are many people in this area with pale patches, but it is due to the water in the well."

"If they come to be tested we can make sure they don't have leprosy. Could you arrange a place for us to hold a clinic?"

"Yes, anna, I'll speak to the schoolmaster. Perhaps you can hold the clinic on the schoolhouse verandah."

"Thank you, anna, I'll speak to Doctor about it and send you a post card when we have arranged the date. I will go and come."

"Go and come, anna!"

As I cycled the twenty miles back to Gollahalli my mind was busy with the problem of the night schools. The sun was sinking behind me as I pedalled slowly up to the top of the range. The steep rock faces of Nandi and Harihareshware rising two thousand feet from the Deccan caught the sun and the green of the fields on either side contrasted sharply with bright red earth and boulders between the fields. What a beautiful country! I thought, when everything is bursting with new growth. I felt in the pockets of my jubba for the seeds I carried, and as I free wheeled down the steep ghat road, braked at each gully running off up the hillside and poked some seeds into the moist soil. Even if one flowering tree survives to maturity it will be worth while.

That night as I lay on my mat I decided the only way to stop interference by the landowners was to take out a court injunction. I would go again to see Ananda Rao and set that in motion tomorrow. When I'd made that decision, sleep claimed me.

Chapter 5

GURUMURTHI

I had been to a village some eight miles south east of Gollahalli and was walking back by another route which took me through Guyelahalli.

After exchanging greetings with a number of people as I passed, some two hundred yards further on I saw a dark shape lying under a fig tree and moved off the path to investigate. The shape moved and a voice said,

"Who's there?"

"It's Sabhapathy. Who are you?"

"Swami, help me - I am Gurumurthi - your father was a man of gold!" He pulled the blanket off his head revealing a shock of white hair above a thin face.

"I remember you. Why are you lying here?"

By this time the stench of his ulcers had reached me and I could see the flies crawling on the blanket, some now trying to enter his mouth and nose.

"I have leprosy, sir, and have become so foul-smelling that people in the village were afraid to come near my house. I was starving to death so I dragged myself out here. The flies are so troublesome I keep this blanket over me."

"How long have you been here? Who feeds you?"

"My relatives bring food but my friends have warned me not to eat it as they have mixed rat poison with it. Some friends bring food but they are afraid to come too close and the monkeys get it before I can reach it. But another friend comes at night and pours milk down my throat."

"How long have you had the disease?

"I first noticed a pale anaesthetic patch on my leg when I was in my last year at high school. I was suspicious, but the only person I knew who had leprosy was our dhobi who washed and ironed our clothes. Then my father died and I had to leave school to look after our land. I went to a private Doctor who said the patch was nothing to worry about, but I began to get stomachaches and bouts of fever and I noticed the patch was growing bigger. When I touched it I felt nothing. It was as large as a rupee."

"What did you do?"

"I went to the Magadi Road Leprosarium in Bangalore. They said I didn't have leprosy, but I was still suspicious."

"Do you have a wife?"

"No, my mother and the villagers wanted to arrange a marriage for me with a girl my mother had brought up but I refused. I was still suspicious of my symptoms, and I felt if troubles come it is better I face them alone."

"So how did you come to get treatment from my father?"

"Three years after going to Bangalore I had more patches so I sold half my land and went to the hospital at Chingleput. They confirmed my fears, but because I was a Mysorean would not admit me, so I returned to Bangalore with a letter and was admitted at Magadi Road. I was only there three months when my relatives came and told me mother was ill and took me home. I looked after her for a year until she died, then I began going to your father for injections. After your father died, I went to a Government dispensary for two months, then felt well so remained here working on my land. For five years I was well, sir, then my strength failed. For the past ten years I have been too weak to leave the village. I told my relatives three years ago they could have my land if they looked after me until I died, but look at me swami."

"You must go to the hospital."

"How can I get there, swami?"

"Did you know the hospital ambulance is coming down the road now?"

"No, sir."

"Who is your friend in the village?"

"Lakkappa."

"I'll go and talk to him."

I walked back into the village.

"Which is Lakkappagaru's house?" I asked a child playing in the street.

He pointed to a house and I went to the door. It was almost dark by now and the villagers had come in from the fields, some sitting talking in groups on the earthen platform under the neem and peepul trees.

"Lakkappagaru" I called.

A tall thin man bent in the low doorway of his house as he came out.

"Namaskaram swami, come in and sit down."

I sat on the mat spread for me. "I believe you are a friend of Gurumurthi's."

"Yes sir."

"Did you know the hospital doctor comes down the road now to examine patients?"

"I had heard of it."

"Can you get Gurumurthi to the road on Wednesday morning?"

"It's difficult sir - people are afraid!"

"Yes."

We sat in silence, his wife brought hot sweet buffalo milk and we sipped.

"Who has a cart?"

"The Reddy sir and one other!"

"Would they help?'

"I doubt it, swami."

Another few minutes passed. Then I had an idea.

"I have a good friend, the Reddy in the next village - he has a cart. I will write him a note." I tore a sheet from my notebook, and wrote on it.

"Take this to him - I will be at Possettihalli at ten o'clock on Wednesday. Bring Gurumurthi then."

"I will try, swami." But he did not look optimistic.

It had become my custom to walk to Possettihalli by 9 o'clock on rural dispensary day. I usually called in at one or two of the nearby villages on the way to escort someone who needed medical attention. The village people were frightened and shy of approaching the doctor, and needed a lot of encouragement. In those early days there were often only one or two patients waiting when the car arrived.

I saw the cart approaching down the road and when the hospital van pulled up both Dr. Graham and Sister Morch were there.

Dr. Graham examined Gurumurthi's ulcers and prescribed tablets. Gurumurthi was unable to get down from the cart for treatment but Sister Morch was waiting with disinfectant, cotton swabs and bandages and brought them over.

"Come on, we'll have to clean you up." she said as she climbed up into the cart.

The stench was so great we felt like holding our noses, in fact some did, but Sister got to work, swabbed the ulcers and bandaged them.

Gurumurthi said to me after the van left.

"They touched me - they were not afraid."

Over the years that followed, in speaking about the hospital to village people, that was what had impressed him most - that anyone could care enough about him to touch him when he was so repulsive.

A number of patients from Guyelahalli came to the hospital with severe hookworm infestation, so Doctor Graham arranged for a team to go to the village one Saturday afternoon about three weeks later. I went ahead to make sure there was a suitable place ready to show the filmstrip. I chose a spot in the street to set up the screen, and mats and benches were lined up for the villagers. They enjoyed the strip of the cat burying its excreta and a talk about wearing sandals in damp places, with graphic sketches on screen of hookworm larvae burrowing into people's feet and travelling through their blood stream. Dr. Graham, Rev. Sleigh, the male nurse and I slept in a hut while the usual occupants moved in with friends.

Gurumurthi came to see the film. Dr. was surprised to see him. "I had forgotten this was your village. How are you?"

"Much better!"

"Are you taking your tablets?"

"Yes."

But it was obvious his ulcers needed dressing again. Doctor was annoyed with himself. "We travelled light! I had forgotten this was your village and haven't brought bandages and disinfectant to treat you."

Sister Morch said, "I'll send someone tomorrow to dress your ulcers."

After their return one of the male nurses was sent by bicycle to dress the sores.

Two months later Gurumurthi was so much better that he walked two and a half miles to the rural dispensary, and six months later walked the eleven miles to hospital.

Dr. Cutting admitted him and put plaster on his legs - his ulcers healed and he became the first resident of the little H.D.ward. He grew vegetables and bananas and delighted in going out with the van on an H.D. round to tell people his story and encourage them to have treatment.

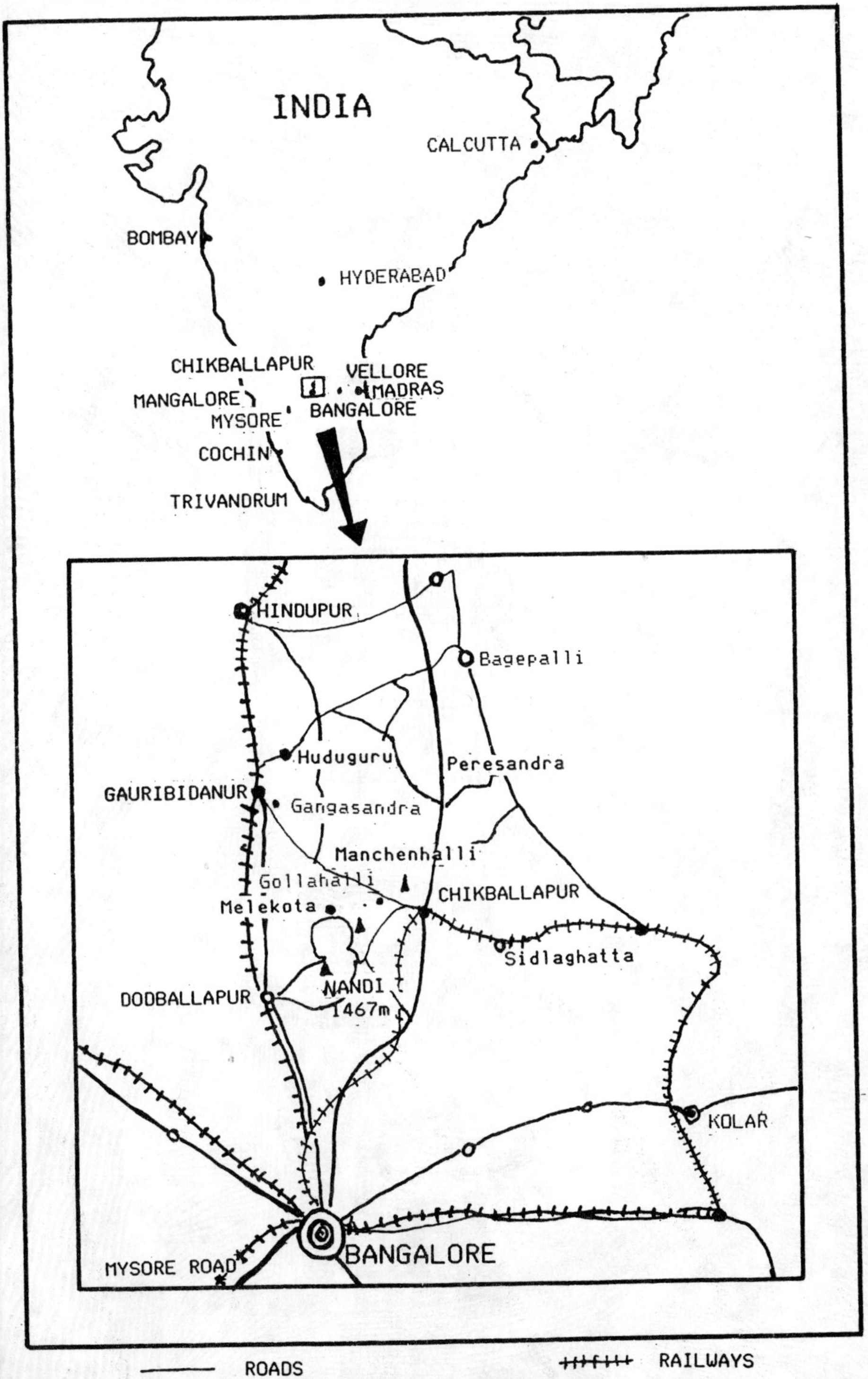
INDIA
CALCUTTA
BOMBAY
HYDERABAD
CHIKBALLAPUR
VELLORE
1
MANGALORE
MADRAS
MYSORE
BANGALORE
COCHIN
TRIVANDRUM
HINDUPUR
Bagepalli
Huduguru
Peresandra
GAURIBIDANUR
Gangasandra
Manchenhalli
Gollahalli
CHIKBALLAPUR
Melekota
Sidlaghatta
NANDI
1467m
DODBALLAPUR
KOLAR
MYSORE ROAD
BANGALORE
ROADS
RAILWAYS

The evening task! Hand-feeding the oxen.

Irrigating the fields.

Is the patch anaesthetic?

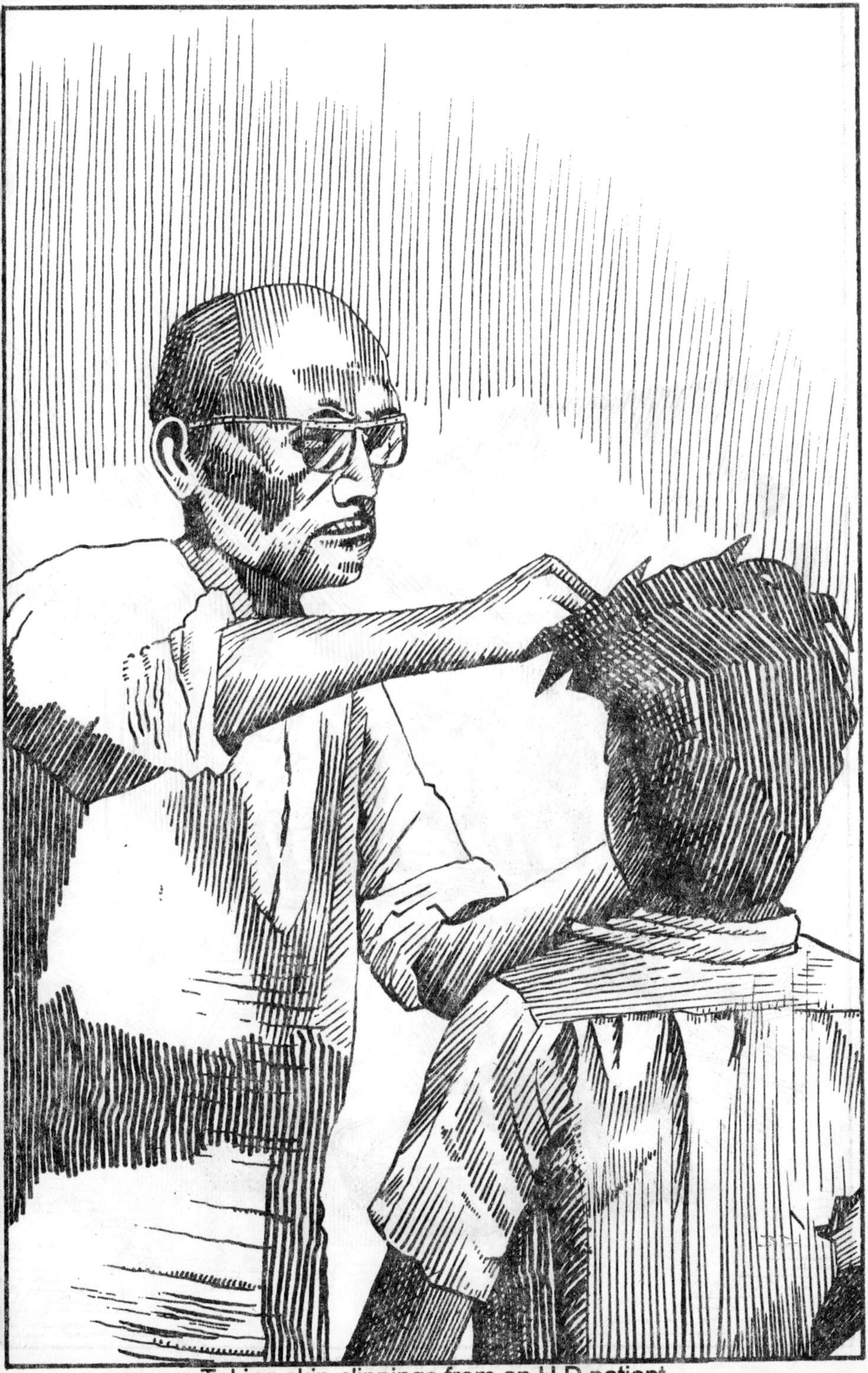

Taking skin-clippings from an H.D.patient.

"Don't muzzle the ox that treads the corn."

Irrigation works Maddurenhalli.

Measuring out the grain.

Lining up for milk powder Rural Dispensary.

Lancing an abscess rural style.

Fruit stall at the bus stand.

Gopuram at Gopal's temple.

Wood to market to buy the day's food.

Bargaining for wood. Note solid wooden wheels.

Chapter 6

RAT'S TREASURE

Although it was still dark I wakened and lay for a while listening to one cock crow, then another. It must be three-thirty and soon time to hit the piece of metal I kept to rouse the villagers for the early morning literacy classes. I got up, folded my bed sheet and blanket and placed them on my mat. The hut was small to accommodate its seven occupants even if one was only a baby. They still slept, their bed sheets pulled up over their heads, resembling a row of corpses. The oxen chewing their cud at one end of the hut had more room than we did.

I stepped gingerly over the sleeping forms, picked up the small brass pot near the door and went outside. The cold air came as a shock and I instinctively turned sideways to the wind and pulled the sleeves of my cotton jubba down over my hands to keep as warm as possible. My pup got up from where he had slept under the haystack and licked my hand as I fondled his ears.

Still no one stirred. This was my half hour to meditate and pray and plan my day as I sat crosslegged on the stone parapet surrounding the well. Looking down between the houses, light from a fading moon caught the water in the tank and threw intermittent flashes back to me. A jackal howled as it made its way back to its daytime lair in the rocky hills.

The day would be a long one as it was rural dispensary and I needed to visit several people before the hospital car came down the road.

I got up and lifted the pieces of iron at the door of the hut, striking them together three times. The village dogs barked, doors creaked open and shadowy figures emerged, crouched against the cold which struck through their thin cotton garments.

I went over to the literacy hut and lit the wicks in the small oil lamps. It wasn't the hour for small talk and soon small groups had gathered around each lamp and were helping one another with the day's lesson.

"Don't forget the car comes today. Pandiananna said he would put louse powder on the children's heads. Be sure to wash their heads before you go and not rub in any oil."

"Yes Maistrulu."

As soon as the class finished I visited two of the homes to remind them about R.D. (Rural Dispensary) and returned to find that Gangamma had coffee ready. I sat on the mat facing the door sipping the hot sweet liquid.

"Don't make food for me this morning, Akka. I must go across to Doddaganahalli to see some of the H.D. patients."

"But where will you eat? Those people have nothing to spare."

"Doctor and amma will have some chapathi and omelette for lunch; I can manage until then."

"You should look after yourself sometimes - you're as thin as a stick."

I was used to her scolding - I took my Gandhi cap from the nail near the door and set out. I walked up past Akkayamma's house, put my head inside and reminded her about R.D. She was sitting grinding Ragi {red millet} to make Ragi ball for the morning meal.

"How's the baby?"

"No good, Maistrulu, he's still making that clicking noise when he breathes."

"Show him to the doctor today then ."

"Yes, anna."

I walked down through the fields of Ragi now bright green. We hadn't had rain for a while so the cattle had been allowed in to graze on the half-grown plants to make the plants spread and produce more heads. Up on to the road - Doddaganahalli was about three miles down. The villagers were Harijans (meaning god's people, formerly called outcastes) and landless, so dependent on daily coolie.

It was our village servant Gangappa's village, and I went first to his house. His wife Aswartamma was there, two of her small children clinging to her sari, another on her hip.

"Gangappa tells me you are not well."

"I feel weak Swami."

"You should go to Possettihalli cross today and see the doctor - he will give you medicine."

"Will you go with me, swami?"

"Yes, I'm going - you get ready and I'll come back in an hour."

Narasimhudu, an H.D.patient lived a few doors away, his wife Pillamma was sitting cross-legged under a nearby tree tossing rice paddy in her winnowing tray. I felt some surprise that they could afford to eat rice, most of the villagers ate red millet and preferred it.

"Are you well, Maistrulu?" she said, as with an expert flick of the wrist most of the cleaned grain landed in a heap in front of her while stones remained in the shovel shaped basket.

"I'm well, amma. Where is your master?"

"He's gone to the fields to collect paddy."

"Oh! I didn't know they'd begun cutting."

"They haven't cut."

"Where will I find him then?"

"Below the tank!" She waved her arm in the direction of the dam another mile in from the road.

As I hurried off I wondered - was he cutting paddy illegally? But he'd hardly do that in broad daylight.

There was no sign of him as I stood on the tank bund and looked across the waving grain in the fields below. Then suddenly a figure rose only fifty yards from me.

"Oh, anna."

"Namaskaram swami," he bent again and disappeared from view.

I climbed down from the bank and walked along between the fields towards the spot. He was busily digging in the edge of a bank.

"I'll come in a moment anna - now I must collect the paddy from this rat's nest I've opened or they will move it to a new nest tonight."

I watched in fascination as he dug a little deeper and exposed a large quantity of grain.

"Hold the bag, Swami."

I held open the mouth of a sack while he scooped the paddy out of the hole with a tin, then gathered the last remaining grains with his hands. There must have been 8-10 seers in all.

He tied the bag and turned to me. "This is how we live, swami - the rat's rice feeds my family and buys a few extras as well. No one else wants it!"

"That's good - I've come to remind you to go to the roadside today to have your blood checked. You haven't had it done for a while".

We walked back to the village together.

Aswartamma was ready, the three children clean and neat.

When we reached the road quite a crowd was waiting under the huge fig trees which made a canopy of shade. They began to gather around me to tell me their problems. One man had a towel wrapped around his head.

"Do you have toothache, anna?"

"No swami, a rat ate my ear in the night"

"Didn't you feel it?"

"No sir, I was sound asleep."

"Had you been drinking?"

"No I hadn't drunk a drop. Where would I get it from?"

Kolar District was dry but illicit brewing went on in the villages, though he probably would have had to walk a long way to get it.

When the doctor examined him he at once took his hand and felt at the elbow for the ulnar nerve.

"His ulnar nerve is enlarged - he has leprosy."

Of course, I thought to myself - I should have realised - a healthy person would have felt the rat immediately.

When I told Doctor about the paddy from the rat's nest he said, "It's a wonder they haven't all died of Salmonella poisoning."

Doctor wrote the name of another leprosy patient for skin clips and said, "You could learn to do these when Mrs. Graham doesn't come it would save the nurse's time." So I went back and watched.

"Doctor says I must learn to do them. How do you know where to take the clippings?"

"You know the saying 'No kushta (leprosy) without pushta (buttocks)' so take from the edge of any visible patch on the buttocks, inside the nose, tips of the ears and if you still haven't got ten, search the back and the face for patches."

I watched as she cut small slits with a scalpel, scraped the raw surface and smeared it on a slide then dropped it into a jar of alcohol to be stained in the laboratory back at the hospital.

It wasn't a pleasant business and I wasn't sure that I relished the job - especially scraping inside the nose which made the patient sneeze.

We had found that many of the patients had been turned out of their homes by relatives, who would not have them back even though told they were not infectious, so now Dr. was issuing a printed certificate after they had had three negative skin clips at monthly intervals. Even this made no difference for some.

Dr. called to Pandian, the male nurse, "There's a man for a tooth extraction."

As Pandian got out the dental forceps, I went over to the patient who was standing anxiously at the side of the road.

"Will it hurt much, swami?"

"Don't worry about it. It will be out in a moment."

Doctor put his finger into the patient's mouth and located the rotten tooth, while Pandian stood by with a kidney dish containing sterile forceps and some pieces of sterile rag.

"Sit down and open your mouth."

The patient squatted on his haunches and opened his mouth, his brow lined with anxiety.

Doctor grasped the tooth with the dental forceps and tugged - it came away without much struggle.

"Spit." The patient spat into the dust. Pandian put some pieces of rag into the bleeding cavity.

"Bite," he said.

Village people can't afford to go to dentists - if a tooth becomes too troublesome, they have it out. Most people have good teeth as they rarely eat sweet things but some who prefer soft food have a lot of problems.

The car moved on to the next stop - it had become my custom to travel with them.

At Kanaganakoppa there was a bandi (ox-cart) waiting. I went and spoke to the young man as he fed some straw to the beasts.

"What's the matter?"

"My wife has a lump in her breast."

"Is it painful?"

"She's been crying with the pain, sir."

"Why didn't you bring her to hospital?"

"The baby is young, it was too soon to leave the house."

I looked into the basket container, the girl lying there was very young. She opened her eyes and looked at me desperately. "Do something, swami!"

"Doctor will be here in a minute."

Doctor came over, climbed up into the cart and examined her.

"You have a breast abscess and a fever. How long has she had this?"

"Ten days swami."

"She must have been in agony."

Her husband hung his head. "Yes swami."

"Will you take her to hospital now?"

"It's difficult sir, the baby is at home."

"Then I'll need to cut open that abscess and give her an injection."

"Do it now, swami!"

Pandian brought the necessary equipment and climbed into the cart with doctor.

When doctor opened the abscess and the pus rushed out, I saw the girl's face relax for the first time.

"Now this will have to have a clean dressing every day - listen carefully."

"Yes, Swami."

"Boil some pieces of clean rag in a dekshi(Indian saucepan) of water with one teaspoon of salt. Do you have a teaspoon?"

"Yes"

"Then boil the teaspoon with the rag for ten minutes, let it cool but don't let the flies sit on it. Wash your hands well with soap. Take off the dressing - lift some of the rag out of the saucepan with the spoon and wipe the wound then put the rest of the rag over the wound and re-tie the bandage. Have someone to keep the flies off while you do it, and throw all the dirty rags into the fire."

Doctor went back to the car and her husband turned to me.

"Tell me again what the doctor said."

I repeated the instructions, then said, "Now you tell me what you have to do."

He repeated them for me correctly.

"Good, now look after her well, and if she has bad pain again bring her to the hospital."

"Yes sir." He walked over to bring his oxen back to the cart and harness them up.

"How are you feeling now?" I asked her.

"Much better - the pain is less."

"Anna, we're leaving." Pandian was holding the door open ready for me.

Shortly afterwards we turned off the main road to the right. By this time it was 2 o'clock and our next halt, apart from some brief stops to deliver Dapsone tablets to men who had come to the roadside to get their month's supply, was at Minakanagurki for lunch.

As we travelled between the fields, with rows of corn almost ready for harvest and the heads of the millet beginning to fill, the broad expanse of dry river bed was to our left, with just a narrow trickle of running water.

A bit further to our right was a thick grove of mango trees which almost hid a small temple on a hill behind them.

Samanna drove the car off the road into the shade and we all got out and washed our hands from the water bottle. We sat in a group on the bare ground and opened our tiffin carriers. Dr. always brought enough omelette and chapathi for me as well. As we sat eating, a monkey suddenly appeared without warning and grabbed the chaplain's tiffin carrier. Dr. threw his container at it and it dropped the carrier, but got away with a chapathi, and sat at a safe distance, grimacing and chattering angrily as it ate.

Fortunately we were nearly finished because we could not relax after that.

Amma said "I'm going up to look at the temple."

"It's really a tomb." I said.

She set off up the hill through the trees until she disappeared from sight and returning a few minutes later said,

"That's an interesting place - the tomb inside the temple is beautifully decorated with fresh flowers. I met the Poojari and he told me the story of the Yogi (holy man) who asked to be buried alive for twenty-four hours but when they dug him up he was dead. They've been keeping vigil there ever since."

Our next stop was at Huduguru, quite a large village of many well-built stone houses with its own school building.

I had introduced the team to this village, as one of the leading merchants, Gurappa Chetty, was a very old friend of mine. He was a Theosophist. A small, slim, energetic man who did a lot to help the village. He arranged for us to hold the clinic on the schoolhouse verandah.

There was one Christian in the village, an elderly man called Kondappa, the only Christian member of his family. He helped with organising the patients and was well respected in the community.

After the patients had been examined, we all went to Gurappa Chetty's house for coffee and light eats, sitting in a row on mats along the hallway which was open to all four rooms on one side. His wife and teenage daughter served us.

About a year later after a clinic during the hot weather the daughter was not there.

"Where is your daughter?".

"She was stung by a scorpion a week ago, and died."

"Ah yo! Why didn't you bring her to hospital, there is good medicine."

"We didn't know, sir."

People who die from scorpion sting usually drown in the fluid which builds up in their lungs. It was the same with snake bite: the villagers accepted it as the will of God not knowing that there was anti-venom at the hospital. It takes a long time for such information to penetrate the villages.

We headed for home. By now the light had faded and we drove through the wide bed of the Pennar river in semi-darkness, our headlights illuminating villagers, with bags of grain or bundles of grass on their heads, on the track through the sandy river bed. Samanna kept in the wheeltracks of previous cars and drove steadily, trusting that pedestrians would get out of his way, for if he swerved or stopped we would have to spend the next half-hour digging the car out of the deep, soft sand.

Now the main lure of home was a 'bana' of hot water to wash off the patina of dust and sweat before we ate.

Chapter 7
GANGASANDRA

Since going to live in Gollahalli I had seen the young children grow from toddlers to early school age and was concerned at the lack of discipline and direction in their lives. There seemed little hope of much education or change from the lives their parents lived and with each generation the area of land owned by the average family decreased.

Although at times I had rebelled against the discipline at boarding school, in hindsight I could see it had been good for me.

Two or three of the children seemed to me very intelligent but they attended school very irregularly and the teaching, was often poor. Mrs. Graham was now involved with the village boarding school at Gangasandra, so I decided to ask her next time I saw her, if Gangasandra would admit some of our children.

I was waiting by the roadside at K.T.Ramaiah's hut when the van pulled up on Wednesday. Amma was in the car, so as she was giving milk powder to the children, I said to her, "Amma, these children should be at school but their parents don't send them regularly and they are becoming disobedient, I would like to see them admitted to Gangasandra school. Is that possible?"

She moved along the line of children scooping milk powder into their tins according to the number of family members. When she reached the end of the row and had put the lid on the tin she tucked the end of her sari into her waist and said, "We receive a government grant and one of the conditions is that children should be admitted irrespective of race, caste or creed. I'm not sure whether we have any Hindu children at the moment. I'll put it to the management committee."

"Thank you, amma."

"How many children were you wanting to send?"

"Two girls, Padma and Jayamangali, and three boys, Muniangini, big Krishna and little Krishna."

"I've been wondering about those children on the range - there's no future for them there."

"They may be a bit old."

"The two little ones anyway - the girl would only be six or seven."

I left it with amma. I knew she would follow it up.

Three weeks later when I went to the bungalow for lunch after Leprosy clinic, amma was there.

"Good news about the children! The committee has agreed to admit them. I'll give you some application forms."

Now I had to work on the parents. To send their children away to boarding school would be a new idea for them. Padma's father was a very devout Hindu who did 'Puja' every day at the little shrine above the village and made himself responsible for its repair and maintenance - he would be the most difficult to persuade.

As I cycled from village to village delivering the Dapsone tablets and checking up on the patients I gave a lot of thought and prayer as to how to convince Venkatappa that Padma should go to school. On my return as I went up the path to their house I began to feel more confident - I was sure her mother would help to persuade him. Theirs was one of the two larger houses in the village with a courtyard, separate bathroom and storage shed. The mingled smells of fresh hay and cow manure met me as I entered the courtyard where Padma's father was just settling his cattle for the night in their covered stalls - giving them each a good helping of ragi straw. He was a lean man of medium height with an intelligent face.

"Namaskaram swami, how are you? Have you just come in from the villages?"

"Yes, how are you and your family?"

"We are well, come in and sit down."

He would know my visit had a purpose but as custom demands he did not ask me why I had come. His wife, a tall fair-complexioned woman came to the doorway.

"Come in Maistrulu." She laid a mat along one wall then disappeared into the kitchen to prepare coffee.

Venkatappa and I sat down and Padma, a quiet little girl with long black plaits and big brown eyes, came and sat down beside her father.

"That rain we had was good. Is it in time to save your crops?"

"It's good, anna, we may get an 80% crop." We discussed the weather further and the coming elections.

Nanjamma brought coffee, then I broached the subject uppermost in my mind.

"I have observed that Padma is a very intelligent child."

"Yes, she is anna - even now she is a great help to her mother in the house and has already taught herself to read with some help from us."

"If she had a good education she could become a teacher or a doctor and look after you both in your old age."

"That would be good anna, but it is more important for her to become a good wife and mother."

"Education would make her a better wife and mother."

"Perhaps."

"I am able to get her a place in the village boarding school at Gangasandra. There she could study up to 7th standard."

"That is the Christian Boarding school?"

"Yes"

"I will think about it. What are the fees?"

"The fees are very small, only five rupees a month. Please consider it and let me know. I have some application forms."

We sipped a few more minutes in silence then I rose.

"I will go and come."

"Go and come anna."

I knew Nanjamma had heard the conversation and that they would discuss it later.

I took food then walked to Chikkahanumantudu's hut. When I told him I could get Muniangini a place he was delighted.

"Anna - I want my son to study so that he can do things I've never been able to do. I only learnt to read and write here two years ago."

Krishna's parents made no difficulty - Akkayamma and Avalappa were happy to see their second son have such an opportunity as their eldest boy had epilepsy and was not able to add much to the family income.

Before she went on holiday amma told me to take the children down to school on June 6th. In addition to making sure the two young children from our household had a small trunk, bed sheet, towel, a change of clothes, slates and pencils, I made sure the others were also ready. The requirements were basic but even these were a struggle and text books would also have to be purchased.

A good crop had been harvested and now we looked anxiously for the rains, the fields were baked a hard dull red in the hot sun. The children, dressed in their new clothes were excited and even the last minute instructions from their parents to 'listen to the master's words' didn't dampen their spirits as we left the village. A trunk on each black head, the children followed me to the main road.

When the bus arrived it was crowded, but to my relief, it stopped. The cleaner climbed on to the roof and I handed up the five tin boxes, as the children squeezed in between the legs of the standing passengers. I had to stand with the cleaner on the back step.

The passengers did not look the usual crowd - many more young men and women - dressed in their best. I said to the cleaner, "Is there a festival somewhere?"

"No sir, it's Monday - many childless couples go to the shrine near Gauribidanur to pray for a child on Monday."

Then I remembered hearing of the shrine, which was quite near Gangasandra.

When we got down at Gauribidanur we had two and a half miles to go. The boxes weren't heavy, so we decided to walk. The children took out their towels and rolled them into a round pad for the tops of their heads then placed their trunks on top and we set out. I carried the girls' trunks turn about.

Within a few minutes we came to the Pennar river. Here it swept in a wide curve and even at this time of day the sun reflected off the wide expanse of sand hurt our eyes. We could only just walk in the hot sand and when we reached the small trickle of water on the far side we spent a few minutes standing in it before climbing up the bank and continuing our journey.

The dirt road was busy with jutkas passing to and from the fertility shrine. It stood back from the road in a grove of Pongamia trees, rich with the smell of honey and the humming of bees hard at work collecting nectar. We passed through the two rows of houses and one shop, comprising the village, and on to the school where the children were already in class. We found the boarding house deserted. It was a small whitewashed cottage, verandah across the front, large living room and back verandah enclosed either end to provide kitchen and bathroom. Behind this cottage to the right was the headmaster's house and to the left the borehole latrines enclosed by upright granite slabs. Further still to the right was another house occupied by a teacher and the girl boarders.

The boarding house catered for children from more distant villages, while the school also had pupils from Gangasandra village and others nearby.

"You stay here on the verandah with your boxes."

I walked across to the school, a long low whitewashed building with classrooms and an office, and knocked on a classroom door. All eyes turned to stare although the chanting of tables didn't miss a beat. The teacher came to the door.

"I would like to see the headmaster."

He called one of the boys to take me to him.

"Excuse me for interrupting, sir, I have brought the children from Gollahalli."

"That's all right, many of the boarders are still to come. Where are the children?"

"On the boarding house verandah."

"I'll come across and show them where to go." He turned back to the classroom and put one of the boys in charge of the class, then we walked across to the boarding house.

The children all made namaskaram as we approached. They looked so neat and polite I felt proud of them.

Visweswaraiah, the headmaster, showed the boys where to keep their boxes and then we all went across to the girls' boarding house and deposited theirs.

"We have twenty-four boys and twelve girls boarding this year, so we are very crowded, but we have been promised money from OXFAM to put up a new boarding house - that will be a big improvement."

Yes, I thought to myself, there must be barely enough space for the children to lie down.

"Have the children brought money for books?"

"No, please write me a postcard to let me know what they need and I will purchase them and bring them down myself."

As we left the girls' house and walked towards the school, a boy emerged with a large bell which he rang vigorously. Almost immediately the children began streaming out for recess. I didn't see any sign of the children from the foothills, but the children of Doramma who had been amma's cook saw me and came running over.

"Namaskaram sir," they beamed at me.

The eldest, a good-looking intelligent boy, took charge of my lot.

"Don't worry sir, we'll look after them."

I made my farewells and left, taking a short cut through the school orchard at the back and across the fields towards the Gauribidanur road. It would cut a mile off my walk but the question was whether any bus would stop for me. The sun beat down and the fields were hot, bare and deserted. I was glad to reach the shade of the roadside trees. I began walking towards Chikka, my ears alert for the sound of a bus behind me. I hadn't been walking long when a lorry overtook me. I held up my hand. It drew to a stop and the man beside the driver opened the door. I climbed up into the cabin.

The driver, a young man in a red checked turban leant across and smiled.

"How are you Swami? Do you remember me?"

"What village are you from?"

"Neralaghatta sir - some years ago you were in our village when I was bitten by a snake, you looked after me and took me to hospital."

"Yes, I remember, I didn't recognise you. You were only a boy then."

When we reached the Gollahalli turnoff he let me down and wouldn't take any money.

We missed the children. So Gangamma, Nanjamma and I went down one Sunday to see them. They were happy and we returned content.

They came home for a few days at Christmas and we were all amazed at their changed behaviour. They cleaned their teeth and combed their hair each morning without being told and entertained us in the evenings with songs they'd learnt. What pleased their parents even more was that they were more obedient and helped willingly with household tasks. I felt very happy for I knew it would be easy now to persuade other parents to send their children.

I knew amma had a constant battle to raise enough money for the running of the school and that she was concerned about their food so I asked people to donate ragi {red millet} and on several occasions received baskets of vegetables which I delivered to the school on the back of my bicycle. The children were always glad to see me and came running.

Easter was drawing near and as I pushed my cycle up to the road I met the postman, his bag slung over his shoulder.

"I've a card for you swami."

He lowered his bag and drew out a bundle of letters tied with pink tape. From among them he pulled one of the buff coloured postcards used by most people for cheap communication.

It was from the children asking me to come down and watch their Easter program.

It was easy for me to organise my tablet distribution for that area to fit in with a night spent at Gangasandra. I set out early. The air was crisp and clear and the fields on either side of the road green with ragi, corn and pigeon pea. As I travelled further down the road this gave place to sugar cane, its blue grey plumes of flowers waving like a mysterious sea. Further on the sea turned to yellow as I passed fields of turmeric in blossom and almost ready for harvest. Even the cash crop, tobacco, was in flower and I thought to myself, we'll see more wounds to the roadside trees as the curing barns light up again.

I turned off the main road on to one which wound like a red ribbon through the green landscape. An ox-cart stacked high with freshly cut cane creaked slowly along and ahead, a column of grey smoke told me that sugar crushing was in progress. As the thatched roof of the boiling shed came into view I could see steam-shrouded figures hovering over the wide shallow pans of bubbling sugar juice as they stirred it with long wooden paddles. A mound of cane lay near the roadside, and the noise of the motor which drove the crushing machine drowned out my voice as I shouted a greeting to the man absorbed in feeding the stalks into the jaws of the crushing wheels.

I dismounted and put my hands together in greeting.

"Namaskaram ayya," I shouted above the noise.

He nodded to acknowledge my greeting and his lips mouthed a namaskaram.

"How is your son?" I bent close to hear his answer.

"He is well swami. He is at school, the Christian school at Gangasandra."

"That's good. I'm going there now. I wondered if you'd give me some cane to take for the children."

He waved his head in the direction of the pile, his eyes never leaving the greedy wheels as they crushed the juicy sticks . "Take what you want, swami."

I made namaskaram and collected an armful which I tied lengthwise to my handlebars and rear rack. It made cycling a bit uncomfortable but I had only a few miles to go. As I cycled on, I thought of the day his son had his head caught in those wheels and had been brought to the hospital. Doctor had spent a long time in the theatre picking splinters of bone out of his brain. It must have been the fact that his head was a bit too big for the wheels to grip firmly, that had saved him.

I called at three villages to visit H.D. patients and make sure they were taking their Dapsone tablets. In one house the patient's wife greeted me and I could see him lying on his mat a bedsheet pulled over his head.

"What's the matter with your master?"

"He's no good, swami!"

Muniappa pulled the sheet down and I could see his puffy red face with swollen ears and eyebrows making him almost unrecognisable.

"Has fever come to you?"

"Yes, Maistrulu."

The picture was familiar. "I think the Leprosy germs are fighting. Sometimes it happens. You must go to the hospital and get a new medicine to fight back."

"Yes swami, I'll do that."

As I continued on my way I thought how lucky it was that he had lands and could afford to pay for the drug, which was much more expensive than Dapsone.

As I approached Gangasandra I saw two schoolboys, their cloth bags on their shoulders, coming towards me. I realised one was the sugar crusher's son. I braked and stopped beside them.

"Namaskaram sir."

"How are you?" I said as I put my hands together in greeting.

"I'm well sir."

"What are those for?" I indicated the two small leaves he had stuck, one outside the corner of each eye.

"I put those on to stop my eyes pricking."

"Good, I am glad you are well. Your father gave me this sugarcane to take to the boarders. I will go and come."

"Go and come sir."

As I approached the school I could see that the foundation slab for the new boarding house had been laid and the brickwork for the walls stood a metre high.

As soon as the children saw me coming they surrounded me and took me to Mr. Benjamin's house. By this time Benjamin was in charge of the school and the boarding, and very popular with the children. His wife Vimala welcomed me and as she served me with coffee said, "Graham ammagaru is here, she is just taking a bath."

Just then Mrs. Graham emerged from the hallway. "Namaskaram Anna, I didn't know you were coming down."

"Padma wrote me a card."

"Padma and Mohan are to be the stars of the Easter play. They both have beautiful voices."

"Ammagaru has been mending the children's clothes and the older ones have been helping her."

"Some of the shirts were more hole than whole, and there were so many buttons off that I sent one of the boys to buy a gross and only have about thirty left."

I enjoyed the evening's entertainment. When children are acting, even the things that don't turn out as planned, usually add to the delight.

Vimalamma had prepared food for both amma and me. A very welcome meal as she was a very good cook and put lots of green chillies in the yoghurt chutney, just as I like it, although it doesn't always like me.

I said to amma, "It is good to see the Boarding school going up at last."

"Yes! What a relief! I couldn't make out why the contractor didn't get on with the job and finally tackled him about it and discovered he was waiting to find out what cut I expected. When he realised I didn't expect anything he began work next day."

Benjy and Vimala's three small children ate with us, then went off to bed, while Benjamin gathered up two mats and a pillow and took us across to the school to sleep in one of the classrooms.

He gave me a mat, pillow and bed sheet and spread the other mat for amma near the windows, then said, "I will go and come."

Amma had begun to take her bedsheet and small pillow out of her bag as we heard the bolt on the outside of the door shot into place. Amma froze and looked at the barred windows and I wondered if all those green chillies I had eaten would leave me in peace until we were released. Did amma's thoughts run along similar lines I wondered.

We lay down on our mats and slept.

When morning dawned we heard the bolt drawn back and Benjamin stood there with two cups of steaming coffee.

"Did you realise you'd locked us in?"

"Ah yo! I'm sorry, I just bolted the door automatically!"

We took the coffee and amma put hers on the window sill then disappeared out the door. I followed her outside and watched which way she went then took the opposite direction.

Later, as we took breakfast in Benjamin's house Amma said, "I didn't realise how cold those stone floors are. I usually sleep on the table in the office when I come down, and that's not too bad. The children don't even have mats. I'll write to the Church at home and ask them to send some money for mats and blankets."

Within a few weeks amma purchased mats and blankets with the donation she received from Brisbane.

Chapter 8

INFANT HEALTH

For the second time that night Muniamma's baby was crying. I turned over on my mat to ease the pressure on my hip and waited for peace to descend again on the occupants of our hut.

I hàd observed over the years that the village babies were beautiful until they reached nine months but after that they lost weight, so that by the time they were eighteen months they were very lean and often had running noses or ears and became ill very easily. Of course they were breast fed; for unless mothers were able to breast feed them they had little chance of survival.

Gangamma's grandchildren were the same and I said to their mother, "You should give her other food, not just breast milk."

"She doesn't like our food!"

"Make something different for her then."

"What to make, Maistrulu?"

"Oh, something soft and bland." but as I sat and thought about it I realised I wasn't confident about telling her what to feed to her baby.

The problem had been at the back of my mind for some time but Muniamma's words "What to make?" had made me realise I should do something about it - Amma (Mrs. Graham) had raised four children, and she knew the foodstuffs available in the villages. I would ask her to teach the women. They were also interested in Christianity, perhaps amma would also tell them some Bible stories and pray with them.

On Thursday after the Leprosy clinic. I cycled across to the bungalow to take food as was my custom. As I pushed open the big wooden gates and wheeled my cycle through I was surprised to see Padma, dressed in her new Gangasandra uniform of gold jacket and green skirt, come running towards me followed by the compound children.

"Namaskaram Maistrulu" she said with her wide smile.

"What are you doing here?"

"I had bad diarrhoea, so amma brought me here on the back of her motor bike. I'm better now!"

"That's good. What are you doing?"

"We've made a shop with all the seeds from the trees."

After taking my meal I knocked on the front door. Amma was there.

"Come in and sit down anna - will you have coffee?"

"Thank you."

"Did you see Padma?

"Yes, she came running when I came for my meal. She told me she feels much better."

"Yes, she was quite sick yesterday so I thought it better to bring her here. They did some tests, nothing identifiable but we'll keep her here for a few days to be sure she's alright."

"Amma, I have a request to make."

"Yes, What is it?" she smiled and gave me a quizzical look.

"Could you come to Gollahalli and teach the women?"

"What do you want me to teach?"

"About germs and cleanliness and how to feed their babies and their children and for a long time I've wanted to give them teaching about Christ so if you could tell them a Bible story and pray with them it would be good."

"The prayers would be very simple - I'm not really up on prayer language in Telugu."

"Simple prayers will be best. They are unaccustomed to prayer language.

"When would you like me to come?"

"Could you come one afternoon each week. Now that you have the motor cycle you can be independent of buses."

"Yes, it makes a huge difference."

As we sat sipping our coffee the big black and white cat came and purred loudly as he rubbed against my legs. I broke off a piece of my biscuit and gave it to him.

"He's a beautiful cat, I've never seen such a big one."

"He's become a big problem. He has killed two hens in the last week, one of them the gateman's. Those hens are too valuable to be destroyed like that, so I took him down to the vet and explained the situation but he said he couldn't put down such a beautiful animal. Now I really don't know what to do."

"Why not give him to me, amma? I'll take him to Gollahalli and he will keep down the rats."

"But what if he kills the village hens?"

"There are plenty of rats and bandicoots which eat our grain. He would be an asset."

"Well, if you're sure you know what you're doing. I really would hate to kill him but I can't keep him here."

Amma's visits to Gollahalli became a regular event. The women enjoyed them.

I was there for the first session. I remember amma said "You grow peanuts - they're a very good food."

"Oh no, amma they give the babies fits!"

"If you prepare them well, they won't cause fits.? It's your custom to grind up your curry spices isn't it? Grind the peanuts on the curry stone as though you are making peanut chutney but leave out the chillies - mix the ground peanuts with a little soft wet rice and feed it to your children."

She told them how to prepare the jungle fruit and the weeds that they gathered after the rains. If I had told them these things they would not have listened but because amma told them they believed her.

When amma came to the village I liked to have something for her to drink, so I cycled to Doddaganahalli where some of the people kept buffaloes for ghee. The milk from the animals was collected and boiled slowly for a very long time until the ghee rose to the surface and could be collected. By this time the milk was dehydrated and very rich; my friends gave me some and I returned with the brass 'chembu' of milk on my handlebars.

On one occasion, when I reached Gollahalli I could sense a tension. Everyone was unusually quiet and some of the men followed me into the hut.

"Anna, have you been near the Gollahalli turnoff today?"

"No, I cut across to the road and down. Why?"

"There's a corpse under the Lantana up there."

"Ah yo! Who put it there? Do you know who it is?"

"He's a stranger, Maistrulu. Narasimhudu got off the bus and smelt it. He went to see what it was, then came and told us - three of us went and looked. He must have been there since yesterday."

"Did you touch him?"

"No sir, we wouldn't do that!"

"We must go to the police and report it."

"No, Maistrulu, don't go to the police, they will blame us and beat us."

"But we can't just leave him lying there the jungle animals will eat him."

"I wish they'd eaten him yesterday, then we wouldn't have this problem."

"The crows and the kites have been at him already."

"Ugh! Do any of you know anything about it?"

"No, Maistrulu - we swear we don't."

"We've never seen him before."

"I think we should go to the police."

"No anna, please anna," the women begged me.

I kept quiet but I didn't feel happy about it. I understood their fear of being beaten to extract a confession.

It was about time for amma to arrive, so I gave the chembu of milk to Muniamma to heat up and went to Nanjamma's house for some raw sugar to add to it. The men went back to their huts and the women gathered in Gangamma's house.

Soon we heard the put-put of amma's motor cycle as she came carefully down the hill in low gear trying to avoid the ruts.

Gangamma went to meet her at the foot of the hill where she parked her cycle near Avalappa's house and they walked through the village together.

As she approached to greet me her cat appeared, sat by the corner of a hut and began to groom himself.

"Oh, there's Mitz, he looks very sleek I hope it isn't because of a diet of hen."

"The only time we ever see him, amma, is when you come. He must live in the jungle and hear your scooter from a distance."

Amma removed her sandals, bent her head and entered the hut. After she was seated on the mat and drinking the hot milk, she said,

"There was an awful smell at the top of the track - like someone dead."

I saw the women look at one another then one of them said,

"Will we tell amma?"

"Yes, we can trust her."

"There is a dead man under the Lantana bush but we don't know where he came from."

"Ah yo, have you told the police?"

"No, we are afraid to tell them."

Amma was silent - I guessed what was going through her mind - she would understand their fear.

Akkayamma said "Please don't tell them amma."

"No, I won't tell them."

After amma had gone we discussed the matter again. I said, "If someone else reports it to the police and they know we have kept quiet it will direct their suspicion at us."

"That is true, Maistrulu."

"I think it is best that I go to the police station and report it. They are reasonable men."

"Perhaps swami, but we don't have much faith in them."

"I will go, it is better to do that." By this time it was already late so I set out early next day. It was cold and I was shivering so much I could scarcely push the pedals but the exertion soon warmed me. When I reached the top of the range and looked down towards Chikka the world was a sea of white, occasional trees or rocks rising from it like islands, their shores surrounded by wisps of foam.

When I reached the police station the sergeant greeted me.

"What can I do for you, Mr. Sabhapathy?" I was known to him as I had acted as mediator in a number of disputes where the police were involved. I explained the situation to him.

"I will come with you now, but first we must hire a cart to bring in the body."

He took his cycle from where it was leaning against the wall, put a large padlock on the door and we cycled down to the bus stand. Baskets full of carrots were being taken off a cart and put on to a Bangalore bus.

"We want to hire your cart."

"Yes Sahib."

"What will you charge to Gollahalli and back?"

"Twelve rupees, sahib!"

"You'd be joking! I'll pay six!"

"Ah yo swami, what about the range? What do I have to carry?"

"Find someone else!

I finally persuaded three of them to return with me and called to the women, "Heat bath water ready for our return."

The cart was there when we reached the top of the hill and the sergeant took charge, ordering the driver and the three men to lift the body into the basket.

That was the last we heard of the matter officially but through the grape vine we learnt that the murdered man had already been reported missing in Gauribidanur. He had been seen getting on to a lorry. He was carrying money to Chikka in payment for a pair of oxen. A lorry driver was later charged with the murder.

Chapter 9

A.I.

Dispensary was over for the day and I pedalled out through the hospital gate and along the road, the huge rain trees casting welcome shade. The big wooden gates into the bungalow compound were open, Samanna must be out bringing in a patient.

I cycled to the back of the bungalow to take my food out of the hot case on the back verandah, and met amma crossing the lawn.

"Come and see what I've got!"

She led me to a shed in the corner of the compound.

"I bought 200 day-old chicks from the government poultry farm at Hessaraghatta."

We watched them for a while as they scratched busily or drank from the earthenware water bowl. "They are unsexed and we won't need many cocks except for meat. I've been reading the poultry books, and they say the cock is most important for upgrading poor stock. Perhaps we can arrange some swaps."

"I can probably bring in a village cock for one of yours."

"Yes, that's what I hoped."

A few weeks later when I saw amma she was downcast. "The chickens have a deficiency disease and many are dying every day."

"What are you feeding them on?"

"I got a formula from the poultry farm, I even bought riboflavin powder at a terrific expense, but I decided there must be something wrong and finally rang them yesterday to check. One thing had been left out, a teaspoon of shark liver oil per 10 pounds of mixture so I went straight to the dispensary and got some - now I'm waiting to see what happens - only one dead this morning and they are looking better already."

On Wednesday when the hospital car came down for rural dispensary I asked about the chickens.

"They're fine, I haven't lost any more."

It wasn't long before they were almost full grown and I began taking roosters from the villages, slung over my handlebars when I went into town, then returning with good roosters in exchange. That worked well, because, by using the roosters only, we did not weaken our stock or lose the village hens' ability to raise chicks, and in each generation the egg size increased and so did the number of eggs laid.

I went often to see the vet, who at that time was a very conscientious and enthusiastic Muslim. He said one day, "The Government has a free animal artificial insemination program."

"How does it work?"

"When your animal comes into season bring it to us and we'll send the peon to pick up a Jersey bull or Murrah buffalo semen in Bangalore."

"Do you come out to the villages?"

"No, you have to bring the animal in here. You will also need a vacuum flask to carry the semen."

It sounded good. I went into town and spent the last of my money on a vacuum flask. As I cycled the long climb up to the edge of the plateau, the cattle were being driven in from the hills where they had been grazing during the heat of the day. The herdsmen with them hardly needed to crack their whips, and as the cattle came into the town, individual animals left the herd of their own accord as they came abreast of their houses.

I was so absorbed in thinking about the A.I. program and what it could mean to the villagers, that I cycled into the middle of the herd scarcely noticing, until an animal ran across my path and I had to swerve sharply, almost coming off in the dust.

I shouted to the herdsman, "Look after your animals!"

He shouted back, "You look after yourself! If you ring your bell they'll get out of your way, they don't see you coming."

When I reached the top of the range I went flying down the ghat road across the bridge and past the temple, finally reaching the Gollahalli turnoff where the deeply rutted track down to the village necessitated more caution unless I wanted to land on my head.

Gangamma and her husband were in the hut, as well as their son and his wife and children, the men having brought the village cattle in from the jungle. I removed my Gandhi cap and Nehru jacket and sat down. While Muniamma prepared coffee for me, I told them about the scheme.

"Do you mean to say you don't take the cow to the bull?"

"No, they give the cow an injection of the bull's semen."

Old Premadasappa was sitting as usual in the corner near the door in his shirt and G-string, his knees drawn up with his staff beside him. "It's not good swami, it doesn't sound natural."

"But it means our cows and buffaloes will produce good calves, and they'll give more milk."

"It's not good to go against God's laws."

Even his son looked doubtful and my spirits were dashed. Admittedly Premadasappa was a man of the old school, but I realised his reaction probably foreshadowed the views many would put forward.

As I lay on my mat that night I realised it would not be easy introducing something like this - I'd have to get my case together to be convincing.

My fears were realised, and as I travelled around the villages delivering Dapsone tablets to H.D. patients and trying to persuade sick people to go for treatment, I met with a lot of opposition to the A.I. plan. But some were interested and I felt sure once a few villagers brought their animals and saw the benefits, others would follow suit.

It wasn't long before a man appeared at our hut late one evening.

"My cow is calling, sir!"

"Good! Can you drive it to the veterinary dispensary by noon tomorrow? I will go early and make arrangements."

I set off on my cycle before first light — at least it was cooler pushing the cycle to the top of the range. Once there I hardly needed to pedal all the way down to Chikka. The vet wasn't due at work until 9am so I went to his house. He came to the door, still in his loin cloth.

"Sahib, forgive me for coming so early but one of the men from Guyelahalli has a cow in season."

"Ah yo! The peon has taken three days' casual leave and I have only one assistant, I can't spare him to go to Bangalore."

What a blow! After all my build up of the programme to the villagers, the first time they were willing to try it it was going to be a failure. Surely there was some way around the problem.

"If I go to Hessaraghatta myself, will they give me the semen?"

"They will if I give you a letter."

"Please do that, sahib."

We rode our cycles down to the office together, and he wrote me a letter, stamped it with his official seal and gave it to me. I didn't have any money for bus fares, having spent my last on the flask, so I rode the 40 miles. Fortunately the road to Bangalore is not too hilly and I made good time and soon covered the extra five miles to Hessaraghatta. The farm was on high ground looking towards the huge expanse of shimmering water which was Hessaraghatta tank. I was glad to sit down in the office when I got there and very grateful for a cup of coffee and the cool breeze coming over the water, while they organised collection of semen.

"Would you like to come down to the pen and watch, ayya?"

As we went down to the pen to watch them at work we saw the Murrah buffalo bull in his enclosure, a huge animal with shiny leathery-looking skin. One of their workers untied him as we passed and led him down to the dam for his daily bath.

The Jersey bull in his pen seemed bad-tempered and they treated him with respect.

"These Jersey bulls are dangerous, unlike the Brahmin or Sindhi bulls, which are very docile."

Finally, with the semen safe in my flask, slung in the cloth bag over my shoulder, I set out towards Bangalore, but by the time I had crossed the city it was midday, and I was hungry and very thankful for the shade of the avenue trees as I cycled out along the north road towards Chikka.

An H.D patient who was an old friend of mine lived in a village beside the Bangalore road some ten miles on, and I decided to call in there, as my head was beginning to spin from lack of food.

He had had leprosy for many years before commencing treatment at the hospital.

As I rode off the road towards his whitewashed stone house I heaved a sigh of relief, threw my leg over and braked to a halt. He had a pleasant walled courtyard in front of his house with healthy drumstick, tamarillo and Sampangi trees providing shade as well as fruit and flowers. I walked up to the open door and knocked. "Ayya, are you there?"

His wife appeared in a green cotton sari and smiled in recognition, for I had been a regular visitor with Dapsone tablets for many years.

"How are you, swami? Please come in, the master is here. I will tell him. Please sit down." She waved me to a chair.

I sat down thankfully, took the vacuum flask out of my bag and checked to make sure it hadn't broken.

Venkatappa came into the room and greeted me warmly. I looked him in the face with some difficulty; he was not a pretty sight for the leprosy had destroyed his nose which had collapsed, leaving two ugly holes.

"I haven't seen you for a long time what brings you so far?"

"I have been to Hessaraghatta to get Jersey semen for a cow in Guyelahalli."

He was interested and I told him about the scheme. His wife appeared with coffee for both of us.

"Have you taken food, anna?"

"No, I haven't!"

"Ah yo, sir, you must be hungry."

She disappeared into the kitchen,

A girl of about eighteen appeared in another doorway. Her father called, "Lakshmamma, come and greet Sabhapathygaru."

She approached and made namaskaram.

"What are you doing now?" I asked

"She completed matriculation a year ago and is now at home."

Lakshmamma made namaskaram again and left us.

Venkatappa leant forward. "I have been trying to arrange a marriage for my daughter ever since she matriculated but as soon as the matchmaker comes to make arrangements and sees me, the plans fall through."

I looked at him. It was understandable.

"They find me repulsive and are afraid, even though I tell them I am not infectious, as you know."

"Have you been to see Grahamdoctoru about it? There might be something he can do."

"But my nose has gone, sir."

"Yes, but doctor has had a little girl in the hospital who lost all her upper lip and part of her jaw through measles and he made her a new lip with part of her arm."

"Will you go with me?"

"Yes but I'll ask Doctor about it beforehand and if he says it's useless we'll drop the matter."

His wife brought ragi ball and split pea curry and I ate thankfully.

Shortly afterwards I took leave and continued my journey. I didn't want to be longer than necessary as the semen is most effective when fresh.

When I arrived at the veterinary dispensary the villager was sitting on his heels outside watching for me and his cow was tied inside the compound waiting.

We both watched carefully as the vet and his assistant inseminated the cow. I thought to myself, "We would only need a large syringe to do that ourselves in the village."

After that, I arranged A.I. for many village animals. I managed to borrow a syringe from the vet, to make the long slow walk to the dispensary with the animals unnecessary.

After the first calves were born, many people were won over and the program became even more popular as they saw what good animals were produced. It wasn't all gain, for although the cows were better tempered than our village cows, the bulls had to be handled with great care; but as time went on the increase in village milk production made it well worth while.

The following Wednesday Dr. Graham came down with the car for rural dispensary and I seized the opportunity to ask him about Venkatappa's nose.

"I would need to see him to be sure but I could probably build him a new nose."

"The bone is gone, doctor."

"That is no problem, I can use a piece of his rib for that but his general health must be fairly good or the graft may not take."

I was anxious to take the news to Venkatappa, so arranged my tablet distribution in a wide circle, finishing up at his house that night.

"Doctor says he must see you to make a final decision but thinks he can rebuild your nose."

"That is very good news, sir."

"I must be at the hospital for Leprosy clinic tomorrow morning. You can accompany me."

Venkatappa had surgery a few weeks later, which was so successful that, a year later, we were all invited to his daughter's wedding.

Chapter 10
CHOWDAPPA and THIMMARAYAPPA

After delivering tablets in the Dodballapur area I spent the night in the home of the stonemason then set off before dawn. I cycled towards Nandi Durg (Bull Mountain) which rises two thousand feet above the three thousand foot elevation of the Southern Deccan.

The local buses skirted Nandi to the south but when walking or cycling I took the short steep road to the north through Sultanpet. It really climbs over the gap between Nandi and Kalawara.

Since the 1939-1945 war the hillsides have been reafforested with Australian eucalyptus hybrids raised in the government nursery at Sultanpet.

I pedalled as far as I could up the steep road then dismounted and pushed my cycle. Although it was late in the year and the weather comparatively cool, I had still produced a generous amount of sweat by the time I reached the top.

I lifted the ends of my pancha (loin cloth) and tucked them in at the waist, then mounting, freewheeled down past the huge granite bull. Each time I pass it I look at it closely, for the Hindus believe it grows each year, nourished by their offerings of ghee which have made its surface glisten black under the roof of the shrine. It certainly is a huge mass of stone, I thought, I wonder who carved it and how many thousand years ago. If it is growing it should have outgrown the shrine by now. Commonsense told me it was impossible and yet every time I passed it I looked at it speculatively.

The small village of Sultanpet lay, a cluster of houses on either side of the road, sprawling a short way up beside the two thousand odd steps leading to the top of Nandi. Many of the people working on top of the hill live there and climb up and down the steps each day to work.

The Eucalyptus nursery was just to the left; acres of seed beds, the huge counterpoise beams of the wells brooding over them like hovering predators. I debated whether I would call in and ask for some eucalypt seedlings. I had my carrier, and they would wrap them in hessian for me. Before I'd made a conscious decision my cycle turned in the gate and I rode through a grove of tall eucalypts, the light passing through the branches making dancing patterns on the ground around me.

A workman was weeding a nearby bed. "Do you have any spare seedlings?" I asked.

"I don't know, swami. Ask the boss."

An office was set among the trees, the forest officer seated inside working on some accounts.

"Can you spare me any eucalypt seedlings today?" He knew me well as I had already collected and distributed several hundred trees around the villages near Gollahalli.

"For you, sir, I can find some." He rose and came outside.

"Hassan Sahib" he called to a nearby worker. "Give the sahib fifty seedlings."

Soon I was on my way again. My next halt was a small village hugging the road to Chikka some miles on.

As I approached the village the click, clack of the looms reached me from a long low shed running parallel with the road. Its thatched roof was shaded by huge Tamarind trees. I looked in but there was no sign of Chowdappa.

"Where's Chowdappanna?" I asked a man, his hands busily moving the wooden toggles that lifted and lowered the frames.

"He's at home!"

When I called at his doorway he was sitting on a mat in a corner of the room. I hadn't seen him for a month and I was shocked at his appearance - he looked haggard.

"Namaskarappa! Are you well?" I asked.

"Yes I am well." He looked down and sat in silence. I sat down on the mat near him uninvited - there was obviously something wrong.

"Where is your wife?"

"She has gone to do 'coolie'."

"I looked in at the weaving shed but you weren't there - they said you were at home."

"Yes, I am at home but I would be better dead!"

He held out his hands in front of him, his fingers curling inward in clawlike fashion. "Look at these hands - I can no longer grasp the toggles - I'm useless."

I sat in silence. "Dear God how can I help him." His family had been weavers for generations, he knew nothing else. Could Doctor do anything for him I wondered.

"Don't despair anna - keep on taking your tablets and I will speak to Doctor- perhaps he can do something."

I couldn't really imagine what doctor could do about it but he was obviously very depressed, and it might give his spirits a lift until we searched other avenues.

I gave him his tablets and cycled on towards Chikka, exploring in my mind ways in which he could earn a living but his hands were almost useless and I could not think of anything.

I looked at the sun - it was well up - and pedalled harder - there was a Taluk Board (Shire Council) meeting at 10 am and Mr. Muniraj had invited me to come and speak to them about a grant towards purchase of tablets for treatment of Leprosy patients in the Taluk.

The previous Thursday after I had passed the last patient on to Doctor at the Leprosy Clinic I had spent another two hours working through the books making a tally of the leprosy patients in the Taluk receiving treatment. Now I was armed with up-to-date figures.

When I reached the huge block building that housed the Rural Development Project, I propped my cycle against the wall and went up the stone steps. I looked in the door of the long building. After the sunlight outside I could see nothing, then gradually shapes emerged, and I saw there were a number of people already seated at the huge wooden table. They looked at me in some surprise but greeted me politely as I was known to all of them. I was about to launch into an explanation of my presence when Mr. Muniraj arrived. He was a tall good looking young man of about 40 years and as local Congress M.L.A., had their ear.

"I invited Sabapathyayya to come today to tell us about the work which is being done for Leprosy patients in our Taluk. Mr. Chairman, if we convene the meeting, perhaps we could hear what he has to say first, then he will be free to leave while we deal with other matters."

I spoke to them giving them a list of villages where H.D. cases were to be found and the numbers in each village. After I had finished speaking one of the members said,

"A government doctor I was speaking to recently told me there was practically no leprosy in this area."

"The incidence is certainly low compared with some areas of Andhra and Tamil Nadu, but I can assure you all these people have returned skin clippings positive for Hansen's bacillus, as the lepra bacillus is now called."

"Thank you Mr Sabapathy, we will discuss the matter and decide what help we are able to give."

"Thank you. I would also like to mention that we are forming the Mahatma Gandhi Leprosy Association to deal with help and education for leprosy patients and their families in this area.

"Good, we will be glad to hear how it progresses."

I made namaskaram and left, riding on to the bungalow next door to tell ammagaru's cook I was in Chikka unexpectedly. Having done that I went across to the hospital hoping to see doctor. I was in luck, he was in his office.

"Sir, I delivered Dapsone tablets to Chowdappa this morning. He is a weaver and his fingers have such bad contractures that he is now no longer able to grasp the toggles. Can anything be done about it ? He is very depressed."

"Well, as a matter of fact, Dr. Paul Brand, a doctor in Vellore, has recently pioneered an operation for that. He transplants the undamaged tendons from the back of the hand so that movement is restored."

"Could we send him to Vellore Hospital then?"

"I'm hoping to go down to Vellore to learn to do the operation here, but before raising his hopes I would need to examine him. Do his fingers appear undamaged apart from that?"

I conjured up a picture of his hands held out in front of me. "I am fairly sure he has not lost part of any finger."

"Tell him to come to the next clinic then, but it will be a slow process as he will need special massage and exercises for some weeks before and after surgery. Mrs. Graham will go down with me to observe in the Physiotherapy department while I'm with Dr. Brand."

"Thank you doctor."

As I mounted my cycle to ride back to Gollahalli my spirits soared, and I alternately sang and hummed "Praise to the Lord, the Almighty, the King of Creation" as I pedalled up to the top of the range before speeding down around the bends of the ghat road.

When Doctor examined Chowdappa he said "Your hands are suitable for surgery. Come back in two weeks time and we will admit you."

Doctor and amma went down to Vellore and on their return Chowdappa was admitted. It was a lengthy process, first his hands had to become supple enough for the surgery to be successful.

Amma began the treatment, each day dipping his hands into hot wax, putting them in padded mittens for half an hour then giving them massage and exercises.

One day when I went to the bungalow amma said "Today is a red letter day!" and looked very happy.

"Is it some anniversary for you?"

"No, Chowdappa smiled for the first time. For two weeks I've been working with him and today was the first time he actually smiled and answered more than yes or no to a question."

"He has been very depressed."

"He can move his fingers a little bit now and will have his 'op' in two weeks time."

Chowdappa's operation was a success and he returned to his village with hope in his heart.

About this time I discovered through my friend the veterinary officer that the government was providing a small number of sheep to villagers on application. These were Bannouri sheep, an excellent meat animal, and one that was reasonably hardy in village conditions.

I put in an application for thirty sheep, each person to receive five, then I set about going through the lists of patients to decide whose need was greatest and who would benefit most. We had by now formed the Mahatma Gandhi Leprosy Association and I submitted a list to them for a decision.

It was decided Krottapalli Thimmarayappa should be one of the recipients. He was a tall thin man with a shock of curly black hair, whose habitual dress was a heavy army coat which reached just below his hips. A G-string completed his attire. In spite of bouts of weakness and sometimes reaction to Dapsone, he worked hard and was always cheerful. The danger was that he would damage his hands or feet unwittingly, causing ulcers and resultant loss of toes or fingers. If he could build up a small flock of sheep it would be a big help.

I had asked the vet to let amma know when the sheep arrived. The children were home from school on holidays so amma sent a message to me, then went down to the veterinary office with the children and Gopal, a young boy from the foothills who was living with them. Between them they drove the sheep up the main street, through the town to the bungalow and put them in the buffalo shed.

I sent messages to the people involved to go into Chikka to collect their sheep. The six men went in and we divided them up, a ram and four ewes to each. Some of the ewes were already in lamb.

Thimmarayappa was delighted with his, and his family between them were able to graze them as well as do coolie or cut firewood. In time he hoped the flock would grow.

Doctor decided that he would also be a suitable candidate for tendon transplant surgery. He was admitted so that amma could give his hands wax baths and massage in readiness for the operation.

When his hands had become sufficiently supple doctor operated on him, then amma once again gave him daily treatment. The result of the surgery was good and his hands became useful once more.

When doctor discharged him he said, "Remember you must protect your hands and feet, and watch for any injury - they won't tell you if they are hurt. And get yourself a cat!"

"A cat, swami?" He looked surprised.

"Yes! A cat, to eat the rats so that they don't nibble at your toes in the night."

"Yes swami!"

I reiterated the warning next time I saw him.

"Don't forget what Doctor said about looking after your hands. Remember you can't feel pain, so don't burn them or damage them by working too hard or too long. If you do hurt them, come immediately to the hospital for treatment."

"Yes, anna"

I looked down at his feet, encased in special sandals hand made by the Chakla (Cobbler) who attended leprosy clinic each Thursday to make shoes for the patients whose need was greatest. This had been made possible by donations we'd received from a former missionary nurse and a church in Brisbane, Australia.

"Remember to look after your feet also."

A few months later I went to his village - one of his daughters was watching the sheep in the field as I approached.

"Is your appa at home?"

"No, appa's not here, he's gone away."

"Oh! Where has he gone?"

"I don't know, he didn't say."

I felt puzzled - he was not the type of man to walk out on his family.

"Is your amma at home?"

"Yes, she's cooking."

I went on to the house and knocked. His wife appeared from the smoke-filled kitchen area wiping her watering eyes on the corner of her sari.

"Amma, is your master here?"

"No, he's not!" She looked defensive and did not meet my eyes.

"Has he gone out?"

"He's gone, swami!"

"When will he be back?"

"You tell me, swami." She looked down and turned to go back to the kitchen.

"Is he alright?"

"Yes, and so are we if he stays away. We don't want his disease."

So that was it!

"But he's not infectious, he's been having treatment for a long time. Doctor even gave him a certificate to say so."

"Perhaps. Who can be sure, swami."

"They've done tests at the hospital. Do you know where he's gone?"

"No, I don't!"

I left it there.

Some weeks later Thimmarayappa turned up at the Thursday clinic - his feet were a mass of ulcers and he could hardly walk.

"Where have you been? I saw your wife and she didn't know where you were."

"I left home sir. My wife told me to go. I got a job as a railway ganger in Bangalore but my feet got bad and I had to come here."

Doctor was shocked when he saw his condition. "You people must look after your feet and hands!"

"What to do, swami - I had to eat."

He was admitted to the little leprosy ward, his feet dressed and put in plaster until the ulcers healed, but the damage was done and his feet and hands would never be fit for work again. He was condemned to live as a beggar, a bitter pill for a proud and independent man like Thimmarayappa.

Chapter 11

PIGS

My companion, Chikkahanumantudu and I set out on our cycles at 5-30 am. There had been good rains and the hills ahead of us glistened green in the first rays of the sun.

As we approached the ghat, the corn and ragi in the fields was a sea of green and under the Jambu trees the road was stained purple with fallen fruit. We stopped and collected some, putting them into the baskets we had brought to carry the piglets. They were refreshing to eat as we rode.

Just above the temple we dismounted and began the long push up to the top of the range. At that time of day the sun was pleasantly warm on our backs. At intervals I leant my cycle against the parapet at the edge of the road and walked a few yards up a gully or on to a bank to push some seeds into the moist earth. I had been collecting seeds of flowering trees to plant along the hill road, to give some relief from the dominating Lantana and wait-a-while.

When we finally reached the top, we mounted our cycles and coasted the three miles down into Chikka.

Amma was ready and waiting under the porch of the bungalow, and all three of us waved goodbye to the children and set out. It was still cool enough to make the eighteen mile ride pleasant. The first ten, along the Bangalore road, then off across the fields on foot tracks, skirting a tank (reservoir) and on to a small village, a group of thatched houses with a larger, flatroofed one of vertical granite slab, nestling near a grove of Pongamia trees. As we cycled past the trees, our ears were assailed by the deafening hum of bees feeding on the nectar in the tiny mauve flowers. Several small children, baskets on the ground and twig brooms in their hands, were busy sweeping up the flowers to add to their family compost heaps. They stopped work and stared at us as we passed. They had probably never seen a white woman before.

We smelt the pigs before we heard them, and the owner came to join us as we stood looking over the mud wall into the sty. A huge pink sow lay there, with eight little piglets battling for feeding stations.

"Namaskaram Sir! Come inside and sit down."

We followed him into the larger whitewashed stone house and sat down to strike a bargain, while his wife supplied us with coffee. We agreed on 10 Rupees per piglet and I handed him the money, then we went out to make our choice. Anna and I each had wide-mouthed baskets strapped to our luggage racks.

The owner of the pigs called to a boy "Get into the pen and catch the piglets!" He climbed in, keeping a wary eye on the sow.

"After the sow gave birth she was very fierce, none of us could get into the pen, but now she is quieter!"

The boy caught the piglets of our choice, two females, handed them to us and we tied their legs firmly, then put them into the baskets.

"We'll go and come, ayya"

"Go and come, swami!"

When we reached the bungalow the children were sitting on top of the compound wall waiting. They jumped down and came running after us as we cycled to the back of the house. We lifted the piglets out and untied their legs to give them a run.

"Mummy, can we keep them here?"

"They are Sabhapathyanna's pigs; he'll take them to Gollahalli."

"Please anna, can we keep them here while we are home on holiday?"

"If your mother doesn't mind. I'd like to leave them here for a few days until we finish building their sty."

"Mum, please!"

Amma said "Alright!" I could see she was as keen to keep the piglets as the children were.

We took the piglets and put them in the chicken run.

"They look hungry. What can we give them to eat?"

Amma said "Mix some of the chickens' food with water and pour it into that wooden trough."

We turned to leave.

"Please take food before you go, Sahib has cooked for you."

We left the children totally absorbed in making the piglets happy, while we washed and ate before setting out for Gollahalli.

Anna and I returned to Gollahalli and went to work on the sty. We had only eight inches of mud to put on top of the wall. The women mixed the mud and carried it to us in baskets while we slapped it on top.

Chikkahanumantudu, a tall lean man, his hair tied in a short pony tail, was our village carpenter, and although untrained, soon made a sturdy frame from some forest wood, then lashed branches across it to make the door.

Three days later we returned to collect the pigs. The children were still in love with them but amma said "I'm glad to see you, those piglets are real Houdinis."

"Yes,"said Greg "they escaped every time we shut them up. They pushed under the wire of the hen run; then we put them in the hen house and they tore a hole in that; so we tried the old kitchen, and they jumped up and got out through the window. We nailed boards over the gap then they found a loose board on the other shutter and pushed through that."

"Each time they escaped the children and I had to chase madly around the compound until we caught them again. I haven't had so much exercise for years!"

As we secured the piglets again in the baskets I felt anxious - would our sty be secure?

The children kissed the piglets goodbye and we rode off.

The village children saw us cycling down the track from the road and came running to meet us gathering round so closely that we had to dismount.

"Can we help you look after them, anna?"

"Yes, but remember they need to be looked after everyday."

"We'll do it every day, anna!"

We put the piglets in the pen and watched anxiously as they investigated means of escape. They pushed their snouts between the wood on the gate and jumped at the walls but couldn't reach the top.

Chikkahanumantudu said to two of the boys "Take this mattsu and go to the gully for more vines."

Ramu, one of the older boys, was watching "Ramu, help me catch the piglets and tie them so that anna can strengthen the gate." We climbed into the sty, caught and retied their legs to a chorus of piercing squeals.

"Jayamma, go and bring some peanut cake and a pot of water and soak the cake in that pan."

By the time Hanumanthu had the gate secure and we released the pigs, the peanut cake had swelled to a sticky mess and they shoved their noses in and ate with rapid grunts of delight.

While the children were on holiday I had plenty of willing helpers and the pigs soon became accustomed to their sty and when out of it followed me or the children like dogs.

Each day we took them down to the tank and bathed them. They loved the water and frolicked in it with squeals of delight. When school recommenced I took them down below the village by the tank each day where they grazed and poked around in the mud. I sat and read my library books or prayed while watching them. Premadasappa and the other men often collected jungle fruit for them while out with the cattle and I begged tamarind seeds from my friends in surrounding villages. After the peanut crop was harvested I took them to snuffle out any that remained.

I regarded the pigs as a village project, a means of increasing village income so when I came home late after delivering Dapsone Tablets to find no one had bothered to take the pigs out to graze and that they had not even been fed or watered, I was angry. I called out to the group of men sitting on a slab near the well.

"Couldn't one of you have spared the time to take the pigs out to graze? They are hungry and thirsty too. When I'm away it's your job to feed them."

The village women were always busy. They rose early, drew the day's supply of water from the well, cleaned the grain and ground it, cooked and served the food, looked after the children and even bathed their menfolk when they came in from the fields or jungle. If there was harvesting or weeding to do they did that as well. The men had more time, many of them sat around before taking out the cattle then relaxed and gossiped on their return.

One of the women took a pot and went to draw water while Gangamma appeared in the doorway with a winnowing basket of peanut cake.

"We'll do it Maistrulu, don't worry."

"Aren't you ashamed to sit there and watch the women work."I shouted at the men.

"Drawing water is women's work, anna." said one of the men.

It would take more than a few words from me to change that attitude, I thought, as I walked angrily back to the pig pen. The village people were not used to looking after pigs, Pigs looked after themselves!

In spite of these periods of neglect the piglets thrived so I thought I'd better approach the veterinary officer about a boar.

I cycled into Chikka, and down the main road, past the Bangalore circle and the High school to the Veterinary office. The vet was watching his assistants castrate a pair of bulls. I stood and watched as he placed the huge pincers above the testicles and clamped them tight. The sight of the tied bulls struggling in pain made me feel sick and I turned away. Surely there was some more humane way of doing it.

The vets voice at my side roused me with a jolt and I realised I had closed my eyes.

"What can I do for you, sir?"

"I would like to apply for a 'jati' boar.You told me some months ago the government had a scheme to supply pedigree boars to villagers who were rearing sows."

"Yes, come inside and I will give you an application form."

We went up the wooden stairs into his office where his desk was placed under a ceiling fan at the centre of which hung a long string from which a piece of milkbush dangled. As it was mango season and the rains had come, the branch was a seething mass of tiny black flies. He sat down and pulled out a drawer where after a quick search he came up with an application form and handed it to me. I began to read it.

"There's no hurry, bring it back tomorrow."

"I'll fill it in now. It will save me another trip in from the village."

Before the boar arrived, I had to go to Vellore Hospital with a friend from one of the villages who needed heart surgery and was afraid to go alone.

I said to Chikkahanumantudu before I left "If either of the pigs becomes ill, go and tell amma."

Two mornings later when he went up to feed the pigs, one of the sows was lying on the ground, flushed and panting.

Hanumantanna rode straight into Chikka and knocked on the bungalow door. Fortunately amma was there.

"Amma, the sow is sick."

"Ah yo! What's wrong?"

"She is lying down and breathing heavily and I think she has a fever."

"I'll go and tell the vet."

By this time amma had purchased a Lambretta so that she could cover the 23 miles to the rural boarding school more easily.

She went to the Veterinary office to be told the vet was in a village some 8 miles out dealing with an outbreak of blackwater fever, so she continued on to the village to find the vet sitting with the village elders almost tearing his hair out in frustration.

"I have a big problem. All the animals with fever have been destroyed and the bodies should be burnt but the people here won't accept that because it means they won't be able to sell or eat the meat."

"I can understand that. What a terrible loss!"

"It's necessary! If they don't, thousands of cattle may have to be destroyed. I'll come to the bungalow as soon as I've sorted out this problem. I'll have to put someone reliable in charge to see that none of the animals is smuggled out."

Amma returned to the bungalow and waited. At about 9pm the vet arrived in his jeep.

"Did you manage to convince them?"

"Yes, I myself supervised the burning."

They drove to Gollahalli. The vet looked at the pig, gave them a thermometer to take its temperature, then filled a large syringe with Benapen (long-acting Penicillin) and handed it to amma. "Please give the injection."

Amma was taken aback but then remembered the vet was a Muslim.

"Where shall I give it?"

"Under the foreleg where the skin is soft."

Amma stabbed the pig and managed to get the fluid in.

By morning the sow was much better and when I returned the following evening seemed almost normal.

We received the boar and some months later the sows farrowed. We sold some of the piglets and kept the rest.

In the summer holidays the children, home from Gangasandra, offered to watch the pigs as they grazed near the tank. They did this each afternoon and it left me free to do other things.

One afternoon I had not long returned to the village when I heard screaming. The children came running, shouting and crying with fear, "Seil kukulu! Seil kukulu!" (Jungle dogs).

A number of us grabbed implements and ran, but by the time we reached the tank the pigs were dead and most of the flesh had been stripped from the bones. The dogs had heard us coming and were gone.

I was just thankful the pack of jungle dogs had gone for the pigs and not the children for they have been known to strip a man to his bones in five minutes.

That was the end of my venture into pig-keeping.

Chapter 12

TRIPLE ANTIGEN

I had just taken food and stepped outside the hut to enjoy a cooler breeze which came over the tank. It was full moon and what appeared to be a ball of fire was glowing in the south east as the moon showed itself beyond the water, bathing the land in that mysterious light which revealed the trees as gaunt silhouette on the horizon.

Two figures appeared, village men, their towels tied turbanwise, their panchas tucked in at the waist for freedom of movement.

"Namaskaram swami."

"Namaskaram. What brings you here so late?" They were men for whom I had helped to arrange an allotment of a good breed of pigs through the veterinary officer.

"Swami our 'jati' boar is sick."

"Ah yo, what's wrong with it?"

"It has fever sir, and is panting, we are afraid it will die."

"You'd better take it to the animal doctor in Chikballapur."

"It won't walk sir. How can we take it?"

"Do you have a cart?"

"No sir."

It was a very valuable animal. What could we do? I sat in thought for a few moments.

"The hospital car comes down the road tomorrow." I was thinking aloud. Would the Doctor be angry if presented with a sick pig? Which doctor would come with the car tomorrow, I wondered? "Can you bring the boar to the roadside?"

"It's very heavy but it would only be a few hundred yards. We could put slings under it and carry it on a pole."

"Do that then and I will persuade the Doctor to look at it."

"When the car arrived at Possetihalli next morning I was there. Doctor Graham was in the car and called me over,

"Sabhapathy, we need your help."

"Yes doctor, what can I do?"

"Glaxo Laboratories are sending us a batch of Triple Antigen which is almost out of date. It is a great opportunity."

"What is Triple Antigen, Doctor?"

"It gives protection against Whooping cough,Diphtheria and Tetanus and is particularly good for young children as they are the ones who most often die or are seriously damaged by these diseases. Even if we can prevent a few cases it will be worthwhile. It's no good giving the Antigen unless it is done properly and this means that all the children done should have two needles six months apart. Do you think that would be possible?"

"Yes, Doctor. I think so, because mothers have a great fear of those illnesses."

"I don't think we could do it without your help because we don't have the manpower to send around the villages and organise all the parents to bring their children on one day. Besides, if we sent a nurse, the parents wouldn't have faith in him."

"How many children can you vaccinate?"

"We have enough for 200 children."

"Yes doctor I can do that. In any case I will be travelling from village to village delivering the Dapsone tablets and could organise this at the same time."

"How about a Saturday three weeks hence. We'll bring a team down to Possetihalli by 9am."

"I have to ask you a favour, Doctor." I told him about the pig.

When we reached Kanaganakoppa there was the pig, his large white body lying in the grassy ditch by the roadside .

Doctor said "We'll get this over first." and climbed out of the car stethoscope in hand. The pig was lying, flushed and breathing heavily. Doctor put his stethoscope into his ears and bent over the pig, listening intently to its chest.

"It has Pneumonia. I don't know the dosage for pigs but it is a huge animal so we'll give it a very big dose of long acting Penicillin. Prabhakara, bring me your biggest syringe and needle and a bottle of Benapen."

Doctor searched for a spot where the skin was not too tough and injected the dose. The pig lay mute, too ill to complain even when its grateful owners lifted the pole and staggered off with it. Within a few days appetite restored, it was grunting and wallowing with its harem.

After leaving Possetihalli we followed the narrow strip of bitumen, which was a patchwork of light and shade under the huge avenue trees, through to the wealthy little village of Manchenahalli surrounded by fields of sugar cane, waving tall and topped by feathery mauve flowers. At this stop we always had a few patients suffering severe anaemia due to hookworm infestation, for all the fields were irrigated.

As we drove further on, the dominant crop became tobacco. What was referred to as a 'cash' crop, with here and there a field of turmeric, its bright yellow flowers making a patchwork of gold. We could see the tall rectangular mudbrick tobacco-curing barns before the smaller village houses became visible.

I saw that the potters' kilns had been fired, and went fifty yards along the road to look at them, burning with a glow visible even in broad daylight. The pots had been stacked in rows, one above the other, to form an igloo shape, then they were covered with layers of straw and the whole mound sealed over with clay, apart from draught holes in the bottom and top. The heat coming from the kiln was so great I could not go within five yards of it.

To reach Halehalli we had to cross the dry sandy river bed twice. Samanna drove the old Austin A40 in at a good speed and went steadily but about halfway across the rear wheels began to spin and we all got out. Samanna tried to move on while we pushed. It was useless, and we had to dig the wheels out several times before the car finally moved off. We cheered and ran after it. We were hot and sweaty and covered with sand which stuck to us persistently. There was no water in the river to wash it off. When we climbed the steep bank on the other side, Samanna had parked the car under the shade of a tree.

Thankfully, we sat on the bank of the river to eat lunch, then travelled on between fields of peanuts towards a dense 'tope' of trees. This was one of my favourite villages - perched high on the bank above the river, the whole village seemed sheltered by trees .

The biggest landowner of this village, Angadi Chikkanna, was a cheerful, philanthropic man of powerful build. He came to greet us.

"Doctorgaru, how are you? Anna, how are you?"

"We are well, how are you?"

Angadi Chikkanna had a servant with him carrying a stainless steel pot of hot sweet coffee and some stainless steel tumblers. He filled them one by one and handed them to us - it was very welcome.

We held the dispensary there, under the trees, looking down on the sandy river bed far below. On the other side, the tall trees appeared to be laden with large black fruit until the chitter and the smell made one realise they were fruit bats.

One of the nurses once asked if he could bring a party to shoot.

"Oh no! Certainly not! These bats are sacred to us. If you shot at these bats it would bring bad luck to the village."

"How is your daughter?" doctor asked.

"Very well thank you."

"Do you have good news of your son?"

"Yes thank you Doctor." His son was a post-graduate exchange student studying Agricultural Engineering in Australia.

A few minutes later he drew me aside. "Please tell doctor I would like to make a donation towards the building of a new ward as a thank you."

"Doctor will really appreciate that, but you tell him."

"No, I would like you to tell him later."

Doctor examined patients. A lady came up, Doctor asked the usual questions.

"What is your name?"

"Lakshmamma, sir."

"How old are you?"

"You tell me,Swami."

"Amma, don't you know what year you were born?"

"No, Swami." Muslim patients always knew their year of birth, whether the year of the rat or of the dog etc.,but the lower caste Hindus often had no idea, so doctor had to work it out.

"Do you have children?"

"Yes."

"What age is your oldest child?"

"Fourteen years, swami."

Under' Age' doctor wrote 30.

"What is your problem?"

"I feel listless."

Doctor bent forward and pulled down her lower eyelid. On her chit he wrote Haemoglobin %.

"Do you have a cough?"

"Yes,swami."

"Do you cough up anything?"

"Sticky stuff, sir."

"Does it have blood in it?"

"Sometimes!"

Doctor took his stethoscope and put it on her chest under her sari. "Breathe in! Out! In! Out! How long have you had the cough?"

"Six months, Swami."

"You need to come to hospital to have more tests done."

"Ah yo! It's impossible!"

"Why?"

"I have five children to look after."

"Then it is very important you come to hospital. Who will look after your children if you become very ill? Are your children well?"

"My small boy has lumps!"

"What sort of lumps?"

"Like mumps in his neck."

"How long has he had those?"

"One month Swami."

"Can you come to the hospital and bring him too?"

"Ah yo! Swami! What can I do?"

"It's important you come to hospital and bring your son. Now I'll give you some tablets to give you strength and you must eat vegetables and eggs and meat." Poor woman she probably couldn't afford any of them.

"Sabhapathy can you persuade her to come to hospital - I believe she has open Tuberculosis and it sounds as though her son has tuberculous glands of the neck. Perhaps you can talk to her husband. If she were in hospital it would at least reduce the risk for the other children."

"I'll see what I can do. If her eldest daughter is fourteen she may be able to look after the family while the father works."

"They would both need to be admitted but it might be best just to persuade them to come to hospital first."

I went with her to the back of the car. "What is your husband's name?"

She was embarassed. A woman does not call her husband by name. A small boy had appeared beside her."

"Is this your son?"

"Yes sir, my eldest son."

"Nayana, what is your father's name?"

"Venkatappa sir."

"What does he do?"

"Farming, sir."

I explained to her again how important it was for her to go to the hospital, for her sake, as well as the family.

"I'll speak to my master, swami."

I left it at that and decided to visit their village on my return from distributing Dapsone tablets.

After leaving Halehalli we went to Gudibanda which is a fairly large village built on steep ground. The 'Gudi' or temple at the top of the hill is hewn out of a huge lump of granite and the houses cluster just below, rubbing shoulders with the large granite boulders of which they are made.

There were numerous monkeys in the village and perhaps because of the scarcity of trees they tended to be aggressive.

We stopped the car as usual below a huge fig tree growing out of a raised platform built around a stone shrine.

A man came up at once with a child on his hip - her hand bound up in some strips of cloth.

"What has happened to your little girl?"

"A monkey bit her sir."

Doctor unwound the bandages to reveal an angry looking set of teeth marks.

"Was it a good monkey?"

"Oh, yes sir, it was just angry - it tried to take a banana she was eating."

"That's good, you haven't seen any mad dogs or sick monkeys in the village lately have you?" Rabies is an ever present fear with animal bites.

"No sir."

Doctor wrote - Clean and dress wound, Tetanus Antitoxin and Benapen - then called back to Prabhakara.

"Give her just a small drop of the anti-tetanus serum now and wait ten minutes to see if she has any reaction, if she is O.K.give her the full dose."

A woman went up to amma and began whispering in her ear. Amma brought her to Doctor.

"This woman says her little girl has a heavy white discharge. She says she won't bring her here or let you examine her."

Doctor said to Amma "You'd better go and look at her then, as you're the only woman in the party today."

Amma went off to their house. When she came back she described the symptoms to Doctor who prescribed a large dose of long acting Penicillin.

He said to Amma "You'll need to give the injection into her thigh and make sure you don't contaminate yourself - it's probably Gonococcal!"

As doctor examined patients here, the village children played games of tig or hop scotch on the platform above and to our left, while in the fig tree overhead twenty or thirty monkeys played their own games. All were harmonious as long as nothing edible was in evidence.

As Prabhakara finished counting up tablets for the last patient the children lined up on the edge of the platform ready to wave as the car moved off. This was in marked contrast to another village we visited for a while where the children lined up along the road out of the village ready to pelt stones at us as the car drew abreast.

"Samanna will you please put me down at Dodballapur Station, I want to visit the stonemason there to give him his Dapsone and from there I will return across country on foot delivering the tablets." Samanna pulled the car over and stopped. I got down.

"Go and come, Anna."

"We will go and come." The car drove off and I crossed the road to a stone house opposite.

"Ayya!" I called.

The wife Papamma, came out of the kitchen to greet me.

"Namaskaram, swami - the master is not home yet but should be here soon. Come and sit down."

"Thanks amma."

She spread a mat and I was glad to sit and relax. We'd had a busy day and although I had not done much I had not had time to sit down except for the half hour we had spent eating our lunch.

A small window in the kitchen cast a beam of golden light from the setting sun through the doorway into the living room. I could hear Papamma grinding masala on the curry stone and soon the tempting smell of fried onions and spices reached my nostrils and I realised I was very hungry.

A shadow blocked the fading light from the outer door and Govindappa walked in. I rose to greet him.

"Are you well, swami?"

"Yes and you?"

"I am well. The hospital car just dropped me off after Rural Dispensary ."

"Ah yo! You should have brought doctor in for coffee."

"They were anxious to return to the hospital."

He always spoke very loudly and stood very close to me speaking into my face. I unobtrusively edged back a pace away from the spray and he took another step towards me.

"Sit down swami, please sit down."

I sat down thankfully and he went into the kitchen returning with a cup of coffee in one hand, a plate of crisp chakli in the other.

"Since that day doctor and amma had coffee here I have been careful not to put my fingers in the coffee as I carry it - I felt very embarrassed."

"Doctor did not mean to embarrass you but for your own family's sake and others it is necessary for you to take precautions and not pass on your disease to others."

"Yes, I understand."

His wife brought him coffee and we sat quietly. I handed him his month's supply of tablets. He was fortunate the Hansen's Bacillus had not caused any deformities and provided he took his tablets regularly he should be alright.

"I will go now." I rose to my feet.

"Please take food with us."

"I would like to reach Aredeshanahalli before nightfall."

"It is too late, swami."

Certainly there was little light left and I had no torch. The track was rough and shaded by trees.

"Thank you, I will take food and leave early in the morning."

A teenage boy and girl appeared from the small room adjoining the hall, made namaskaram and went into the kitchen to take food.

"They are studying for exams."

Papamma called "Will the ayyagaru take a bath? I have put water there."

Govindappa showed me to a flat stone slab outside the back door, screened by mats. A 'bana' of hot water and dipper awaited me and although I had no change of clothes I poured the hot water over myself until I felt refreshed.

When we had both bathed, Papamma set stainless steel plates before us and served us with chapathi, rice, dhal curry and curds.

Chapter 13

OLD CUSTOMS DIE HARD

The people of Gollahalli had appointed a young man called Gangappa from the nearby Harijan (formerly called outcaste) community to work as their village servant, and put in money to buy him khaki shorts and a green shirt. He was a good-looking young man who always kept himself clean and neat.

Although I had visited a number of villages on my way back from Dodballapur I still had many people to see and decided to take Gangappa with me.

I'll admit I had a double motive. Firstly I was glad to have his company although it meant I could not ride my cycle, but most of the villages were only two or three miles apart. Secondly I wanted to make a point.

We took early coffee and set out at dawn to meet people before they went out to the fields or forest.

The tank below Gollahalli still had plenty of water in it and sparkled in the early light as we walked down the grassy slope and skirted it, coming out on the cart track the other side. The Pongamia trees had set seed so I picked a few and put them in my pocket.

"It looks like a good seed crop, Maistrulu."

"Yes there'll be plenty of oil for the lamps this year." Pongamia trees are a valuable asset - the leafy branches are cut and put into the rice fields as green manure - the small flowers make excellent compost and the oily seeds are bought by the itinerant oil seller each year in exchange for oil which lights the village lamps.

It was almost an hour before we reached our destination - smoke rising through the thatch showed cooking in progress.

"There are young children in this house."

I stopped in the doorway of a larger house with stone slab walls and called "Ayya".

A woman emerged through the smoke from the little kitchen at one end, a small child on her hip, another grasped her mother's sari firmly, and peered shyly from behind.

"Namaskaram swami." She smiled, her hair was neatly done and her gold chain and earrings showed that they had some substance.

"Is your master here?"

"He's gone to water the cattle but he will be back soon. Come in and sit down."

She looked at Gangappa.

"This is Gangappa."

"What village is he from?"

"Doddaganahalli."(A Harijan village)

She waved him towards the slab bench outside the house.

"Sit there."

We both moved over to the slab and sat down.

"You come inside swami - master will be here soon."

"Gangappa and I are together, we'll take coffee here."

She did not know how to handle the situation and after a moments hesitation went inside to return a few minutes later with coffee for both of us.

We sat and sipped but before we'd finished her husband appeared.

"Namaskaram swami. What are you doing there? Please come in and sit down."

"May we both come in?"

He looked at Gangappa, then at me - I had known Venkata Reddy for many years.

"Yes, come in."

We entered and Gangappa sat cross-legged near the door.

I greeted the old woman sitting in another corner pounding her betel nut in a small stone pestle and mortar. I sat on a mat with my host.

"Have you eaten?"

"No."

"Amma, bring food for Sabhapathygaru and his friend."

After eating I broached the matter of triple antigen.

"I have come because the Doctorgaru has a good medicine to prevent Whooping cough, Diphtheria and Tetanus. I know you have young children and thought you would like to have them protected."

"That sounds good, anna, but what sort of medicine is it?"

"It's needle medicine."

"But they are not sick."

"This injection is like smallpox vaccination. It stops them getting those three diseases."

"Will they never get them?"

"They can have another injection after five years but it is most important now when they are young because you yourself know how often those diseases kill small children."

"Yes. What will it cost?"

"It's free, but you donated grain to the hospital last year and we'll be glad of donations at harvest time."

"I'll give gladly, sir."

I made a note of his children's names and ages, their parents names and their village.

"Now I need your help - can you tell me which families in this village have children under five years?"

"My wife can answer that better than I can. Amma come here."

His wife came and put the baby into a large wooden cradle suspended on chains from a beam near the old lady then handed her a short length of rope attached to the cradle which she began to pull at regular intervals to keep up a swinging motion. The baby gave a couple of whimpers then settled contentedly, sucking his thumb as his grandmother rocked the cradle.

His wife said "I will show you the houses, swami."

"Good, we will take leave, ayya."

The Reddy's wife came outside and pointed out several houses.

Gangappa and I walked along the village street to a thatched hut. I paused in the doorway then saw that the master of the house was taking food so turned away but he had seen me and called out.

"Who's there?"

"Sabhapathyanna - forgive me, we'll go and come."

"Never mind, come in. Have you eaten?"

"Yes, we've eaten."

A small boy of about 4 years had followed us to the house and I noticed he had two Pongamia seeds, hanging from a string around his neck. Now he went through to the kitchen calling

"Amma, amma."

His mother appeared in the kitchen doorway.

I took the Pongamia seeds I'd collected from my pocket and held them out.

"You have these seeds tied around your son's neck to prevent dog's cough but the doctor at the mission hospital has a much better medicine which will prevent not only dogs cough but cattle fits and diphtheria as well."

I told them about it and with their consent took the names of their three children and told them to come to the roadside Saturday, two weeks hence.

After visiting the remaining houses with similar results I went back to the Reddy's house and asked him to remind the others nearer the time.

Gangappa and I walked from village to village for three days. It was a slow process but such things cannot be rushed.

In one village I went first to the Patel, well known to me , but he refused to allow Gangappa to enter his house so I left him and went to another friend in the village. At first they did not like Gangappa entering their houses or taking food with them, but as time went on they came to accept it and I hope it influenced their behaviour towards others of the Harijan community. Customs which go back hundreds of years cannot be changed quickly even when the Government legislates against them.

Doctor had said that the van would be at Possettihalli by 9am so I left Gollahalli by 7-30am making sure the young children and their parents came with me or would follow shortly. I had hoped to group the children according to their villages but that proved impossible as many arrived late.

The old Austin A40 arrived with the team, Dr. Graham, Dr. Charlotte, a male and female nurse. They immediately set up two little spirit stoves to boil needles after use. With two people innoculating and two people keeping up the needle supply they worked quickly. I was kept busy finding and ticking off names and making sure they knew to come back in six months time.

By the time we finished it was after midday and we stopped for coffee and biscuits.

Doctor said "That was well organised - it must have been a big job preparing all those lists."

"I will visit them all again just before the second injection doctor."

"Yes it's important they come again - we can't expect 100% but even one injection will give some protection."

"Six months later some 85% returned for their second injection. For village India that was a very satisfactory result."

Chapter 14

JUNGLE WALK

The bus shuddered to a stop at the Gollahalli crossing and I got down clutching a cloth bag in each hand. I had been to Chikka to buy some tomatoes, potatoes and dhal, ready for the evening meal when we expected Dr. and Mrs. Graham to spend the night in our village.

A few weeks earlier I was sitting with the Rural dispensary team on the banks of the Pennar, high above the sandy river bed as we ate our chapathis and omelette for lunch when Doctor said "Sabhapathy, Mrs. Graham and I have not had a holiday this year so we are planning to walk through the jungle to Lepakshi to look at the temple there. I believe there are very beautiful frescoes on the ceiling. What do you think would be the most interesting route?"

"Doctor, why don't you first climb Kalawara Konda, then walk along the range and spend the night in Gollahalli? We can accompany you from there to Ketenhalli and on to Lepakshi if you wish."

"That sounds a good idea. How far would that be?"

"About sixty miles doctor."

"That would take us about four days."

"Yes."

Now, as I hurried down the hill, the countryside was a patchwork of varying shades of green; peanuts, ragi, corn and pigeon pea but in spite of the fact that this was the cold season the sun was still hot.

When I reached the hut Gangamma was busy pounding paddy to remove the husks. I handed my purchases to Muniamma and she deposited them in the kitchen then spread a mat for me.

"Take food, Maistrulu, the sun is high and you haven't broken your fast."

As I sat eating, shadows fell across the doorway then disappeared. When I rose and went outside to wash my hands two men from another village were waiting for me.

"Maistrulu, you must come. Venkatappa has called Narayanappa a thief and accused him of driving cattle into his field of Ragi. He and his friends are very angry. Now Narayanappa says he will burn Venkatappa's haystack unless he eats his words - please come quickly, sir, before something worse happens."

"All right, I'll come. But first I must make some arrangements here. The doctorgaru and ammagaru are coming tonight to stay."

A number of people had gathered so I gave them all instructions. "Akka, see that the night school hut is cleaned out well. Tomorrow morning we will hold our class in Narasimhappa's house. Don't make that tomato and potato curry too hot, reduce the amount of chilli powder."

We hurried off as we had three miles to walk. I hoped they had not yet come to blows. They were still shouting at one another when we reached the village and I made them all sit down while we tried to find out exactly what had happened. It seemed a small boy had been left to watch the cattle. He had seen a jujube tree nearby and gone to look for fruit. He forgot time as he climbed and ate, and when he came back the cattle had strayed. When the accusation was made he was too frightened to own his fault and as the arguments and insults flew had run away and hidden.

By the time peace was restored the sun was sinking and as I hurried back to Gollahalli I thought Doctor and amma would surely have arrived some time ago so I was surprised to see them sitting at the door of the hut removing their boots, with most of the village crowded around them, passing their packs around to marvel at the weight.

"Maistrulu, why do they look like that?"

"What do you mean?"

"Their faces and arms so red."

I laughed "That's the sun, it burns red people and makes them really red."

"Namasakaram Sabhapathy."

"Doctor, you are covered in blood. What happened?"

"The track from Kalawara Konda(mountain) was overgrown with lantana and wait-a-while, we got scratched pushing our way through."

"Akka, is the bath water ready?"

"Yes Maistrulu."

"Doctor, take a bath, water is ready."

Doctor said to amma, "You go first."

The women took amma to Nanjamma's house to bathe her but returned a few minutes later.

"Has amma finished?"

"No she says she will bathe herself." They looked a bit hurt.

"That is her custom."

"Really? That is all right then."

Gangamma had prepared tomato and potato curry, spinach and rice.

"This is delicious!" amma said

Gangamma was pleased, and I was glad I had bought tomatoes for we all enjoyed them.

I went with Dr. and Amma to the hut to help them spread their sleeping bags on the ground, and tie to the rafters the mosquito net they had brought with them.

"That should keep out the rats."

"I hope so."

At 4-30am I hit the gong only once, as I didn't want to disturb them, and we all went to Narasimhappa's house to read.

I took coffee to the classroom at 6-00am.

"How did you sleep?"

"Very well thank you."

"The rats enjoyed the night too, they had a great time using the net as a short cut across the room."

"Forgive me, it is very difficult to get rid of them. Did they keep you awake?"

"Not for long, we were too tired."

Doctor and amma came out of the hut. I met them and two of the women took amma into the fields to squat. I wondered what she would think about that. Even those of us who have been brought up in cities find it difficult, and foreigners even more so. But she needed the women with her to keep off the pigs.

Gangappa, our village servant, and I were to accompany them on the next stage of their hike, so Gangamma and Muniamma had prepared food early. We did not want to delay. The four of us sat on mats while the women served us on fresh banana leaves I had cut especially for the occasion.

Dasappa sat in shirt and G-string by the doorway, his staff in his hand. It was not his custom to eat so early. He would eat at 10am before driving the cattle into the hills to graze.

We were concerned because doctor didn't eat much, but amma explained that since his imprisonment in China during the Japanese invasion he could not eat bulky food, especially rice, as they had had to eat it daily, stones and all.

Doctor and amma refused to let us carry their packs, so we set out with two dogs along the cattle tracks leading out of the village directly towards the hills. When we reached the road we met one of the young men from the huts in the foothills on the way to Chikka.

After he had greeted us amma said "How is your wife?"

"I have no wife."

"Oh what has happened to her?"

"I came home and found her with another man. I cut off her nose and sent her home to her mother."

"Ah yo!"

"It is the custom."

He dived into a Lantana thicket, leaving amma with her mouth open in surprise and shock. He reappeared, swinging a seven foot snake above his head. As we walked on, he continued to swing the snake in a wide circle until amma could stand it no longer.

"What are you doing?"

"I am killing it. If I keep swinging it like this it will die without a blemish and I will get good money for the skin."

We walked on, the snake whirring above our heads. Until at last he said, "I will go and come."

"Go and come," we replied with relief.

It was a good pull up into the jungle and we were hot before we reached the shade of bigger trees but now the walking became pleasant under the canopy.

"This is beautiful country."

"Yes, it is."

Soon we came upon a huge tamarind tree with a crop of ripe fruit just finishing.

"It's very early for ripe tamarind."

"I'll collect some seed and plant it. It may give us an early variety."

"That would be very valuable."

Amma and I both collected some seed. There was plenty of evidence of wild boar and as we walked along the track panther droppings could be seen.

We were aiming for Avala Konda, 3,800ft, but at 2 o'clock came to a stream and doctor decided to take food. We refused to share their food as we knew they only had what was in their packs, and we had eaten well in the morning. We were accustomed to going long hours without food.

One of our young bitches had been dashing off on her own hunting expeditions all morning and now disappeared into the undergrowth.

In a pitted hollow on the rock bank I mixed some milk powder with water from the stream, and the puppy with us drank. When we rose to leave we called "Kappelnakka! Kappelnakka! Oi-i-i-i!" Whistled loudly and waited, but although we called many times the young bitch didn't come.

From the stream the path rose almost vertically, and in many places we were pulling ourselves up, but after an hour's climb we heard an eerie noise.

"What's that?" doctor asked.

As we listened, we emerged into a clearing planted with peanuts and the noise was explained. Kerosine tins hung upside down from trees around the clearing, a piece of iron suspended in the centre so that, as they were blown by the wind they emitted an eerie clang.

We set out across the field, and were hailed from the other side.

"Who's that?"

"We're from Gollahalli, we've brought friends to visit you."

The man approached, carrying a gun, He knew me.

"Namaskaram ayya, I am guarding the crop from pigs, the peanuts are beginning to form."

"By the time we reached the village it was 4-30. I was looking for a friend (Gopalappa) on whose brother-in-law Doctor had operated for cataract two weeks earlier. By the time I found him it was nearly five, and they told us we could not reach Avala Konda by nightfall."

As doctor and amma had boots on, we could not enter the house, so sat on a mat outside the door. We were in a small courtyard used for keeping animals. To our left, against the wall, was a little shed in which an old woman, a poor relative of the family, lived. It was her kitchen and sleeping quarters - she couldn't stand upright in it or see without a lamp, except in the tiny doorway. She sat there preparing some dill for her evening meal, on an open fire. She also had custard apples she had picked in the forest. As she worked she made caustic remarks to us and the men sitting outside.

"Why are you going to Lepakshi?"

"They say the temple is very beautiful."

"Oh, they said to me, 'you must see Lepakshi!' so I went and what did I see? Stones - just stones!! Then they said, 'You must go to Bangalore' so I went to Bangalore and what did I see? - a village, just a village."

Doctor said "You must have something wrong with your eyes, amma."

We had coffee, then went off to the temple where Dr. and amma removed their boots and we sat outside while many of the villagers came and asked us questions.

I discovered my pup had twisted his leg, which was very swollen, so I borrowed one of amma's socks, soaked it in water and bound it up. I went off to make arrangements for sleeping and while I was away a tall man with wild curly hair, a green blanket wrapped around his shoulders, appeared. He had just come up from the creek, and told Doctor he had heard barking down there. Doctor came and found me, and we took the torch and went back down the hill, but by the time we reached the bottom there was no sign of her. Panthers are very fond of dogs, and will always take a dog before they attack a man.

When we got back, the mosquitoes were biting, so we moved across to the schoolhouse as I had arranged. It was newly built and clean.

My friend's wife, Narasamma, brought us rice and potato curry. We all ate, then lay down and slept.

We rose early and I went to the temple to arrange bath water for doctor and amma. Gangappa and I bathed at the well with the villagers.

Amma took a long time over her bath and doctor was impatient to be off.

"What on earth have you been doing?"

"Taking that bath was quite an experience! The Poojari's wife hung a blanket across the doorway into the courtyard so I thought I was safe, but found if I stood upright I was in full view of all the men in the street. I crouched down and was pouring water over myself when in walked the Poojari's wife and began bathing me. She was very thorough, and after I had been soaped and rinsed, she began pouring, what felt like boiling water, over me. She dried my hair on the end of her sari, then kneaded all my muscles before allowing me to dress."

At 8 o'clock, after breakfast provided again by Narasamma, we said farewell to the assembled villagers and Gopalappa insisted on carrying doctor's pack. Doctor said to me in English, "He looks too old to carry it."

I said to him "How old are you?"

"Forty-six, swami."

Doctor laughed, "In that case, he is younger than I am."

Gangappa took Amma's pack and we set out.

The crops in the fields looked green and healthy and with the backdrop of forest and mountain it was a beautiful spot.

As we walked we asked him, "How were the rains?"

"Good! We usually get good rains because of the forest. If we get rain, we get ragulu (red millet). If we don't get rain, we get rogulu (sickness)."

Some distance from the village we came upon an arrangement of sticks tied with twine to the carcass of a goat, which had been killed by a panther. I was glad we hadn't come upon it in the dark. It was a booby trap. When the panther returned to the kill the strings caused guns to discharge and kill it, if all went well.

Narasamma and her husband, Gopalappa, took leave of us at this point and we walked on to climb Avala Konda 3,800 feet. Quite a pull! But when we reached the top the effort had been worth it for we had a view for miles on all sides and sat on a huge rock to take in the mosaic of brown, red and green fields, stretching for miles, with many tanks (reservoirs) dotted at intervals among them. On the hill top was a very ancient temple, rest houses and shrines, carved out of the native granite.

Doctor and amma insisted on going on from there alone, much to Gangappa's dismay as he felt sure amma would not be able to carry her heavy pack.

We took leave and made our way back to Ketenhalli to catch the daily bus back to Chikka.

I had suggested to Doctor that we try to collect ragi for the hospital to help pay for the Dapsone tablets distributed to the H.D. patients, very few of whom could afford to pay.

I had mentioned this to several people the previous night and there were two bags containing some measures of ragi waiting for us beside the little petty shop (a) where the bus pulled up.

When the bus came in, Gopalappa appeared, put the bags on his head, one by one, climbed to the top of the bus and left them among the numerous baskets, bags, vessels and firewood being loaded.

The bus passed the hospital gate going into Chikka, so we got down there, and delivered the ragi to Sister Morch.

(a) A shop consisting of a large wooden box on wheels in which the shopkeeper sits surrounded by his wares. He usually sleeps there at night for security reasons.

Chapter 15

RAMU

I had just finished my early morning coffee and was sitting reading Morgan's "Life of Christ" when a young teenage boy appeared in the doorway.

"Maistrulu, I must talk with you." It was Ramu, one of the older boys in the village.

"Come in and sit down."

The cows turned in their stall and looked at him suspiciously - why was a stranger visiting so early? Deciding he wasn't a threat, they settled again and continued to chew their cud.

Premadasappa, Gangamma's husband rose stiffly to his feet and reached for his staff. He was one of the old school, attired in shirt and G-string, turban on his head. He went outside and spat a stream of brown tobacco juice into the dust. His daughter-in-law was busy preparing the day's food, baby on hip, while Gangamma sat in a corner tossing some ragi in a 'chata'(winnowing basket) to get rid of stones and chaff, ready to make into flour on the grinding stone in the kitchen.

"Sir, I want to go to the farm school at Muttasandra."

"Why do you want to go there?"

"I've passed 7th standard and now I am home looking after the sheep and goats. I don't want to spend the rest of my life doing that."

"You would need to study at the school."

"I want to study sir, and come to know something outside this village."

"It would also be hard work, the students do all the work on the farm."

"I would work hard, sir."

"Well, I'll think about it, and you must prove to me that you are willing to work hard."

"Yes sir, please sir, I will do anything you say."

"Alright then, go and come."

"I'll go and come, sir."

He went off. Gangamma had, of course, heard the conversation.

"It's just a sudden idea he has, anna - you believe too easily. He's never been a hard worker."

"But he's growing up and people change."

I didn't know anything about the requirements for entry into Muttasandra school - I would have to find out. On Thursday after Leprosy Clinic when I went across to the bungalow for lunch I was disappointed because Amma was not there. She had gone to Kolar.

Some weeks previously I had been to the horticultural office to see if I could get some fruit trees to plant on the slope above the tank. Mr Bhaskara, the assistant, was there so I'd asked him. "Is there any scheme to assist villages to plant fruit trees?"

"Yes, there is a scheme for planting on public land in villages - you may submit a request."

We went inside and he supplied me with paper, so I put in a request for thirty fruit trees to be planted on the land above the tank at Gollahalli, to be the joint property of all the village members.

Now I visited the horticultural office again. My trees had arrived! Guava, Jack fruit, Lime, Orange, Mandarin, Pomelo, Grape and Coconut. I was delighted.

"Can you hold them for us for a week or two. We'll need to prepare holes!"

"Yes, they'll be safe here Anna. We'll look after them."

I went back towards the Bungalow and as I reached the corner of the compound wall a child's voice said "Anna, look at me."I looked up to see Heather above my head in the branches of the Tamarind.

"Don't fall!"

"No! Rajanna and Arita and I have a house up here."

"Is Mummy home?"

"Yes, she came on her motor bike and brought some turkey eggs, we're going to put them under a hen tonight."

I went and knocked. Amma was having coffee. She looked a bit depressed as she poured me a cup.

"Have you eaten?"

"Yes thank you, amma."

"I've been to Kolar to try to push our papers through for our Gangasandra School government grant. I haven't enough money to pay next month's salaries. I really should have gone on to Bangalore but it would have been too late to catch the offices by the time I got there. I think I'll get the grant eventually, it's just the delay that worries me. I'll go to the Diocesan office in Bangalore tomorrow and see if they'll give me an advance - people can't live without their salaries, especially the ones with families."

"No!" As I dunked my biscuit into my coffee and ate it I felt concerned. Having worked for years in government offices I hoped the clerks wouldn't hold up the papers too long while hoping for a bribe. I didn't utter that thought as it probably hadn't occurred to amma. Instead I changed the subject.

"Amma, do you know anything about the requirements for entry into Muttasandra farm school?"

"No, I don't really but I could find out. I think Mr. Mason is in charge."

"One of the boys in the village came to me a few days ago - he wants to go there. He has passed 7th Standard."

"I'll write to Mr. Mason if you like and ask him about it. He can send an application form."

"Thank you very much but I am going to test the boy first to see how genuine he is."

"How are you going to do that?"

"I'm going to ask him to dig the holes for thirty trees that I've just been given by the Horticultural office."

"That will be a test - the ground will be hard as iron at this time of year!"

It was two days before I returned to Gollahalli after distributing Dapsone Tablets to the villages.

At 4 am I rang the gong as usual for the literacy classes, cleaned my teeth and went across to the women's hut. Ramu was there waiting.

"Have you heard anything about Muttasandra, Maistrulu?"

"No, not yet, but I have some work for you. We have been given thirty fruit trees and I want you to dig the holes for them."

"Yes, Maistrulu, I will." If he was taken aback he made no sign but walked over to help one of the older women with her reading.

By 8 o'clock he was at my door ready to begin.

I asked him to call the men who were available and we went out to the slope above the tank, paced it out and dug marks with a 'kordawali' (Indian spade) at the site for each hole.

"How big do I make each hole, Maistrulu?"

"Two feet square and two feet deep then we'll put Pongamia leaves in the bottom of each one and I'll buy some dried fish to put in the holes for the coconuts."

He began work straight away and I stood and watched him for a while. The red, rather stony soil, was hard.

"You'll need to use the crowbar."

"Yes, anna."

Even with the crowbar, it was slow hard work. "Perhaps if you dig each hole a bit, then pour in a pot of water, it would be quicker in the long run."

We went back to the village together and he took a brass pot to fill at the tank, a messy job walking out through the mud until he reached water deep enough to submerge the vessel.

Ramu worked at the holes morning and afternoon for two weeks. I was pleased with his persistence and when I was in the village went to encourage him once or twice a day as he laboured, mud caked to his knees and liberally smeared about his person, his sweat making smudged channels through it.

The following Thursday when I went to Chikka for the Leprosy clinic I said to Dr. Graham, "We are having a tree-planting ceremony at Gollahalli on Sunday, I would like you and Amma and the children to come."

"I've heard about the trees - are the holes ready?"

"Yes, Ramu has finished digging them and some of the men are coming up on Saturday to help me take the trees down on the bus."

"We'll come! Even if I can't manage it, the family will come."

Next morning I called Ramu and some of the men and women and we went off with our 'mattsus' to cut thorns. We had to walk several miles, tie them in bundles with vines, then carry them back on our heads.

We returned, scratched and bleeding and put our bundles ready on the hillside. I felt ashamed that I had never learnt to carry a head load and had to leave it to the others.

We spent Sunday morning planting and watering the trees, then the women placed the thorns around them. In the afternoon Dr. Graham, Amma and the children came down. We had prayer and Fiona ceremonially planted the last tree.

A few weeks later I was riding my bicycle down the last slope to the village when Ramu came running to meet me waving a letter in his hand.

"I've got a seat at Muttasandra sir!" His thin face was glowing with excitement as he thrust the letter in front of me.

"That's good, very good. You're to be there in three days time! Have you had some clothes stitched?"

"Not yet, sir, but we've put some money aside, and my amma will go with me to Chikka tomorrow to buy cloth and have it sewn."

Three days later we set off early. Ramu with his padlocked trunk on his head, proudly wearing new drill trousers and shirt. We waited anxiously by the roadside for the first bus - as usual it was overcrowded and went sailing past, but we were lucky - a few minutes later a lorry laden with bags of jaggery {lump raw sugar} stopped. The cabin was full and there were already two men sitting on top of the bags. We passed up the trunk, then they hauled us up to join them. On entering Chikka the driver stopped just before Gopal's Tsattram for fear of being stopped by the police. We handed our bus fares through the back window to him and jumped down, then had to walk on to the bus stand.

I left Ramu in Muttasandra with the farm manager and took the opportunity to visit some of our leprosy patients on that side of Dodballapur on my way home.

On his return to Gollahalli for his second vacation Ramu came to me one evening.

"Sir! I want to become a Christian."

"Why?"

"Well, one of the reasons I wanted to go to Muttasandra was the difference I saw in the children who went to Gangasandra boarding - they were so happy and seemed to want to do things and keep clean and neat. I found out that Yesu swami loves me and I want to love Him."

"Have you thought about the problems it may give you in the future - you know that the Christian community is not classed as backward now so does not receive any of the concessions given to backward communities, in fact they are often discriminated against."

"Yes, one of the men on the farm was telling me about that. He has had trouble getting a place in college for his son and wanted to get his daughter into the public service but couldn't."

"If you've really thought about it and made your decision I'm very happy."

"I've watched you too, sir - you aren't afraid to go and come alone at night. None of the others here would do that, they are too afraid of the devils."

"We don't need to fear, God protects us."

"Yes."

"Have you told your mother and father?"

"Yes, they are happy, but my grandmother is very angry."

"What about the teachers at school, did you tell them?"

"No, I've thought about it a lot but wanted to tell you and my parents first. If it hadn't been for your help, sir, I'd still be watching sheep."

"When you go back to school tell the pastor, and he will make arrangements for you to attend a class."

"Yes sir."

A few months after his return I received a letter:-

Respected sir,

I have been attending classes with some others and we are ready for baptism. The Father Bishop is coming here for the opening of a new church at Hadenhalli on September 20th so we are all to receive baptism in a nearby well, before the service.

I would please request you to come and bring my parents with you.

With thanks,

RAMU

The day we set out was beautiful. There had been rain the night before, the air was crisp and clean, and all the colours washed bright, the red soil contrasting with the brilliant greens of crops and trees.

After the bus drove out of Chikka through the huge arched gateway in the old town wall, we looked over the expanse of blue water in Kandawara tank to Kalawara Konda rising 2000 feet, shimmering blue-green beyond the sparkling water.

We skirted the foot of Nandi hill where the high grey stone walls hid all but the Gopuram of the temple.

Further on the bus pulled up at a small shrine, containing a large brightly painted bas relief of Anjaneya, the monkey god. At once some twenty or thirty monkeys clambered on to the front cabin and the driver got down with a bag of peanuts which he scattered for them, then he entered the shrine, lit incense sticks and prayed, before continuing the journey.

When we reached the village outside Tumkur, the people were assembled waiting for the bishop's car to arrive. Ramu came forward to meet us and made namaskaram. He was almost unrecognisable in new white pancha and shirt and seemed to have gained a new confidence as he took on the role of host to the three of us.

Just then the Bishop's car drew up, and Bishop Sargent stepped out, a huge man in his long white surplice tied with a purple rope at the waist, a shepherd's crook in his hand. The pastors and elders joined him in procession to a large stone lined well nearby, those to be baptised walking behind them, with the congregation at the rear.

We had prayer, and the candidates made their confessions of faith, then the Bishop went down the stone steps into the well, followed by two pastors. The candidates went down one at a time and were immersed backwards into the water held by the strong hands of the Pastors as the Bishop touched them with his crook and baptised them in the name of the Father, Son and Holy Spirit.

Their sopping wet clothes clinging to them as they emerged did not quench the aura of joy that clung to them.

Ramu joined us and we all proceeded to the newly constructed church with its red-tiled roof and freshly whitewashed mud brick walls, a tribute to the enthusiasm of the congregation who had built it themselves.

The Bishop headed the procession which, singing lustily, circled the church three times before we removed our sandals, entered and sat on mats, women to the right, men to the left, while the Bishop conducted a service of dedication.

The congregation had put up a large mat shed close to the church and prepared a midday meal for all present. We poured water over our hands from pots outside and went into the cool interior to sit on mats while we were served. The curry was fiery hot and caught my breath but I could manage it and was soon embarrassed by the remarks made by many of the other guests, some of whom refused to eat it. Surely, I thought, it is not good manners to criticise the food when you are an invited guest - but it often happened.

After the meal Ramu took us to the farm and proudly showed us around. It was his parent's first visit.

Ramu graduated with honours and was employed by the farm as a field supervisor. On one occasion, I met the Diocesan Area Chairman at a funeral and he told me he had been very impressed by Ramaiah's ability. I felt pleased that my faith in him had been vindicated.

Some years later Ramu married a Christian girl from that area and they settled there close to the farm school where Ramu is now a senior supervisor.

Chapter 16

FESTIVAL

We stepped back involuntarily as the bullocks thundered past showing the whites of their eyes. Their drivers, perched precariously on the carts behind them, wielded their whips and shouted to urge them on.

The thrummm...thrummm...thrummm of a drum being beaten added to a sense of confusion. As the cloud of dust settled we made our way round to the finishing line where the noise of the drum became even more deafening.

Men huddled in groups settling their wagers, while coffee sellers had pots of water boiling over blazing sticks, the flames almost invisible in the bright sunlight. A sweetmeat seller carried around a tray of jelebi and mysore pak, waving off the flies with a casuarina branchlet. Bangles, balloons and ribbons were also on sale. A gathering of people like this was too good an opportunity to miss.

This race was an annual event, another of our hot weather celebrations, and I had invited Amma down from Chikballapur to watch it. By the time she arrived on the bus our village women had tied their best saris, put flowers in their hair and some extra bangles on their wrists and were almost ready to go.

We skirted the tank and walked across the bund. On one side the water in the tank had shrunk to a small pool and below us sheep were feeding on the stubble left after harvesting the rice crop. As we reached the level area set aside for the race, some of the bullocks were still drinking from pots held by their owners.

"That's not water they're drinking, it's toddy (fermented palm juice)."

"They seem to enjoy it. They look really proud of themselves with those garlands around their necks and flowers in their harness."

"When they run they're a bit drunk and lose all fear. It's good to keep out of their way."

We made our way back to Gollahalli, and after taking food the women took amma up to the roadside to catch a bus or hitch a ride on a lorry. I'd delayed my round with the Dapsone tablets until after the festival, so now set off on my bicycle due east with the sun beating down on my back.

When I arrived at the first village the sun was still high and I was surprised to see a group of women sitting under a neem tree doing nothing. The heat and glare were intense.

"Namaskaram, amma. Don't you find it hot here at this time of day?"

"Namaskaram ayya, we're waiting."

"What are you waiting for?"

"Muniamma is in labour."

"How long has she been in pain?"

"Nine hours, swami."

"Who's with her to help?"

"No one swami, she's all alone." Their eyes did not meet mine but searched for some point of interest on the ground in front of them.

"Where is the midwife then.?"

"I'm the midwife, but she's not of my caste."

"You must go to her, she may be in danger."

"How can I go, swami! I'll lose caste and become unclean."

"Go and boil water and bring me a bowl." I began to roll up my sleeves. "Bring soap."

The women looked at me in horror. "You, yourself, are not going to her, swami?"

"She needs help, so if there is no one else to go, I must go." My stomach felt like water, I knew nothing about delivering babies but hoped my actions would have the desired effect.

The women looked even more uncomfortable, then the youngest of the three hurried off to her house to boil water while the midwife, the eldest of the three, who was toothless, took out her pouch of betel nut, put a few nuts into her brass pounder and began beating them, each blow making a dull thud on the hard earth.

The third took the pin from her hair and began replaiting it nervously. I squatted on my heels surrounded by heavy silence. Time seemed to stand still as we waited for the water then there was a loud groan from the hut followed by a scream. I got up and began to walk towards the door.

The midwife rose to her feet. "Wait, I can't let you go, swami. I will go to her and may God forgive me."

"I'm sure he will, amma."

We sat anxiously as Lakshmamma hurried across from her house with a pot of hot water. We flinched in sympathy with each groan and scarcely breathed as we waited for the next but at last there was a scream, and then another, and a baby's cry. We looked at each other and smiled with relief.

After delivering Dapsone tablets at one of the houses I cycled on in the direction of Dodballapur. I didn't need the sun to tell me the afternoon was well advanced, for my stomach was crying out. A large Regi (Zizyphus sp.) tree, covered with reddish fruit, was growing among boulders to one side of the track. I dismounted, leant my cycle against a rock and pushed my way through the lantana. The fruit was out of reach but those fallen to the ground looked good. I ate a dozen or so and put more into my pocket to eat as I rode. The slightly astringent apple-like flesh was refreshing. It had been my intention to reach Dodballapur by nightfall and stay with friends, the stonemason's family, but the birth had delayed me and by nightfall I was still in the hills approaching a small village whose inhabitants led a precarious existence grazing a few goats, working a small area of dry land and cutting wood, which they carried ten miles along rough mountain paths to sell in Dodballapur.

As I approached his house Gangudu was just driving the last of his sheep through the gate of a thorn enclosure. He closed the gate and heaped more thorns against it with a pitchfork then turned to greet me.

"Namaskaram, swami, you come late, night is falling."

"Yes, I was delayed."

"You must take rest with us and go on tomorrow. It's not safe to travel these hills at night, there are many panthers and wild pigs and even the bears can be dangerous if you surprise them."

"Yes, I'll be glad to stay here and go on in the morning."

We went to the door of their hut and he called to his wife "Amma, Maistrulu is here and will rest with us."

I felt unusually tired and sipped the tumbler of hot sweet goat's milk they gave me, thankfully, while feeling embarrassed by the sight of their two small children gazing at me from a corner. They need the milk more than I do, I thought.

Gangudu joined me on the mat and Papamma put aluminium plates in front of us. I knew if I ate well Papamma and the children would go without.

As she put a large brown ragi ball on my plate, I said,

"Just a small portion for me, I've not long eaten." I squeezed off a small piece of ball between my thumb and forefinger and handed the rest back to her.

After eating, I was given the mat to lie on, and the family huddled together on the floor in one corner. We'd scarcely settled when my mouth began to fill with saliva and I knew I must get outside quickly, I was not far beyond the door when I was very ill. Gangudu came out with a pot of water and I washed my mouth and face but that was only the beginning.

"I must go to the toilet," I said as I staggered out into the fields.

I vomited and had severe diarrhoea, until I was too weak to help myself. Gangudu carried me into the hut.

"What can I do, swami? You are losing a lot of blood, you must go to hospital."

"Let me take rest, I'll be better in the morning. Just give me water with some salt and sugar in it." I knew from my long association with the hospital that the most important thing was to drink to replace the fluids I was losing. What a fool I'd been to eat those fallen fruit! The flies had probably been enjoying them.

I was barely conscious of the next few hours but came to with the realisation that someone was injecting something into my arm and looked up into the face of Danam, one of the male nurses from Chikka. They put me on a stretcher and carried me to the road. I slept, to waken as they carried me from the car into the hospital.

Dr. George walked across from his house near the gate and was in outpatients almost as soon as I was.

"Is your vomit watery or does it contain blood?"

"I've been vomiting blood all night and my stool is the same."

"We'll get David to check for Cholera but that sounds more like Bacillary Dysentery. Are you in pain?"

"No pain, doctor, just very weak." Even talking was an effort.

"Take Sabhapathyanna to the small ward at the end of the men's ward. I'll come and put in a drip."

My recovery was rapid and by the time Dr. Graham came to do his rounds I was almost myself again.

"I hear you had a close call last night."

"I beg your pardon doctor?" I didn't understand his meaning.

"You were nearly called to heaven. If that villager hadn't sent someone for the car I doubt if you'd have lasted 'til morning. You must take better care of yourself. You're skin and bone. At times like this it is good to have some flesh on your bones to fall back on."

"Yes doctor." It was alright to agree in principle, but I found it impossible to take food from people who were already half-starved.

Chapter 17

CHRISTMAS

The sheep were shy performers and the more the shepherds pulled in an attempt to lead them into the middle of the stage the harder they tried to escape the unaccustomed limelight.

It was the night of the Christmas play at Gangasandra boarding school and some local sheep had been co-opted for the performance, but even with some shepherd's assistants pushing from behind they could not be persuaded to remain on stage. Finally two of the teachers went up the steps to the verandah which was, for tonight, the stage and managed to lead them to a pile of hay where they munched happily in the background.

Mrs. Graham had brought some of the Gollahalli mothers and me down to the school in the hospital car with her four children.

Our Padma took the part of Mary and also sang the solo lead, partnered by Mohan, in the songs, and we felt very proud.

A few days earlier I was telling the Christmas story to a group gathered in our hut. It was cold now that the sun had set and we were glad to huddle together inside to share the luxury of the warmth of some empty corn cobs burning in the kitchen. Those who were lucky enough to own scarves had them wrapped around head and neck.

"I was in the hospital last Christmas, Maistrulu and the Bhajana group came and sang to us."

"What did they sing?"

"Songs about Jesus."

"They do that every year in all the Christian houses." I said.

"Why don't you ask them to come here Maistrulu?"

"Yes, do that anna."

"Alright, I'll ask them."

Next time I was in Chikka I went to the Pastor's house. Rev. Ratnam came to the door, a tall man of very upright stature.

"Anna, the Gollahalli folk request you to send the Bhajana group to their homes to sing Christmas carols."

"That may be difficult to arrange. As you know they're up all night on the 23rd singing in Hindu and Muslim houses then all Christmas eve singing in the Christian homes."

"The Gollahalli people are really interested. It will be a pity if we can't arrange it."

"Perhaps they could go on the 22nd."

"We are going to Gangasandra for the Christmas breakup on the 22nd."

"Could you send a second group on the 23rd, I'm sure Bhaskara and Shanta Kumar and Christopher would come."

So it was arranged.

I had invited Amma's children and foster children down to Gollahalli to spend some days with us. Amma put them all on the bus in the morning armed with sleeping bags and blankets and I met them at the Gollahalli crossroad. They piled off the bus and Ari and Greg climbed on top to throw down the baggage. As we walked down to the village Fiona said, "Mum can't come until tonight she has to drive the Bhajana group down."

"What would you like to do?"

"Can we go for a swim in the tank?"

"We've only had a little rain and the water is very muddy."

"I'd like to look after the pigs. Mum said our pig has eight piglets."

Gangamma had prepared some tindi and coffee so I put some peanut cake to soak ready for the pigs.

After taking coffee we all walked up to the pig pen and gave them the sticky mess. The children watched happily as the piglets squealed and snuffled in enjoyment.

"Oh, look how dirty they are! Can we take them down to the tank and bathe them?"

We managed to pen the sow in her small enclosure then we set out, the children running after the piglets as they scattered. Our children joined in, and when we reached the tank they grabbed the piglets between them and took them in. What a noise! I wasn't sure whether the squeals were delight or horror, as I was too busy keeping an eye on amma's youngest and our little ones who couldn't swim.

After the bath they carefully carried the pigs away from the tank so that they wouldn't get muddy again. I watched with amusement as the piglets headed straight back to have a good roll.

"Never mind," said Fiona "that's nice clean mud."

When the men came in from the jungle with the cattle, the children sat on the stones under the peepul tree and fed them by hand on the hay put ready for them. The men were quite happy to leave them to the task.

Amma was to drive the Bhajana group down and the women of each house were ready with some sweet or savoury snacks as well as coffee in our house and Nanjamma's. We waited expectantly as soon as night fell, but they did not come so the children entertained us by singing songs.

At last we saw the headlights making intermittent flashes as the car jolted down the track from the road.

"I'm sorry we're late, the men had to hire a Petromax and pick up the harmonium."

The hospital chaplain was with the group which of course had to visit each of the ten houses singing carols, followed by a short story and then a prayer and the snacks before they left.

One by one the children crept away so that by the time we finished in Gangamma's house, Heather was the only child awake and all the others were curled up asleep on the floor of the hut occupying all the available floor space.

Amma said "I'll just settle the children for the night then take the Bhajana party back to Chikka and return on my motor cycle."

"I don't like the thought of you coming alone at night on your cycle. Let me accompany you and ride back pillion."

"That's a good idea - I spent most of this afternoon working on the clutch, I'd hate to break down halfway."

Gangamma said "Let the children sleep in the hut. It will be cold outside."

"Never mind, they're used to sleeping outside and have blankets or sleeping bags."

Amma settled the children in a row across the village street, then the Bhajana party, Amma and I set off again in the ambulance.

It was a steep pull up to the edge of the plateau. Amma said "I don't think my cycle would be powerful enough to carry us both from Chikka back to the top of the ghat road. I have to get off to let it cool down before it will take me up, and then I only just make it."

"Let me off at the top then, Amma, and I will wait here until you come back. This jungle bit is the most dangerous and it's almost all down hill from here."

"That's a good idea if you're sure you don't mind waiting alone in the jungle."

So when we reached the top I got down, sat on the parapet and spent some time between meditation and dozing off before I heard the 'put' 'put' of amma's motor cycle.

From there it was an easy run down the steep ghat road, past the temple at the bottom, then up and down through the foothills to the village.

As we came into the village street at 1-30 am, Gangamma was sitting cross-legged, her sari over her head against the cold, keeping watch over the sleeping children.

"Oh, Gangamma you shouldn't have stayed out here in the cold! They would have been alright."

"Amma, take care in the morning, when the cattle begin to move."

"We'll get up at first light."

Amma lay down between Carol and Fiona and we left them, thankful enough not to be sleeping out in the cold ourselves.

I was up at four o'clock as usual and sat on the well parapet to pray and also keep a watchful eye on amma and the children. I was afraid an animal moving down the track might be spooked by the unusual sight and injure one of them in its fright.

About 5-30 the children began to move and amma got up.

"Did you sleep well?"

"After 3am when I discovered a blanket rolled up near my feet."

Gangamma had made chitra annamu {fried rice with tomato}which the children enjoyed.

We were sitting talking in one of the other houses when we heard some altercation at the well and Fiona appeared in the door-way

"I was just drawing some water at the well when the lady came from the big house and shouted at me that I had dirtied the well and tipped the water back again. I said I hadn't dirtied it I had only used Gangamma's water pot but she said I was of no caste, so had dirtied it just by touching it and now they would have to do special Puja to make it clean again. She was very angry."

Fiona was also angry and I felt sad that such an incident had marred their stay but the Reddy's family were still very traditional and we had to put up with it.

By 10 o'clock the sleeping bags and blankets were all bundled and ready to be carried up to the bus.

"You'll put them all on the 3 o'clock bus, anna." Amma said as she began to push her cycle up to the road.

I crossed the road with the children and we all went into the jungle to see what we could find. We came upon a small dragon, very beautifully marked.

Gopal said "Deadly poison!" and picked up a rock.

But we said "Leave it" and admired the vivid green and black and yellow of its markings until it plucked up courage to make a dive into the bushes. We investigated several wild custard apple trees for fruit and found some mature enough to pick.

At 2-30 the children donned their headloads of sleeping gear and we set off up the track to the road. Our Jayamma was going with them to spend Christmas with Amma's children and her grandmother was giving her last minute instructions about good behaviour. We had almost reached the road when Ari gave a strange groan and fell to the ground.

The children shouted "Wai! Wai has come to Ari!"

As I bent over him, I saw that he was indeed having an epileptic fit.

"Has he had a fit like this before?"

"No, anna, this is the first time."

He had hit his head on a rock as he fell and his head was bleeding. The children found a leaf to put over the wound while I fanned him. We heard the bus groan up the hill and go past as we sat with him. He had a drink out of one of the children's water bottles then we made our way up to the road. The next bus was not due for an hour and I debated whether I should go into Chikka with them but Fiona said "Don't worry, anna, we'll look after him, and take him to the hospital as soon as we get home." So I decided to stay.

I had promised to take some of the women and children in to Chikka for the Church service on Christmas morning.

I put on the new Jubba and pancha which amma had given me during their visit. The children and women donned their best clothes. Not being Christians they had not purchased new clothes for the occasion.

It was still cold as we set out for the road, mist lay in the hollows, but was disappearing fast as the sun rose above the horizon.

We waited anxiously as we heard the first bus climbing noisily up the hill.

"Will it stop?"

Thankfully it shuddered to rest beside us, and we climbed aboard, the children pushing between the legs of standing passengers to reach a safe distance from the door.

We were early and the Church was almost empty with two young men still putting the finishing touches to the decorations.

"You're here early!" we said.

"We've been up all night decorating and just went home for coffee this morning and came straight back."

"The church looks beautiful, all those coloured streamers and who made the gold stars?"

"Samuel did those."

Our children were delighted and had time to go around and admire them all. People soon began to arrive. They knew they must be early to get inside on Christmas day.

Two little boys in front of us looked proud of their crisp striped shirts, the trade stamp still on one to authenticate its newness. Their sister beside them wore a bright pink langa and jacket, her hair plaited and sporting large pink ribbons with a strand of woven jasmine flowers like a crown.

There were three christenings, a sermon in Kannada repeated again in English; readings, hymns and lyrics in Tamil and Telugu as well as Kannada, for many of the hospital staff were from other areas and although, by virtue of being in Karnataka state, Kannada was the official language, yet most of the local people regarded themselves as Telugus and many had spoken only Telugu from childhood.

The Bhajana group, in spite of their two previous sleepless nights and being crowded by the large congregation, played with vigour, the drummer matching his head shaking and facial contortions to the rhythm.

At the close of the service we all shook hands and wished one another a merry Christmas. Christmas day and New Year's day are the only times we shake hands, as shaking hands is not an Indian form of greeting.

Chapter 18
FAMINE

Muniamma pulled the wooden bung out of the huge storage basket which took up a large portion of the house, serving as part of the wall between kitchen and living area. The Ragi(red millet) trickled out slowly into her winnowing tray.

"The grain is almost finished, Maistrulu, and still no rain has come."

I finished tying my clean pancha and put on my jubba. Krishna and Jayamma were dressed in their new clothes, their boxes packed.

"Go and tell Munianjini and the others that we are ready to go. It's almost time for the bus."

I went outside and looked at the sky. It was a pale hot blue, not a sign of a cloud.

It was June 1960 and the children were returning to boarding for the new school year. The rainfall in 1959 had been marginal and with an annual rainfall of 14ins the rains had to be above average or very well timed to give us good harvests.

In July we had barely enough rain to plough and sow. The seed came up and daily we searched the skies for clouds hoping for rain but it didn't come and we had to watch as the new shoots shrivelled and died. The tanks were virtually dry so there was no water for irrigation.

Now that the children were older we got down from the bus two miles before Gauribidanur. A boy was perched precariously, high up in one of the roadside trees chopping off leaves for his scrawny sheep and goats which waited hungrily below.

We set off across the fields, the children carrying their trunks on their heads. The ground was dry and dusty, foraging cattle had eaten down every scrap of dry grass. As the children's feet padded along the track little puffs of dust rose behind them. When we reached the boarding house I saw Amma's Lambretta parked outside Mr. Benjamin's house.

Mr. Benjamin came out to greet me. "Come in and take coffee, anna."

"Thank you, I see that amma is here."

"Yes, she's come to paint some of the children with Benzyl benzoate. They've returned with Scabies. A lot of them have it this year because they've been half-starved at home and have no resistance."

"My father used to tell me of the scabies boxes they had in all the village boarding schools in the old days."

"Yes, the whole child went into the box with only a hole for his head then they burnt sulphur inside the box."

Amma walked in."Namaskaram Sabhapathyanna. Did you bring the children down?"

"Yes, amma."

Vimalamma, Benjamin's wife came in from the kitchen.

"Will you take a bath, amma?"

"Yes, thank you."

Later on when we sat down to eat amma said "I had people in yesterday to clean out our well. We had only a few inches of water left."

"The water level here has fallen, but so far we have enough. Chikka would be worse off."

"The hospital is short of water. Doctor has gone to Bangalore to try to arrange for a well-boring team to come out and put down a bore. You can't run a hospital without water."

In the fields on the plateau around Chikka, where most of the crops grown were vegetables for the Bangalore markets, almost every landowner had a large well, pump house and pump for irrigation. Returning from Bangalore at night as we came over the last hill we looked down on a countryside dotted with twinkling lights, for each pump house was allowed to keep one bulb burning. But with everyone pumping furiously to keep their crops alive, the water table fell.

In September, we had some rain and people's hopes were raised. They ploughed and sowed again - those who had already borrowed money for seed tried to borrow more. Our spirits lifted as the brown fields turned green.

Farmers harrowed the crops, ridding them of weeds, and we waited and watched as growth stopped and a few flowering heads were produced - a last effort by the plants before they shrivelled and died.

As I travelled through the villages I saw the effects. Sturdy bright-eyed children became listless, their hair hanging limp and pale, their bellies beginning to protrude.

Amma had been handed the food relief books and supplies when Dr. and Mrs. Cutting left in March. She had wheat, milk powder, cheese and oil, and distributed them to the hospital kitchen and boarding school at Gangasandra, as well as mixing milk daily for collection by poor families near the bungalow.

The hospital staff were aware of people's suffering. According to the Government, no one was dying of starvation. Maybe not, but we had men, women and children dying of pneumonia, tuberculosis and diarrhoea, and children dying of measles who would not have died if they'd been properly fed.

Amma said "If you make lists of families in real need, I'll approach the National Christian Council representative in Bangalore for extra food relief supplies." So I began walking and cycling from village to village making lists of those people in greatest need - landless people, widows with children to support, men too ill to support their families. I wrote the names and ages of each one in my little black book.

Meanwhile Amma made several trips to Bangalore and was finally allocated a good supply of wheat, milk powder and oil. As soon as the supplies arrived she sent a message to me on Rural Dispensary day and I went in to Chikka.

Amma gave me coffee "How are we going to organise this?"

"How many bags have you got?"

"Five hundred, each bag containing about 50 measures I think."

"Perhaps we should start by giving a measure per head with some milk powder and oil. I have told the people on my list to send one member from each family with a bag and two containers when they get word from me."

"Should we distribute it here?"

"Yes, and the best day would be market day, as many come in then anyway."

So it was arranged, and I sent messengers in different directions telling them to come in on Saturday.

Several of the men accompanied me to Chikka on Saturday to help.

"May we borrow your measures please amma?"

Amma brought her measures and a quart jug from her store and we carried a dozen bags from the old cook's quarters and stacked them on the verandah in readiness.

It wasn't long before people began to arrive. I found the names on my list, counted the family members then told the men helping me to give them the required number of measures. Many didn't have bags but tied the grain in a square of rag, and had brought a variety of tins and bottles for their milk powder and oil. We told them to come again in two week's time.

Five hundred bags would not last long at this rate but at least these families would have food for some weeks.

Chapter 19

MADDURENAHALLI

One day when I went to deliver Dapsone tablets at Maddurenahalli two of the men were standing overlooking the steep slope down to the river.

We all stood silently for a few moments.

"The crops are all drying up," one said.

"When we do have rain the water runs off and takes the soil with it."

"Why don't you terrace it to hold the water and the soil?" I said.

"How can we do that, Maistrulu?"

"Well, you've plenty of rocks to use for walls."

"Most of them are too big to use."

"Why don't you cut them?"

"Only Thimmappa can cut stone, he once worked in a quarry."

"Maybe he'd cut the rock and the rest of you could do the terracing."

"We don't have time, swami! We have to walk a long way to get coolie and without cooli we'll starve."

I left it then. I could see their point, but surely something could be done. The problem continued to prick my mind as I walked from village to village. Next time I went to Chikka I visited the agricultural supervisor to ask his advice.

"They need a pump and some polythene pipe."

"They have no money to buy such things."

"I'll lend you a book - I've seen one in our library on terracing and lifting water."

I took the book off in triumph, and spent the next few days reading it as I watched the pigs graze. It looked like a lot of work, but during the dry weather the men of the village would not be able to find coolie and could work together.

Each Thursday I attended leprosy clinic at the hospital and went to Dr. Graham's bungalow for lunch. Sometimes I ate lunch with amma but if I was very late she did not wait for me, but served me when I came in, then sat with her slow loris on her shoulder and we talked as I ate.

"I'm worried about my food relief grain: the weevils have got into it. I asked my merchant in the bazaar what they do to keep weevils out and he said they mix Gammexane with the grain. That sounds awful to me and almost puts me off eating. What do they do in the villages?"

"They spread it in the sun."

"That sounds much safer. It's difficult with a large quantity though."

"I'll get some of the Gollahalli women to come and do it. You'll need a flat patch of ground."

"The old tennis court might do."

I had no trouble finding volunteers among the women. The hot weather was upon us so coolie was scarce. Some of the women had already gone to other villages for wedding ceremonies.

Akkayamma volunteered.

"What about the children?" I asked.

"I'll take them with me, Maistrulu."

"No,you'd better stay at home - amma will have six extra mouths to feed, we don't want children as well."

On Wednesday night I sent Gangamma to tell the women to take their winnowing baskets and we were climbing the hill to the road at first light.

The bus stopped for us and we pushed our way in. When we reached Muniamma's hut in the foothills the driver stopped and her eldest son Rajanna began to climb aboard. His shirt was blood-stained, his face pale, and one arm hanging useless as he pulled himself into the bus with difficulty. When he saw me he seemed a bit put out.

"Namaskaram ayya." He greeted me and looked away.

We managed to clear enough space for him to sit on the floor.

"What happened to your shoulder?"

"I was out shooting last night and my gun went off as I was pushing through some Lantana."

"Ah yo! That was bad luck. Are you in much pain?"

"The pain is bad, swami. I'm going to the hospital"

"Where were you shooting rabbits?" Gangamma asked.

"At Jakkalamadugu tank."

When the bus reached Gopal Tsattram we got down and went to the bungalow. Amma came to greet us.

"Please show us where we can spread the wheat and we'll prepare a patch."

Amma led them to the old tennis court between the two bungalows.

"There are a few weeds here but it's ant bed underneath."

The women got ready for work, lifting the back hems of their saris and pulling them up between their legs to tuck into the waist in front so that they looked as though they were now attired in baggy knee breeches.

Three of them began to weed and sweep.

"Can we get some cow pats from the shed?"

"I'll go and get the 'bindige'(brass water pot) so that you can draw some water from the well."

When amma returned with the pot Gangamma put the loop of the well rope around its neck and lowered it into the well.

"The well is very deep; and there are only two or three feet of water. We'll need to have it cleaned out again if the rains don't come soon."

The fresh manure was put into a garden bucket and the water poured to make a thin gruel, just right for spreading.

Amma and I stood and watched as they spread the liquid manure making a glistening patch on the clean surface.

"Somehow I love that smell of hot wet manure," amma said, as the sun beat down and we watched the steam rising from the green brown surface.

"It makes an excellent surface to keep down the dust. Now we'll have to wait for it to dry."

"Come and have coffee then, while you wait."

We all went into the bungalow and amma spread mats on the dining-room floor.

"Please sit down."

Amma put leaf plates in front of us and served us with puri (thin deep fried chapathis) and potato palyam, then gave us all coffee.

"We may have enough room on that patch to spread the grain from twenty bags." They were bushel bags and the heaviest work was carrying the bags of grain from the store.

I watched them as they spread the grain, putting the empty bags on the hot path to kill the weevils. The wheat had to remain in the sun for two hours being stirred occasionally by hand.

I looked at the sun, it must be time for clinic.

"I'll go and come, amma."

"Go and come, anna. We will wait for your return before we take food."

Rajanna was waiting with the other patients in the outpatient hall. I heard him tell one of the men next to him about his shooting accident. The nurse on duty came and took him in to be examined as he was the person who looked in greatest need.

I was about to register one of the H.D.patients from Jakkalamadugu. He leant forward, "That's his story!"

"What do you mean?"

"Gangudu disturbed a man trying to steal his sheep last night and shot at him. He heard a shout and believes he scored a hit. That Rajanna and his family belong to the criminal tribes, he would be wise to keep his mouth shut."

I had heard similar rumours myself.

When I returned to the bungalow two of the women had their winnowing baskets high above their heads while the others were collecting the winnowed grain or sweeping away the dead weevils which had been blown to a pile on one side by a gentle, if hot, breeze.

The work took two days, but, as amma gave the women good food, as well as sleeping accommodation, they were all happy with the arrangement, and went home with several seers of wheat each, to help feed their families.

This exercise gave me an idea so I broached the matter of Maddurenahalli with amma.

After explaining the situation I said "Could you give wheat to help pay these people while they terrace and make wells."

"I'm not supposed to give wheat as wages, but are these people poor?"

"Yes, they are poor."

"Then I could allot wheat to them. If they are doing work to make the community self-supporting, I don't see any harm in that."

I went to Maddurenahalli and asked the Panchayat to call a meeting of the village people.

"If you terraced your lands and built wells, you could make this land productive."

"How can we, swami?"

"Thimmappa could cut stone and perhaps teach another to help him, and the rest of you could build walls."

"How would we eat?"

"I could get grain and give you two seers per day to feed your families."

One of the younger men said, "That sounds good, Maistrulu, but we don't know where to build the walls."

"I have a friend who has promised to make a plan - he's an engineer so you can trust him. We can also build wells to hold water for irrigation."

They began discussing it among themselves; then one of them said.

"It's good - you make the plans."

"It will be hard work! And only those people who do the work will receive the wheat."

They agreed, and an air of excitement could be felt as they gathered in small groups discussing it.

My next task was to contact my engineer friend and bring him down to the village. He brought with him a young surveyor. Between them they measured and calculated, drawing up a plan for terracing the whole hillside and placing a series of wells and catchment tanks up the middle to catch water and run it on to the fields. At last we were ready to start work. It was agreed that they would commence work each day at 4am, work until twelve, and receive two measures of wheat.

When mother refused to feed us, after the incident at the police station following father's death, for many years I did not go to her house for food but after I sought forgiveness for my part in the quarrel the scars were healed and we were reconciled.

After retirement from her position as a teacher in the Government Middle School my mother worked from 1960 as a teacher in the Municipal Nursery School at Chikballapur. Philip, due to the brain damage resulting from Epilepsy, remained in her care and my youngest half brother Prasanna, having graduated B.Sc.,Dip.Ed.was employed as a Physics and Maths teacher in the High School.

In 1965, on retirement from that position, mother found it too expensive to continue to live in Chikballapur so we built a small house on our site in Gollahalli where the men's schoolhouse formerly stood, and mother came with my half brother Philip to live there. She agreed to help distribute grain and keep records in

Maddurenahalli when I was absent. This meant she had to live there until the work was finished.

The villagers toiled for months, but, by the time the work was completed, they had a system of wells, catchment dams and channeling, 101 constructions in all. This meant that their land could be used for most of the year and changed the standard of living in the village forever.

We were all very happy with the results but awaited the visit of the area supervisor from C.A.S.A. with some trepidation as our distribution had not been strictly according to rule and Dr. and Mrs. Graham had gone to Australia on furlough.

I met the supervisor in Chikballapur and he accompanied me to Gollahalli where we went through our record books, then walked the 9 kilometres to Maddurenahalli.

When we showed him what had been done he was very pleased and said to me "Have you trained up anyone to take over the task of distribution?"

I had thought about it so I said "Yes, I have someone in mind."

"It is necessary to have a man of some education to keep accounts and be in charge."

Mr. K.T.Ramaiah, a devout and sincere Hindu who lived in Chikka, had lands around Gollahalli, including some wet lands below our tank. So when we organised a meeting at D'palya for World Leprosy Day I invited him to accompany me.

On reaching the schoolhouse where the meeting was to be held, the organizers had tacked many posters up on the walls bearing slogans used to educate people about the disease. Mr. Ramaiah jotted down a number of slogans including a couple which indicated that a person earns much 'punyam' (merit in heaven) caring for a leprosy patient. He was very interested. Some time after this I broached the subject.

"Ayyagaru - I need an educated man to be in charge of relief food for leprosy patients. Would you be willing to act in that capacity?"

"It's a big responsibility; I will think about it."

Next time we met I said, "What's your decision?"

"Yes, I'm willing, but I would like you to be present at distribution whenever possible."

"Good, that will be a great help to me."

After that when he was about to leave for his lands he went to the bungalow and collected a number of bags of Bulgar wheat and some tins of oil and had them put on the bus.

He had been acting as distributor for some time and got to know the village people in the area. However some of the villagers were going back to their old ways of stealing sheep to cut and eat and had also been persuaded by rascally leaders in the area to cut large branches from the roadside trees to sell to the owners of the tobacco barns as fuel for curing the leaf. Mr. Ramaiah came to know of this and gave a report to the police.

The first inkling I had of trouble was when I received a complaint from some of the members of the Leprosy Association, asking that Mr. Ramaiah be removed as distributor because he was taking the wheat to Chikka and selling it.

I felt very upset. I had had complete faith in him.

I made some discreet enquiries of people in the area. Some said " He is an honest man, he is doing a very good job." Others I asked said "He is not to be trusted he is taking the food to Chikka and selling it." But I heard from another source that those who complained had been involved indirectly in the sheep stealing.

One day I just happened to be at Gopal Tsattram when Mr. Ramaiah got down from the bus and unloaded some bags labelled Bulgar Wheat. My heart sank. The rumours must be true then!

"Good morning anna - are you well?"

"I am well. And you anna?"

"Yes, I am well thank you."

He was a good friend and I felt very awkward but after looking at one another in silence for a moment, I said,

"Anna, may I check the contents of your bags?"

"Yes. Check them anna. I will be pleased."

He bent and proceeded to untie the twine from the neck of a bag.

I looked inside - it was paddy (unhulled rice) and the next one was the same.

He said "Feel the third, anna."

I stooped and pinched the third bag. I could feel the ridged edges of the paddy grains, rough between finger and thumb. I straightened up with a sigh of relief.

"That's good, very good! Some people have been circulating rumours about you - I just wanted to put them to rest, in my mind, at least!"

"I know, anna, some of the people are angry with me because they have guilty consciences."

"We all have to live with our consciences. Let them live with theirs and leave ours alone."

Chapter 20
HEALING

I put my head around the door and knocked loudly on it. "Prasanna, may I come in?"

"Come in and sit down, anna." he called from the kitchen.

I had cycled into Chikka on Wednesday night, and went to the rooms my youngest brother Prasanna rented in the town. He had completed a Science degree and was working as a teacher in the High School. Unless I had other business in the town I caught the last bus in, for by that time Prasanna would have returned from school, made his purchases in the bazaar and be about to cook his meal. As many people did, he prepared enough food in the morning before commencing school and took his main meal then. In the evening he heated the curry and rice and perhaps added an egg or some vegetables.

"I've brought some weeds, the area around the tank is covered with them since the rains and the women picked a large basketful yesterday." I handed him the weeds which Gangamma had wrapped in a leaf plate and tied with cotton.

"They are washed and ready to throw in the pan."

"That's good, I'll fry them with some garlic and ginger, they'll go well with the dhal curry. Sit down, anna."

Ignoring the rather uncomfortable looking chair at his desk I took a rolled mat from a corner, spread it and sat down.

"How's school?" I asked.

"Good, I'm busy designing some experiments for our open day which we're holding next month."

A few minutes later he brought two cups of coffee and as we sat drinking he said suddenly "Anna, I think it's time I got married."

The remark took me by surprise, he had never mentioned marriage before.

"Have you spoken about it to mother?"

"Not yet. As my elder brother you should make the arrangements."

"I'll do anything I can. Do you have anyone in mind ?"

"A new teacher has come to the school this year, she's very beautiful."

"Do you think she would agree?"

"Yes, she seems to like me, but I don't know about her parents."

"Is she a Christian?"

"No, that's the trouble, she's a Brahmin."

My heart sank. "Are they conservative?"

"Yes, I'm afraid so. But Lalithamma is well educated and has moved away from that sort of prejudice I'm sure."

"You know how difficult it is for a girl to go against her parents. I'm sure mother or I could arrange a marriage for you with a beautiful Christian girl."

"Thank you, anna, but I only want to marry this girl."

"You'd better get her to try to persuade her parents then. She is more likely to be sucessful than we are."

When I lay down on the mat to sleep that night, although I was tired, sleep did not claim me for a long time. What troubles had Prasanna got himself into. He had as obstinate a streak as any of us and had obviously made up his mind that this was the girl he wanted to marry.

The H.D.clinic commenced at nine so at eight-thirty I cycled along the road to the hospital - I liked to be there in time to talk with the patients before Doctor arrived.

The 'chakla' (shoemaker) was already sitting cross-legged on the ground outside the door of the outpatient hall.

"Namaskaram swami" palms together he greeted me.

"Are you well, anna?"

"Yes, by God's grace, I am well."

His small daughter was playing 'knuckles' in the dust beside him, using small stones in the absence of bones.

"You've made Gangappa's sandals?" I said, pointing to a pair of shoes in his basket. Our H.D.sandals were distinctive, having leather uppers and a strap behind the heel to give more protection.

"Yes, swami, they're ready."

"I've told a man from Hosahalli to come in today - I think Doctor will want him to have a pair."

I walked up the stone steps to the door. Just then Doctor came in from the registration hall and looked around.

"Good morning Sabhapathy. We've got a good turn out today. You must have been busy."

"Yes, doctor, I went to some of the villages west of here - I hadn't been there for a while. Some had not been taking their tablets regularly and some have not had their blood haemoglobins checked for a long time so I told them to come in."

"That's good, we'd better get to work. Is the Chakla there?"

"Yes doctor, and I asked a man from Hosahalli to come in - he drives the cattle to the forest and already has a small ulcer on his foot."

The clinic got under way. One of the women had burnt her hand and I heard Doctor say

"You shouldn't be doing the cooking, can't you get someone else to cook?"

"What can I do swami? My husband's out farming and my children are too young - there's no one else."

"Sabhapathy, would you talk to her about B.C.G. Vaccine for the children? They seem to think it gives some protection."

As I took the woman to get her tablets I said "Amma, this disease you have is catching. Doctor can give your children needle medicine which may stop them catching it. Can you bring them next week?"

"Yes swami, I'll bring them."

It was after one when I went across to the bungalow for food then set out on my cycle towards Bangalore intending to turn off to the east and work my way back to Gollahalli across country, visiting villages as I went.

As I turned off the main road I suddenly found myself going one way, my cycle another. I picked myself up, no real damage done, but I was puzzled and examined the road for stones or gravel - nothing obvious.

Two weeks later I fell again for no apparent reason. This time my arm was bleeding, but as I was nearing Gollahalli I made for home.

Gangamma was drawing water at the well.

"What have you done to yourself Maistrulu? Your shirt sleeve is covered in blood."

"I fell off my cycle."

"Ah yo! What made you do that?"

"I don't know!" I said

"I'll wash it and put on some leaves."

"You'd better boil some rag strips in salt water, as Doctor tells the patients to do and wash and bind it with that."

I didn't tell Gangamma I'd fallen twice, but as I sat and drank coffee while the salt and water cooled, it began to prick my mind. Why had I fallen off? I'd been riding for years without an accident.

Over the next weeks I had more falls, not only from my cycle, I began to have dizzy spells and headaches so I took the bus to Chikka and went to outpatients. Dr. Graham had recently gone to Kavutalam Hospital 200 miles to the north. Dr. Purushottam was on duty and gave me a thorough examination.

"I can find nothing organically wrong but perhaps you should go to Bangalore and see a nerve specialist."

I'd prayed for many people over the years but it was a long time since I'd prayed for myself - now I began in earnest.

One day when I went to the Horticultural office Mr. Bhaskara said,

"You're not riding your cycle, anna."

"No, I'm having problems with dizziness and I fall off."

"That's no good - have you seen the doctor?"

"Yes, he suggests I go to the special hospital in Bangalore. I don't want to do that."

"I've heard that there's a faith healer coming to Bombay soon - why don't you go there?"

As I walked to the bus stand and waited for my bus I was scarcely conscious of the children around me begging, or the hawkers selling trinkets and ribbons, my mind was occupied with what Bhaskara had said. A faith healer! Did I believe in faith healing? I believed God was all-powerful and I believed in the Biblical miracles. If God is all-powerful then why don't we see miracles today? I remembered my father's great faith and how early one morning I had gone looking for him in the hospital and on pushing open the door of his office had found him kneeling with mother in prayer on a buckskin. I quietly closed the door again feeling an intruder. After that I realised they disappeared together early each morning.

I knew it was the custom in the operating theatre for the team to pray before the commencement of surgery and certainly the patient recovery rate was excellent but did I believe in straight out miracles? I'd like to!

A small grimy hand in front of my nose roused me from my thoughts and I said rather abruptly "Por! Porvair!" (Go! Get out!).

The bus came in, and as I fought for a seat one of my friends greeted me.

"Namaskaram anna, I spoke to you before but you didn't hear me."

"Forgive me - I was deep in thought."

We chatted of trivial events as the bus climbed up to the gap and went rattling down the other side, but after I got down at the Gollahalli cross my mind switched back and I decided that, as I believe in a living Christ, then I should also believe in miracles - I would go and see Bhaskara again and get more information.

A few days later I went to Chikka and made my way again to the Horticultural office.

Bhaskara was busy selling some grape vines to a customer. I wandered around the little nursery section until he was free.

"Anna, tell me more about the healing meetings in Bombay."

"I don't know much, I just know that someone with the gift of healing is coming from Australia and big meetings are to be held at the racecourse."

"Is anyone going from here?"

"Yes, Satyanandam and two or three others."

"I've decided to go."

"Then I will take leave and accompany you, anna."

"Thank you, I'll be glad of your company."

Apart from visiting the doctor in outpatients some weeks earlier I had not sought further medical advice neither had I mentioned my symptoms to anyone else. I think I had an inward fear of what I might find out, and a hope that if I ignored the symptoms they might go away. In fact for days at a time I would feel perfectly well, then become dizzy and have a headache for some hours.

I had to organize some money for the fare. That done I went to tell Dr.Graham that I would be away for a week, but he had gone to Diocesan Council in Hyderabad so I went across to the bungalow to tell amma who was still in Chikka.

When I knocked she invited me in for coffee.

"I'm going to Bombay."

She looked very surprised so I explained

"A faith healer is to be there next week, I'm hoping to be healed."

"I'd heard a rumour that you weren't well. What's the matter?"

"I don't really know but I'm having dizzy spells and have fallen off my cycle many times so now I'm walking to the villages."

"Ah yo! That must make you very hot and tired - but shouldn't you have more medical tests done?"

"No, I've decided to go to Bombay. Please explain to Doctor and please look after the village children in the boarding for me if they should need anything."

"I will and I hope you have a good journey and are healed."

Bhaskara and I went to Gauribidanur and caught the night train - we'd have had a better chance of a seat if we'd gone to Bangalore but the extra fares made us decide against it. We were lucky, as four of the people in our compartment were leaving the train at Penukonda to visit their Guru, Sai Baba, at his ashram. When they took their luggage off the rack, Bhaskara said "Climb into the rack and have some sleep anna, we've got tomorrow night as well."

"I wouldn't feel happy up there - you go up and I'll lie on the floor."

Bhaskara climbed up and was able to have a few hours sleep. I spread my one bedsheet under the seat and crawled under, covering myself with another- I was so tired the rattling of the wheels on the tracks and the rocking motion of the carriage served as a lullaby, and I knew nothing until I wakened to something brushing against my face. When I opened my eyes a cockroach as large as a mouse scurried across my face and disappeared into the woodwork. I lay for a minute watching giant cockroaches making forays into the compartment then sleep once more overcame me. The next day passed slowly - the flat almost treeless plains of the deccan a patchwork of fields, dark green of cotton, bright green of sorghum and blue green of chick pea. Shepherds waved as they grazed their animals beside the track.

The second night I slept sitting up, to wake frequently with a crick in the neck.

We stayed in Bombay with friends of Bhaskara's. Next day when we reached the racecourse I was amazed at the thousands gathered there; for only 3% of our population is Christian. I hadn't seen such a gathering since the Billy Graham campaign in Bangalore many years before.

As the Bhajana group began to play, a hush fell over the crowd until a young man led us in song from the makeshift stage.

The audience joined in the simple choruses obviously known to many of them and even though unfamiliar to me they were easily learnt.

A middle-aged man next to me sang lustily then in a pause turned to me.

"What is your village?"

"I'm from Chikballapur in Karnataka."

"I'm from Gudur in Tamilnadu."

"You must have been travelling for more than two days then."

"Yes."

As I looked at the people around me I decided though most of them would know English there were probably many who didn't.

The speaker spoke about the Holy Spirit. I had always believed in the Holy Spirit but not been conscious of His power in a personal way. The speakers at this conference seemed to know the Holy Spirit and be filled with His power. I'll admit at first I watched the proceedings with some scepticism, but I had noticed a child pushed in a home made wheel chair - her legs were like sticks - the result, I imagine, of infantile paralysis, which is a common cause of death or permanent disablement.

When the speaker finished his address he asked those who wanted healing to come down to the area in front of the stage. As the bhajana played and the people sang, many hundreds began pushing forward. I found myself close to the child in the wheel chair.

Teams of young counsellors then came to each one, laid hands on them and prayed. As I waited my turn I observed that many of the people prayed for seemed to lose consciousness and fall to the ground, to get up a few minutes later and walk away.

When my turn came a young man asked me.

"What is your problem, sir?"

"I am suffering from headache and giddiness."

Three of them laid hands on me and he prayed.

"Holy Spirit come in all your power and heal this man - take away all giddiness and headache and fill him with your power. In Jesus' name, Amen."

As he prayed a wave of heat swept through me, and I felt myself sway but managed to remain upright - peace engulfed me.

Just then a great shouting, laughing and crying broke out beside me, I heard voices exclaiming "Praise God!"

The crush of people was so great I found it difficult to make out what was happening but as I peered between the people beside me I saw the child who had been in the wheel chair, standing - her mother embracing her and weeping.

I made my way back to my seat with difficulty.

Bhaskara said "How are you, anna?

"I believe I am healed!"

"Praise God!"

"You noticed that child in the wheel chair over there - I think she's healed!"

We watched the group still out in front, begin to make its way back, this time to our amazement, the child was walking unsteadily and the father pushed the wheel chair. I looked at her closely - was it my imagination or were her legs looking stronger already?"

My heart sang with joy as we finally made our way back to Bhaskara's friend's house.

Our train trip back to Chikka was as tedious as the previous journey - this time I was bold enough to hoist myself into a luggage rack - it was an old carriage and the wire rack left it's mark upon me, but that was a small price to pay for the comfort of stretching out in comparative peace.

Chapter 21

FAREWELL

There was a lot to do on my return. Dr. Graham was shortly to leave on furlough and I wanted to make out a complete list of patients undergoing treatment for H.D. before he left. This meant checking up on those I had not visited recently to make sure they were still taking their tablets regularly. A common attitude was, "I feel better so I haven't been taking them!" The end result was greater damage, as the bacilli quietly multiplied.

Before their transfer to Kavutalam, Mrs. Graham had been coming down to Gollahalli each week on her motor cycle to tell the women a Bible story, have prayers and speak to them about infant health or some other health problem. I wanted to give her a farewell which was different from the usual coffee and tindi (Bhuga Mix.) She had also made the irrigation works carried out in Maddurenahalli possible through the supply of relief food, but had never seen the end result, so I wrote asking her to come and visit Maddurenahalli when next she came to visit the Boarding school at Gangasandra, and to let me know in time.

As I walked between villages one day I looked at the surrounding countryside, steep hillsides covered with huge boulders, tortured trees struggling to survive, an occasional one rising above the others when its roots found some hidden source of nourishment. Bee-eaters swooping drew my attention to a huge honeycomb in a thorn tree, and I thought of John the Baptist in the wilderness eating locusts and wild honey.

"That's it," I decided, "have a farewell party in the jungle with locusts and wild honey - maybe not the locusts, they would be hard to find - but we could gather honey and have fruit."

When I returned to Gollahalli, and a group of us sat in the hut talking, I told them of my idea. They didn't sound enthusiastic.

"Do you think amma will like that?"

"Yes, I believe she will - I know she likes the jungle."

"It doesn't show much respect, Maistrulu, perhaps she'll be offended."

"No! I don't think so." I outlined my plan.

It was 'Santa' (market) day in Melekota when we arrived there to meet amma. The area of dry earth near the bus stop was crowded with people with sheep and goats for sale. Around the edge of this hubbub sat women with baskets full of flowers, puffed dhal or vegetables. Woven mats were propped against a tree and a stack of freshly fired pots sat in a corner. A copper smith sat beside a pyramid of brass pots gently tapping to push the metal to fill a small hole in a pot while the owner watched.

The bus came in, laden high with more merchandise, fowls in crates, bundles of blankets and seemingly bursting at the seams with its overload of passengers. I spotted amma near a window and went over to catch her zip bag as she dropped it out.

"How are you Sabhapathy? I was afraid I wouldn't be able to get on when I saw the crowd - but I managed it."

"I had forgotten it was 'santa' day."

I knew amma had caught the bus at midnight so had brought a 'chembu' (screw-lidded brass pot) and had it filled with coffee at the hotel.

Chikkahanumantudu, amma and I set out. We'd left the others four miles along the track, so after walking for an hour we came to the spot I'd chosen, where the jungle thickened giving us shade, and the track overlooked a steep rocky gully.

There the men were waiting with two large honeycombs and one of the largest Jackfruit I'd ever seen - it must have been at least two feet long and nearly a foot in diameter, its green prickly skin just beginning to take on a slightly yellowish tint. Even in the open the stench of the fruit had reached our nostrils long before we saw it.

Two of the women had come and stepped forward to garland amma. Then we all sat down on the ground.

"Where's the oil for the knife?" Avalappa asked.

I took the small medicine bottle of oil from my pocket and handed it to him. Had I forgotten the oil, cutting the fruit would have been a very messy business, as the latex in the skin sticks to everything and after a cut or two the knife becomes so coated it's virtually useless.

He cut open the Jackfruit and two of the men cut the honeycomb and began squeezing the honey into a 'dekshi'(saucepan).

I handed the first piece of fruit to amma and said "Dip it in the honey before you eat it, amma."

Amma dipped the yellow segment of fruit into the honey and began to eat. I could see she was enjoying herself.

"Please put the seeds in the bag." I had brought an old Bulgar wheat bag for the purpose and as we ate we threw in the large brown seeds. They would be good boiled and eaten next day, their nutty flavour a real treat for the village children . I would keep a few to plant near the tank.

When we had eaten enough, the women whispered together and disappeared into a clump of bushes to reappear with a leaf-tied bundle holding a new red and green handloom sari, a coconut and some flowers.

Amma took it, looking a bit overwhelmed.

"Ninda Namaskaram"(grateful thanks) she said as she put her hands together and bowed. We all watched as she untied the cotton.

"Oh, a sari, a handloom one too! You shouldn't have done this."

"The women insisted on giving you this, amma, so that you can remember them as they will remember you."

"I will never forget them!"

The sun was halfway towards the horizon and we had another hour's walk before reaching Maddurenahalli. Some of the men gathered up the remains of the Jackfruit and honey while another picked up the torches.

"How do you make those torches, Sabhapathy? I've always wondered."

"The women saved pieces of old sari, soaked them in Pongamia oil, then wrapped them in many layers around those four foot poles. They will burn for several hours."

To reach Maddurenahalli we had to descend a steep stony track into the sandy river bed. The four foot wide trickle of water being easily crossed, we began the steep ascent to the village. As we went I pointed out to amma the stone lined basins on the side of the hill, to which water was thrown in baskets, stage by stage, until it was finally thrown into the holding tank, also of stone, at the top. From there the villagers had constructed irrigation channels to supply the fields. These works had transformed the village, which had previously been dependent on the sparse rainfall, although the river was flowing fast below.

By the time we had taken coffee in the Reddy's house the sun had sunk below Kalawara Mountain, which looked blue black against a burnished sky. We set off in single file, the torch bearers in front and in the middle, the flickering flames casting dancing shadows on the uneven track; the only sounds an animal scurrying off into the night, or the rattle of a loose stone, accompanied sometimes by a low curse as a toe made painful contact. The shadow of Kalawara loomed high above us cutting off the last glow of the dying sun. A cloud of fruit bats flew in a silent wave overhead, off to the night's feeding ground - an orchard perhaps or jungle fruit.

Chapter 22
PRASANNA

I stood on the bank of the tank and watched as Chikkahanumantudu and his family worked, mud to their thighs, building a dam across the small pool of water which remained near the outlet to the reservoir.

His bid had won the contract for the fish that now gave the muddy water touches of silver as they swam wildly; disturbed by the sudden invasion of their privacy.

"Come and help us, anna." Hanumantudu called as he waded through the water and emptied a basket of mud on top of the wall they had almost completed.

I laughed, "I have to go into town and haven't a clean change of clothes." I had been walking since dawn after delivering Dapsone tablets in the Melekota area.

"That's your good fortune!"

Hanumantudu, the dam complete, now tied ropes to the handles of a closely-woven basket, and he and his wife began the slow task of tossing the water from one side of the small dam to the other. As the water became shallower the fish became more desperate, twisting and turning in their diminishing pool.

"I'll need to bring these fish into Chikka to sell as soon as I've sorted them."

I left them using an old sari as a net to catch the fish and went up the hill to the village.

When I reached the hut Gangamma greeted me.

"Your brother Prasanna has come, he is with your mother."

Prasanna did not often visit the village even during school holidays and I wondered what could have brought him down. I walked across to mother's house. Prasanna was sitting taking coffee, my mother trying to tempt him with some peanut 'laddu' she kept for special occasions.

"Namaskaram anna. Are you well?" I greeted him.

"I am well, anna, and you?" The heaviness of his voice and a lack of his usual animation belied his words.

Mother came out of the kitchen with more coffee and offered me a laddu as well. I didn't refuse. The rich sugary balls were a real treat for me.

"You haven't forgotten how to cook, mother. These are delicious!"

"After bringing up so many of you, I'm not likely to forget."

Mother went into the kitchen to prepare the meal.

Prasanna sat gloomily drinking his coffee.

"Are you going to stay for a few days anna?"

He made no reply but continued to sit in silence. After a few minutes he said "Remember that girl I told you about."

"Yes,"

"She loves me and is willing to marry me. She said when she returned to her home for the holidays she would mention me to her parents. Yesterday I received this letter."

He pulled a sheet of paper from his pocket and handed it to me. I read,

Dear Prasanna,

Today I spoke to my parents about us. They are very angry. They say you are not a suitable person for me. You are not of our caste and you are a Christian. They have forbidden me to see you again and have made me ask for transfer to another school. I will always love you but cannot go against my parent's wishes. Please don't write to me or try to see me.

Yours sincerely,

Lalitha

I reached out and covered his hand with mine.

"It's a shame, but a lot of parents still think in that way, and nothing will budge them."

"How can she just agree to their wishes like that! Doesn't she have any courage! Any mind of her own!"

"A dutiful daughter obeys her parents. You know that, anna. Don't blame her, she is just doing what she feels is right."

"But what about me? I think if she really loved me, she would marry me in spite of her parents."

"I'm sure she loves you, but you know very well that parents still have the last word when it comes to marriage and usually the partners they choose are more suitable in the end. Mother and I are responsible for your marriage and I am sure we can find someone who is beautiful, well- educated and would make you a loving wife."

"I've told you before I don't want anyone else."

"You feel like that now, but after a few months have passed we'll talk about it again."

We sat for a while in silence. Mother came and gave him the latest news of his sisters.

"I'll go and come, anna. I have to go into Chikka but I'll be back in a couple of hours."

I walked across to Premadasappa's house. Gangamma was waiting.

"Come and take food, anna."

"I'll take food later. I have to meet someone at the Tahsildar's office as witness to a property transfer at ten o'clock so will have to go now. Mother gave me coffee and laddu."

I took my Gandhi cap from the nail near the door and set out for the main road to catch the bus. My friend was waiting as arranged, and we took the documents into the office and signed them in the presence of the clerk, who then attached his official seal.

"Come and take coffee, anna."

"Please excuse me, I would rather return to Gollahalli I have some work to do."

"That's too bad, but go and come, anna."

"I will go and come."

I chafed at the delay as I sat waiting for the bus. The sun was high and the old bus made heavy going of the pull up to the edge of the plateau. We made the descent down the steep ghat road and the conductor still hadn't taken my fare.

"You haven't taken my charge, anna." I called out.

"The boss says you are to have free travel wherever you want to go."

I could hardly believe my ears. " Please give him my grateful thanks." Since my illness I had been unable to ride my cycle and often had to walk for lack of a fare. The bus ground to a halt at our turn off and I hurried down the track to the village. I was somehow relieved to find all quiet. Mother would be resting at this time of day. I ducked my head and entered Premadasappa's hut.

Gangamma's daughter-in-law was there to serve me and two-year-old Bhagia came and sat beside me on the mat.

"Bring a plate for Bhagia and I'll give her some of my food."

"She's had her's, anna!"

"Never mind, it won't do her any harm. Children always like to share someone else's food."

Muniamma brought another tin plate and I broke off some of my ragi ball and scooped some dhal over it with my fingers.

Suddenly a shot rang out. It sounded as though it came from mother's house. As I leapt up I instinctively looked up at the rafters.

"Where's my gun?" I shouted as I ran out the door.

"Your brother came and borrowed it half an hour ago." Muniamma said as she swept Bhagia into her arms.

I felt sick with foreboding as I reached mother's door.

Prasanna was lying on the floor in a pool of blood. As soon as I saw him I knew there was nothing I or anyone else could do for him. Mother was weeping loudly. I put my arms around her and led her to a chair. The room had become dark as though night had fallen as the villagers filled the doorway, looking on in horror as I brought a bedsheet and covered Prasanna.

My worst fear was realised and I had not had the foresight to prevent it.

Chapter 23
SURGERY

After my visit to Bombay, I believed I was healed and felt so much better I even began riding my cycle again.

Imagine my disappointment when I had my first fall and then another. I realised I would need to seek medical help so went in on Wednesday afternoon to attend outpatients.

Dr. Purushottam again examined me.

"Some of your motor responses are impaired. It suggests damage to your eighth nerve. We don't have the facilities here to do further investigations. I really feel you should go to the Special Hospital in Bangalore without further delay."

I was disappointed but this time my fear was gone and I decided to go in on Thursday afternoon after H.D. clinic to be at the hospital early Friday morning January 1967.

The doctor who examined me said "I need to admit you to do further tests."

"Yes, Doctor." His words came as no surprise, in fact I had brought some reading matter with me and some writing materials hoping to write some letters to family members during this period of forced inactivity.

On the third day the doctor detached an x-ray from the clipboard at the end of my bed and held it up against the light. He pointed his finger to a spot on the left side of my skull.

"Mr. Sabhapathy, this x-ray and the tests we've done indicate that you have a tumour of some sort on your eighth facial nerve."

"Oh!" I didn't know what to say as my mind grappled with the shock. "What does this mean doctor? Is it malignant?"

"Probably not, but we can't be sure until we examine it. You will need to have surgery."

I sat in silence trying to take in all the implications.

The doctor continued, "A conference of Neurosurgeons is being held in Delhi next month and a surgeon from Edinburgh who is a specialist in this type of surgery is to visit us here. I will put you on his list."

"Thank you, Doctor."

I was discharged and told to come back in a month.

During this time Dr. Graham returned from furlough and I continued visiting villages and distributing Dapsone tablets until the time came to go to Bangalore.

On admission to the Special Hospital they said I was too weak for surgery and proceeded to feed me up with nourishing food. It was fortunate for me that the visiting neurosurgeon was spending some time in Bangalore.

The day before I was to have surgery the neurosurgeon came to examine me. I told him how my father had worked for many years with Dr. Cutting who had trained in Edinburgh.

After surgery, on my return to the ward, it was some time before I could attempt to speak or take food by mouth. It was only then that the full extent of the damage was brought home to me.

I had no mirror so did not realise that one side of my face was paralysed, including my throat. This made both speech and swallowing difficult.

When the doctor did his round I asked him by means of signs and sounds whether I would recover.

"The tumour surrounding your nerve was quite extensive and had done considerable damage. It was impossible to remove it without doing more damage but with time the nerves should regrow and you will be able to talk and swallow again without too much difficulty."

That was comforting, although it seemed to leave a rather wide margin of doubt.

Before my discharge the doctor asked me if I had anyone to care for me at home.

"Yes," I said, "the people in the village will care for me."

The Ambulance came from Chikka to pick me up. Samanna said "I have orders from Dr. Graham to take you straight to the hospital."

I felt relief at those words. I had been wondering how Gangamma and the others would be able to look after me with their slender resources.

After a few days in the surgical ward Dr. Graham said,

"You'd better come and stay in the Bungalow until you are stronger. There is plenty of room without the family there and Gopal hasn't much to do."

Gopal was the elder brother of two of the small children who lived with their parents on the range. They all belonged to the criminal tribes and as he was too old to start school Mrs. Graham had taken him in and taught him household tasks as well as some reading and writing. The family owned a very small piece of land, and his mother had Tuberculosis.

I accepted Doctor's offer and moved into the large spare bedroom, with dressing-room and bathroom attached.

The food was good and I was comfortable with plenty of opportunity to read either books from the bungalow shelves or the library just around the corner.

Gopal had become very cocksure of himself and did not like having to spoon feed me. He made the process of eating quite an unpleasant proceeding by spooning the food into my mouth so quickly that I nearly drowned.

I didn't like to complain to Doctor, but the situation resolved itself when Gopal stole some money and disappeared.

Doctor and I were both left in the lurch.

Some missionaries who had been working further north had recently retired and their cook, an elderly man, came down to work for Doctor. He was a good cook, very evangelical and very dirty but he cared for me well and cheerfully.

Doctor invited me to take food with him in the dining room but eating was still very difficult and I often choked on a mouthful. I felt too embarrassed to eat in company with him and took my meals at the desk in my bedroom. I was still looking forward hopefully to the day I would once again be able to eat my favourite dish - pork curry.

I put on some weight and began to go out to the villages by bus visiting patients and delivering tablets.

The drivers on two of the bus routes had come to know me in the months before I had surgery. Now they always stopped and picked me up no matter how overloaded their buses.

The second bus company that served the area was now giving me free travel, so I visited the owners of both companies and thanked them in person.

Mrs. Graham and Carol, the youngest, were due back shortly. I felt concerned at the state of the bungalow. Doctor was too busy in the hospital to notice.

Doctor had the roof of the dining room removed for repairs to be done. He had expected it to be replaced before amma arrived but received a telegram saying they were to arrive in Madras on March 28th. He went by train to Madras to meet the boat and during his absence Samanna driver and I mixed some linseed oil and turps and polished the furniture. He did most of the work. Although it was more than a year since I'd had surgery I was still not up to much physically.

Next day we received a telegram from Doctor asking Samanna to meet them at Bangalore station with the hospital car. They arrived home at 10-30pm and a number of people joined me to greet them with garlands.

Amma looked momentarily shocked at the sight of me then concealed her dismay.

Now that Amma was back I did not use the door between my bedroom and the dining room but walked around to the front door and knocked.

Amma was surprised.

"There's no need to come around here and knock, Sabhapathy, just come into the dining room!"

"I feel awkward about doing that and don't want to intrude, amma."

"We don't mind, it seems strange to come around to the door when you are living here."

"Thank you, amma." I said, but inwardly resolved to continue to go around and knock.

"Doctor says he has asked you to make some lists for wheat distribution. I'll go down to the Boarding school tomorrow and see what they need there. It needs to be distributed as soon as possible. Even if we don't get more, it's better for the people to have it than the weevils."

Grain had been stored in the front bedroom to keep it away from rats and an army of weevils was marching under the door into the sitting room. As we sat and talked I could feel them crawling up my legs and noticed amma scratching surreptitiously.

"It won't be too difficult to amend my lists."

Next day I set off early armed with a plastic container of porridge and a spoon that amma had provided for me. I still couldn't eat solids and the deep plastic container was ideal as the food couldn't escape me.

Almost the whole of south India was in the grip of severe famine. The countryside was brown and hard and the people were suffering. I was careful to go to homes of some substance to take food. In the cities and towns it was just as bad. Sugar, flour and rice were rationed and grains that weren't rationed were either very expensive or unobtainable. Blackmarketeers were flourishing.

When I returned the following noon, amma was sitting outside watching the grain as it lay in the sun on the driveway.

"The weevils are walking away and die on the hot earth. It's given us a chance to clean out the bedroom, and the ward boys will come over to carry it back before the sun goes down."

A few days later Amma's foster children came home from Bangalore to attend the local convent. Arokya Mary said, "Did you know you have to pay 25 paisa for a glass of water in Bangalore now?"

Finally rains came but many people were hopelessly in debt to the landlords and moneylenders.

I began to spend more and more time out in the villages and realised that the room I occupied was needed for the children who were sleeping in doctor and amma's bedroom while they slept on the verandah.

I said to amma, "It is sufficient for me if I sleep on the back verandah when I'm in town."

"You'd have no privacy there. What about one of the bathrooms?"

The bathrooms were large so a bed and table were put in the nursery bathroom and a padlock on the door so that I was free to come and go as I pleased.

Chapter 24
CONGREGATION

Jayanna's head bobbed in time with his fingers as they beat the drums, while Shanta Kumar played the tune on the harmonium.

Christmas had come again and the Bhajana group was down from Chikka for Carol singing.

The Gollahalli folk had put up a mat shed this year so that all who wanted could join in. They sat now quietly, listening intently, as Shanta Kumar sang his latest composition, then, at a wave of his hand they sang it after him, line by line. It was a good tune, and gradually the volume grew as each person sang more confidently.

The night was cold, the Bhajana group all had their heads wrapped up in woollen scarves but many of us weren't so lucky. Those who had blankets sat huddled under them, while even under the mat shed, most of us shivered.

We waved the group off as the hospital car made its way gingerly up the rutted track.

Next day some of the women gathered in Gangamma's hut to talk over the events of the night.

"Why don't we have our own Church?"

"Then we could have our own Bhajana as well."

"Do something about it, Maistrulu!"

"You build a church, and I'll find you an evangelist."

"We'll do that, maistrulu." I was only too happy to do something about it, but I knew there would be some opposition in the village.

Early next day as I set off up the track towards the road, I realised I was growing old. The track seemed steeper and longer than it used to. The Flame tree I had planted at the top of the path down to the village had grown well. I was thankful for its shade as I waited for the first bus from Chikka.

I heard its noisy approach and stepped forward, hand raised. No matter how crowded the buses were, they always stopped for me, and somehow squeezed me in beyond the step. I was grateful for that, and the free travel they gave me.

As we moved off down the Gauribidanur road I could see green fields flash by - millet, corn, peanuts, pigeon pea, then, as we neared Manchenhalli (good village), small boys with trays of cut cane swarmed around the bus hoping to earn a few paisa. It was Monday so many of the passengers were young couples, in their best clothes, making their way to the fertility shrine. They were unlikely customers - hardly the ones to chew on a piece of sugar cane as they travelled. It was no good to me either, for since my surgery I had had trouble chewing and swallowing which had worsened over the years.

In spite of that the boys did well, and, as we moved off, strong teeth bit into sweet fibre and munched happily.

As the bus sped along, a village man, two seats ahead, spat out the window. There was a shriek from a well-dressed woman sitting by the window near me as the fibrous spittle landed on her silk jacket. Her husband shouted, "Watch where you spit! Were you born in the street?" The villager cringed.

I got down before Gauribidanur to walk my usual round trip, distributing tablets. I looked hopefully up the road, but there were no carts in sight. It was too early for the sugar crushing. In my younger days I'd regarded cart travel as too slow but now even a few miles in a cart was welcome.

I planned to reach Chikka by Wednesday night, ready for Thursday clinic. It was now over twenty years since I first began delivering Dapsone tablets to H.D. patients in the area and we had 8 centres in three Taluqs. Altogether nearly 2000 patients on our rolls. Dr. Robinson conducted the clinic and after taking food at the bungalow I caught the bus back to Gollahalli. As I approached the village down the track I saw a new levelled house site. I wondered who could be building there?

A kerosene tin of hot water was ready beside the fire in Gangamma's hut. Gangamma carried it out to the well and I bathed, put on fresh clothes and returned to the hut.

"What is that new house site by the track?"

"That's for the Church."

I was amazed, and my face must have shown it, because Gangamma said,

"You have no faith in us, Maistrulu! You told us to build a church and we are. A lot of us worked all day yesterday levelling that site. When we get a permit the men will go to cut wood for the uprights and roof."

Next day, most of the women and some of the men, set to work carrying water, mixing mud and building walls. The time of year was right; water in the tank, the ground not too hard, and the crops well-grown but not ready for harvest, so everyone had some time to spare.

When we sat down to our evening meal that night we were tired but content. As Gangamma served me she said,

"Have you found us a pastor, Maistrulu?"

"No, not yet."

"We're doing our bit and we'll need a pastor to open the new building when it's ready."

"I'll go and see Chidananda Pastor tomorrow."

Rev. Chidananda had been at school with me in Mysore. He was working at his desk when I knocked on the door.

"Come in and sit down, anna."

I took the chair he offered, while he put his head inside the kitchen door and asked his wife to prepare coffee.

I did not waste any time coming to the point of my visit.

"You know, anna, that some of the Gollahalli folk have been interested in Christianity for a long time. After the Bhajana visit at Christmas they said they would like their own Church. I said if they built a Church I'd find an evangelist for them. Now I've come to ask your help because they are already building a small mud and thatch structure for services. Do you have anyone suitable?"

"Most of the young people who would be suitable are employed by the hospital. The Gollahalli folk need someone to live there and teach them."

"Yes, that's what we had in mind."

"I can't think of anyone. What's more, I don't have any funds to draw on for a salary."

I took leave of him and as I walked automatically in the direction of the hospital, I thought of Bhaskara, so I changed course towards the Horticultural Office.

The huge lemon-scented gums near the Block Development office were a mass of blossom and the heady scent reached me, accompanied by the hum of bees feasting on the nectar.

As I walked past the Sub-divisional office and the Court House I thought how good it would be to plant some trees in the compound.

Bhaskara was in his office.

"Namaskaram, anna. What can I do for you? Are you well? You are looking very lean."

"I'm well thank you, anna. I just have more trouble eating these days and the miles I walk don't grow any shorter. I'm not looking for plants today, but it would be good if you could persuade the people at the court house to plant some trees."

"It would, but it would be difficult to protect them. I'll see what I can do about it?"

"The people enjoyed the Bhajana the other night but it made them want to have their own Church. You are a keen evangelist and I wondered if you knew of anyone suitable to live in Gollahalli and teach the people."

"I don't know of anyone, anna, but Satyanandappa might. Why don't you go to Chintamani and see him?"

I went straight across to the bus stand. A bus from Bangalore to Chintamani was due to pass through in half an hour so I walked across to the library, and spent the time browsing through the last week's copies of the Madras Mail.

When I reached Chintamani, Satyanandappa was at his desk.

"Namaskarappa! How are you? Please sit down!"

"Namaskarappa! I'm well, anna." It was five years since I had attended the meetings in Bombay in his company and I wasn't the only one who had aged.

I sat down in the chair he offered.

"What brings you to this side of the district?"

"I'm hoping you can help me find someone to come and teach the people of Gollahalli. They're building a place for worship and want someone to lead them. They're only a small group and don't have any money to pay a stipend, but they would feed and clothe whoever came."

Satyanandappa looked thoughtful. "I believe I know the very person you need. He's only a young man but he's very enthusiastic and has a great desire to serve God. Tonight he'll come to my Bible class here. Stay and take food with me and meet him yourself."

"That sounds a good idea. Thank you, anna."

After the Bible class Satyanandappa took me aside quietly. "What do you think?"

"I like the young man! I think he would be suitable."

"We'll talk to him now."

The young man remained after the others left and I explained our needs.

"I'll pray about it, ayya, and let you know."

"Good."

I spent the night in Satyanandappa's home, and returned to Gollahalli next day, feeling content.

Some members of the village opposed the building of the hut for worship but many were enthusiastic and worked hard to complete it.

Soon it was ready for dedication. The mud floors were spread with fresh cow dung. To accommodate our invited guests we erected a pandal of Casuarina poles and mats on the path outside and cut banana suckers and mango leaves for decoration.

The pastor and Bhajana party came for the dedication, and commissioning of our young evangelist. The children were home from school and lent volume and tune to our singing.

To me it was a great joy, the more joyful because it was the spontaneous desire of the people themselves.

After the service we stood and watched the car move gingerly up the track, taking our guests back to Chikka. My heart was full and I slipped away quietly beyond the village towards the tank to be alone.

The sky was clear, myriad stars twinkled. The moon made a path of gold across the still water. I thanked God and asked His blessing on us all. Perhaps He would spare me to see the congregation grow and spread the knowledge of God's love to all around us and fulfil my vision of a Church.

Epilogue

Now, as I write this, Sabhapathy's dream has been fulfilled. A local farmer donated land across the main road from Sabhapathy's grave and a brick Church has been built. They are waiting for money to complete the roof. The Diocese is to call it the E.R.Sabhapathy Memorial Church.

I remember the day I left Gollahalli for the last time. Although I was surrounded by people, it seemed strangely empty without Sabhapathy.

A silk factory had been set up not far off which provided employment for some at a wage which was barely worth working for.

Gangamma and some of the women accompanied me to catch the bus back to Chikka. As we were running late we cut across the fields to the road then walked on up the hill towards Sabhapathy's grave.

A woman and two girls approached, laughing delightedly as they twisted strands of jasmine and roses into their hair.

For a moment I was shocked, as I realised the flowers were those I'd laid reverently on the grave a short time before. What would Sabhapathy have thought?

I could imagine his face lighting up with pleasure on seeing their joy at having flowers for their hair. Such a treat for poor village women.

As we reached the Gollahalli turn off we could hear the bus labouring up the hill and we all put out our hands to flag it down but it was already bursting at the seams and rattled past. The cleaner clinging to the bar at the rear door gave us an apologetic wave.

We sat on the red stony earth under the flame tree and talked, until the sound of another motor brought us to our feet.

A lorry slowed to a halt as it came abreast, and two of the men occupying the cabin climbed on to the back to join the passengers already perched precariously on top of bags of grain.

I pulled myself up into the cabin to join the driver.

"Do you remember me? I'm John Venkatappa's son."

"You were only a boy last time I saw you. Is this your lorry?"

"No, I drive for the boss. I started off as a lorry cleaner and learnt to drive by watching and taking the lorry down to the tank for a wash. I've been a driver for seven years now."

"I came to see Sabhapathyanna's grave."

"I often gave Maistrulu a ride. Before he died he became very weak, but he still moved around the villages helping people."

As we drove towards Chikka I thought of the many times I'd hitched a ride on lorries in the past and as we approached the Gopal Tsattram at the entrance to the town the routine hadn't changed. The lorry came to a halt, and all the passengers perched on the load passed a few paisa through the back window to the driver, then jumped down.

"Please take my fare at least" I said as I prepared to descend.

"No amma, I won't take from you." He was adamant.

I turned and waved as he drove off.

GLOSSARY

Akka	Elder sister. Also used alone or as a suffix when talking to or about family or friends.
Almirah	Cupboard (Portuguese origin).
Amma	Mother, also used alone or as a suffix when addressing a woman by name.
Anna	Elder brother, also used alone or as a suffix when addressing family or friends and much as we would use 'mate' in Australia.
Appa	Father (Kan), also used as a suffix on men's names.
Ayya	Sir or used as a suffix to men's names to denote respect.
Babu	Foreman or overseer. Also used as a terms of endearment for small boys.
Bana	Large earthenware pot.
Bandi	Cart.
Betel nut	Seeds of the Betel palm (Areca catechu)
Betel leaf	Leaves of Piper betel.
Bhajana	Band.
Bund	Retaining bank of a tank(dam).
Chakla	Cobbler.
Chakli	Deep fried savoury push biscuits made of chick pea flour and ghee.
Chembu	Small narrow mouthed pot. Brass ones often had a screw-top lid with a small drinking cup inside for use on journeys.
Chikballapur	(Kan, Chikkaballapura) Town of the small measure.

Chutney	Usually freshly ground coconut, tamarind or mint and chillies. There are many different combinations.
Coolie	Manual labour or a person who does manual labour.
Dekshi	Indian saucepan.
Dhal	Split peas.
Dhobi	Washerman or woman.
Doddballapur	(Kan. Doddaballapur) Town of the large measure.
Dorra	Lord. term of respect.
Dosai	South Indian, large, crisp pancake made of rice and black mung dhal and often served with chutney or filled with an onion, potato and tomato mixture.
Drumstick	Seed pods of Moringa oleifera.
Garu	Suffix used as a term of respect for either sex.
Gadapara	Crowbar.
Ghat	Mountain, used to refer to the steep winding road up or through mountains.
Gopuram	Temple tower.
Iddli	Steamed buns made of ground rice and black mung dhal. Usually eaten with a dhal sambar or fresh chutney.
Jaggery	Raw sugar locally made and sold in small balls or as moulded lumps.
Jambu	Purple fruit.
Jati	Caste. Also used when speaking of well-bred animals.
Jinka	Type of small deer.
Jubba	Long-sleeved, high-necked handloom shirt.
Jutka	Pony cart with large wheels and a woven came canopy. The local hire vehicle.
Kanuga	Pongamia glabra.

Karnum	Traditional village surveyor.
Kai	Fruit or seed pod.
Khiru	Sweet spicy pudding made from semolina. Usually contains nuts and sultanas.
Maistrulu	Teacher, master, work supervisor.
Mali	Gardener.
Matey	Cook's assistant.
Mattsu	Large knife used for cutting cane or undergrowth or opening tender coconuts etc.
Mukkeri	Wide-mouthed, shallow basket.
Muruku	Deep-fried sweet push biscuits.
Namaskara	(Kan.) Namaskaram (Tel.) Used in greeting and farewell accompanied by hands placed together as in prayer
Nan	Large flat leavened bread eaten in North India.
Paddy	Rice in the husk.
Paisa	100 paisa = 1 Rupee.
Pancha	Lower cloth worn by men.
Pandal	Temporary structure made of casuarina or bamboo poles and roofed with mats. The Indian equivalent of a tent.
Peanut Cake	The compressed residue left after the oil has been extracted from peanuts. Used as fertilizer and cattle fodder.
Peepul	Sacred fig tree (Fiscus religiosa).
Peon	Office servant or messenger.
Petti shop	Large wooden box on legs used as a shop selling cigarettes, beedis, sweets and snacks etc.
Pi dog	Stray dogs of villages and cities.
Pilau	Rice cooked with vegetables or meat.
Pinugu	Corpse.

Poojari	Hindu priest.
Puja	Hindu worship.
Raga	Tune
Ragi	Copper. Name of the small red millet whch was the main food of Chikka area.
Reddy	Landed farmer.
Sabhapathy	Sabaa'pati. Leader of the congregation.
Saaman	Luggage.
Sambar	Thin dhal curry.
Sampangi	Michelia champaca. Bears fragrant yellow flowers.
Santa	Market.
Seer	Unit of measure.
Shikari	Hunter, hunting.
Swami	Lord.
Tahsildar	The government official in charge of the Taluk.
Tali	The thread the groom ties around the neck of his bride when making his marriage vows
Taluk	Shire.
Tank	Dam.
Tiffin carrier	A many layered container used for carrying food.
Tonga	Pony cart distinctive to Mysore city.
Torti	Small rectangular tank made of cement or slabs.
Tindi	Light eats.
Yogi	Holy man.
Zamkhana	Thick woven cotton mat, usually stripped.